Nigel Gifford OBE is a seasone[...] of the adventure travel compa[...] Green Globe 21 on sustainabl[...] aineering expeditions have inc[...] Himalaya and a solo ascent of Mount McKinley, while as a skydiver he has made over 1,000 freefall descents. He helped set up the Ellie Poo Paper Company, which makes paper from Sri Lankan elephant dung, to the benefit of both villagers and elephants.

Richard Madden is a writer and the Adventure Travel Editor of *The Daily Telegraph*. His travels have taken him to many of the world's most remote corners and cultures and he has participated in a wide range of adventure sports in locations across all seven continents. He has also presented adventure travel documentaries for the Discovery Channel.

The Daily Telegraph

The Adventurous Traveller

THE ONE-STOP GUIDE TO TRAVEL WITH A CHALLENGE

NIGEL GIFFORD AND RICHARD MADDEN

ROBINSON
London

Constable & Robinson Ltd
3 The Lanchesters
162 Fulham Palace Road
London W6 9ER
www.constablerobinson.com

ISBN 1-84119-666-5

A CIP Catalogue record for this book is available from
the British Library

Printed and bound in Denmark

10 9 8 7 6 5 4 3 2 1

'Dreamers of the day are dangerous men, for they may act their dream with open eyes, to make it possible'.

T. E. Lawrence, *Seven Pillars of Wisdom*

CONTENTS

ACKNOWLEDGEMENTS

Nigel Gifford
This book would not have been possible without the help and assistance of a whole host of people. There are those who provided practical support and assistance and those whose encouragement was beyond the call of duty, like Fred King of Stone Allerton, Somerset, a steadfast friend of many years who died recently and who like my father, Frank William Gifford, will not see the book in print.

There were several who teased me nearly to death by goading me with the fear that it would never be finished in time – colleagues from past adventures, the travel world, family and friends all of them.

Of special note is David Browne. Adventure traveller, writer and researcher, who knows more about train and bus travel anywhere in the world than anyone I have ever met. I am indebted to David's attitude of 'creeping excellence' or in other words his penchant for constantly updating and improving all or any aspects of the book. Thank you David, it was such a pleasure working with you and I would leap at the chance again.

Other core 'encouragers' were as follows, and I truly thank them for their support.

While writing in the UK:
Tamsin and Kim Gifford, Julie Riches, Philip Horniblow, Michael Lane, Audrey Salkeld, Bill Morgan, Martin and Sarah Veal, Keith Ruby, Paul Cockhill, Simon Johnson, Rachel Humphries, Henry and 'Tiggy' West, Roy and Christine Clarke, Sue Farrington, Ray McKenna, Phil 'The Phone' Russell, Oag McKenzie, Peadair and 'Min' McKenzie, Matt Hailing – Biggs, Liz Harrall, Rachel and Julian Sims, Sarah and Brent Dodman, 'Ray'dar' Marks and Emma Bulford, 'Navy' Phil, Fiona and Katie Cadbury, as well as Tony Atkins and Jessica Bullock in the offices at High & Wild.

While writing and missing the fun in Austria:
Jenni and Martin Lloyd, Carrie and Ian Bell, Julia Robertson, and not least the Rendl Rabbit – or was it a beaver?

While writing in France:
Peter and Meryl Lilly, James Mutter, Tony and Trish Williams, Keith and Cath Spires.

While writing in Italy:
Carlo Fiaschetti and his team.

And while planning adventures in Nepal:
Suman Pandy, Nima Tamang, Chhudlim Tenba Sherpa and his brother Gaylzen.

And now to thank Alice . . . but how do you thank someone for their love, care and support every day; and for turning your life into a wonderful constantly shared adventure.

Richard Madden

Adventurers adventure, travellers travel, writers write . . . and loved ones make it all possible. Thank you Sarah, my princess, for making it all possible.

PART I
DREAMING THE DREAM

Richard Madden

1
What is Adventure Travel?

Few people ever forget their first experience of foreign travel. A magical doorway swinging open on to other worlds, other peoples, and other often more exotic and exciting ways of doing and thinking about things than our own. A sense of adventure often as hard to recapture as it is to forget. Even in an age of mass tourism, the sights and sounds of an alien culture experienced first hand and for the first time remain indelibly etched on the memory.

For me that moment came as a callow and impressionable schoolboy of 16 finally let loose on the outside world at the start of the long summer holidays. Not only was it my first trip abroad, it was also my first ever plane journey. So far, so normal, you might think. But this was to be no ordinary teenage holiday. The airport for which I was bound was Uganda's Entebbe airport on the shores of Lake Victoria in the dark heart of Africa and I was here to spend the summer with my half-brother who worked in the remote north-west of the country.

It was almost dark as I climbed down the steps of the plane on a humid tropical evening, excitement oozing from every pore. It was plain from the start that nothing here was remotely the same as the cosy familiarity of the world I had left behind. Soldiers in tatty green uniforms lounged around smoking, WWI-vintage Lee Enfield rifles slung cowboy-style across their shoulders. Immigration procedures were conducted in what felt like deliberate slow motion. No questions were asked, the officials simply eyeing me up and down with idle curiosity before languidly stamping my passport.

Emerging triumphant into the arrivals hall, officially at last on foreign soil, I was met by my half-brother's driver, Benja. Around us on the otherwise bare walls were framed photographs of a rotund man in military uniform smiling benignly and looking, to my naive younger self, like an entrant in a fancy dress competition. 'Who is that man?' I rather too loudly enquired, pointing to the largest and most imposing portrait of the man who was shortly to make headlines around the world for his brutality, the Ugandan dictator General Idi Amin Dada.

Benja's response put an instant end to my short-lived innocence of foreign travel. Bundling me out of earshot of the soldiers, he hustled me out of the building into a tropical rainstorm and straight into the pages of a Graham Greene novel. 'You must be very careful, Mr Richard,' he chided me as we drove off into the night, 'please never to ask that question in public again.' During the next three months, a stay that was to include a chance encounter with Big Dada himself, the words 'travel' and 'adventure' became forever fused in my mind.

Which is why, over 30 years later, I still find the question: 'How do you define adventure travel?' so difficult to answer. The label is significant in itself, presupposing as it does that other forms of travel are somehow unadventurous. It also reveals how attitudes to travel in general have changed so dramatically over the last few decades. So in order to understand how the phenomenon of adventure travel has come about, it is important to establish its place in the overall history of recreational travel.

The Origins of Adventure Travel

The concept of travel for pleasure – as opposed to trade, religious or military reasons – took shape with the Grand Tour in the eighteenth century when the British aristocracy set out on processional visits around Europe's cultural highlights. At the beginning of the nineteenth century, the Industrial Revolution massively increased the mobility of Europe's middle class and in 1841 Thomas Cook pioneered the first 'package' holiday taking 570 passengers the ten miles from Leicester to Loughborough and back by train.

During the following hundred years, most travel beyond European borders was in the interests of the colonial powers and included many now famous expeditions to the world's unconquered wildernesses including the Himalaya and the Poles. In the early decades of the twentieth century, the more exotic forms of recreational travel – across Europe on the Orient Express or across the Atlantic on cruise liners like the *Mauritania*, for example – were largely the preserve of the rich and famous but the writings of adventurers like Wilfred Thesiger and Patrick Leigh Fermor were to inspire a whole new generation of travellers.

As the privations of WWII gradually receded, the increasing popularity and affordability of the package holiday sparked the modern era of mass tourism. But cheaper air travel and the 1960s youth revolution also spawned a new breed of independent traveller who saw travel as more of a rite of passage than something you did on your summer holidays. Overlanders like Tony and Maureen Wheeler, the founders of the iconic Lonely Planet series of guidebooks, saw themselves as neither 'explorers' nor 'holidaymakers' but 'travellers' following in the treadmarks of the American 'Beats'. These were the natural heirs of writers like Jack Kerouac, author of *On The Road*, who in the 1950s had made the act of travelling not just a way of life but a philosophical statement.

By the 1970s, taking a year or two out after university to follow the overland trail to the Indian subcontinent and beyond had become something of a birthright, but the increasingly competitive climate of the 1980s put an end to all that as for many people the equation between time and money went into reverse. Whereas once, time had been plentiful and money in short supply, now the reverse was often true. At the same time planes could whisk us further and more cheaply than ever before. If it was possible to take two weeks off work and go to the other side of the world, why waste all that time getting there in a clapped out old bus?

But the more widely travelled we became, the more we began to realize that one tropical beach looks much like another, however far from home it might be. People also began to feel they were missing out on the one thing they had taken for granted all along – a sense of adventure. As more and more of us became used to regular infusions of exotic cultures – and conversely more and more exotic cultures became used to Western visitors – travel to a far-off foreign location was of itself no longer enough to be called an 'adventure' per se.

The Adventure Sports Phenomenon

At the same time, an explosion of popularity in what were dubbed 'adventure sports', fuelled by advances in technology which produced ultra-strong, ultra-light and ultra-efficient materials from carbon fibre to Kevlar, had captured the imagination of a wider audience of young travellers bored with beach culture and thirsty for thrills. When, in June 1987, the New Zealander A.J Hackett jumped from the Eiffel Tower with what appeared to be no more than a piece of elastic tied to his legs, the archetypal adventure sport of bungee jumping was born.

Worldwide publicity for the stunt caught the imagination of a new breed of daredevils and proved that leaping off bridges a hundred and more metres over a ravine was not only safe but also a viable commercial proposition. The Kawarau Bridge jump, near Queenstown in South Island, New Zealand, opened soon after. Adventure sports holidays had arrived with a vengeance and operators were soon filling the pages of their brochures with ever more energetic alternatives to the traditional beach holiday.

A Need for Challenge

As more and more people went in search of an extra dimension to their forays abroad, psychologists were wheeled out to explain how this had come about. One popular explanation was the 'flight or fight' mechanism, our primeval response to predators, which in the modern age has been sublimated into a need to relieve the stress of modern life with regular doses of adrenalin. Leaping off bridges, swimming with sharks, or flying Icarus-like in an armchair suspended from threads of Kevlar were the perfect way to simulate the adrenalin rush and heightened sense of reality of being hunted by a predator – only this time without the inconvenience of actually being killed.

Another theory suggested that the need to take risks may be hard-wired into our DNA. Israeli scientists discovered a gene known as D4DR, the so-called 'thrill-seeking' gene, which they claimed had a longer sequence in personality types predisposed to getting their kicks from regular doses of adrenalin.

But alongside these theories, there was also a social explanation: the influence of the physical and psychological environment in which people live their daily lives. The increasing mental pressures of growing up in a modern, industrial society have been well documented but this has occurred during a period of unparalleled material prosperity when a whole generation has reached middle age without having to fight a major war. In an era when, mercifully, few young British men or women have friends or family who have been killed in action, paragliding may seem extreme. But compared to our grandparents' generation, some of whom were required to fly unarmed, unmotorized gliders over enemy territory, the risks are tiny in comparison.

Desirable as it may seem, living in a society whose exposure to everyday risk is at an all-time low is not necessarily what evolution has programmed us to expect. This may go some way to explaining why it is that so many adventurers experience the sensation of feeling more fully alive when they are exposed to risk than in the course of their everyday lives. In a world where material comfort is the norm, deliberately seeking out the more extreme range of human experience with all the risks that this entails is a deep-seated need for many people. In order to push ourselves to the same extent as our forbears, we need to perform ever more death-defying feats.

Climbing Mount Everest has long been a metaphor for this risk-taking approach to life and the conquering of seemingly insuperable odds. In the 50 years since Hillary's first ascent in 1953, more than 1,100 climbers have reached the summit as a small industry has grown up of elite mountain guides charging tens of thousands of pounds to sometimes, almost literally, drag their clients to the summit. Tragedy also played its part when, on the infamous 1996 expedition described in Jon Krakauer's masterly account *Into Thin Air*, eight climbers died after a ferocious storm set in. Stories abound of climbers so obsessed with 'summit fever' that they have left fellow climbers in trouble to their fate rather than forego their own attempt on the summit.

All this is a paradox in societies where so much effort is put into the minimization of risk. Whole sectors of the economy have been built on the desire to insure ourselves against an uncertain future, safety nets that in the past simply did not exist. Risk itself has become the drug we seek to avoid the mundane routines of everyday life. Paradoxically, this ultimately vain attempt to eradicate risk from our lives works against an in-built psychological drive to face and overcome the fear of danger – a process which many believe is profoundly necessary if we are to become fully-developed human beings. Experience tells us that if we are not allowed to test or stretch our limitations, our sense of self-esteem falls.

It may also go some way to explaining a phenomenon often noted by adventure travel operators when in the aftermath of tragic accidents, demand for the holiday or activity in question sometimes rises rather than falls as one would naturally expect. Examples include a gruesome incident in the mid-1990s when a tourist was eaten by a crocodile on a Zambezi canoeing holiday and the Columbia Space Shuttle disaster of 2003. Following the latter, enquiries to Space Adventures, the American company pioneering space tourism, rose dramatically.

These are very extreme examples of what many adventure guides have described to me as an unspoken, or even unrecognized, need in many people to extend personal boundaries. Taking us out of our individual 'comfort zones' by taking on physical and psychological challenges that once we would have thought of as beyond our capabilities can be an important tool for personal growth.

A Thousand Different Adventures

While for many, travelling in a team is an important part of an adventure experience, Nicholas Crane, whose book *Clear Waters Rising* described his epic 6,000-mile walk along the chain of mountains which stretches across Europe from Cape Finisterre to Istanbul, believes in the importance of self-reliance.

> My understanding of adventure travel is derived from my own enthusiasm for bold, low-impact, self-reliant journeys. That usually means travelling solo with minimal equipment and learning to live off the land and, more importantly, with its people.

Rebecca Stephens, the first British woman to climb Everest, emphasizes the excitement of the sense of discovery.

> Ski touring for a day is great, but ski touring from one point on the map to another over a period of several days

or weeks is a real adventure, never knowing what is around the next corner. It might be on foot, on skis, on horseback, on a bike or a canoe – anything that allows you to be in contact with the landscape and the people. And it doesn't really matter how long the journey, or where it is, so long as there's a feeling of exploration and discovery.

My own career as an adventure traveller began as an addicted Himalayan trekker and long-distance cyclist in the 1970s and 1980s seduced, like Crane and Stephens, by the lure of dramatic, sometimes hostile, landscapes and interaction with the people whose lives I briefly shared far away from established tourist hot-spots. By the 1990s, I was also hooked on adventure sports and over the years became in turns a keen diver, horse rider, mountain biker, sailor and, more recently, paraglider.

Some incredible memories stand out: watching the northern lights while streaking across the Yukon with my own team of huskies in −25 °C; playing at being David Attenborough with a family of gorillas in the mountains of Uganda; negotiating swollen rivers, crumbling mountainsides and sublime scenery on a journey on horseback through the Hindu Kush; rafting Tasmania's notorious Franklin River; diving with sharks and manta rays in Indonesia; clinging to the yardarm of a square-rigger in a Force 8 gale. The knowledge that sweat, cold and discomfort were part of the price that had to be paid for many of these memories makes them all the sweeter.

As I hope this book will demonstrate, there are many types of adventure travel and many destinations and activities through which it can be enjoyed, both solo and in groups. While everyone has their own definition and expectations, adventure travel in the widest sense of the term is a journey both physical and psychological, during which the thrill of breaking new ground can only be won by taking on, living with and ultimately learning from, the new, the different and the unknown.

2
In Search of Adventure

Trekking

If there can be said to have been an 'original' adventure holiday, trekking must surely be it. Essentially the same as hiking or walking – 'tramping' as they call it in New Zealand – trekking involves travelling by foot off the beaten track into mountainous terrain for anything from a few days to a few weeks and first became popular in the Himalaya in general and Nepal in particular. The term itself was coined from an old Boer word meaning 'a journey by ox wagon' and the first Himalayan trekking agency was the brainchild of an Englishman, Colonel Jimmy Roberts. A retired Gurkha officer and mountaineer, Roberts was one of the first Westerners to explore Nepal which remained closed until well after the end of WWII.

Roberts ran his inaugural commercial trek in February 1965. After obtaining permission from the King of Nepal, he recruited Sherpas from the Solo Khumbu region as guides, cooks and porters. The Sherpa people were already world-famous for their mountain skills following Tenzing Norgay's ascent of Everest 12 years previously alongside Edmund Hillary. The five-week trek, escorting three American women, was a great success and Roberts' trekking agency, Mountain Travel, soon established what was to become the model for trekking tourism throughout the region.

The joys of trekking are self-evident to anyone who loves wilderness walking, but it is often as memorable for the unique cultures and peoples encountered in the world's remote places as for the inspiration of walking through its most sublime landscapes. While there are numerous classic treks around the world – the Lost City Trail in Colombia's Parque Tayrona, the Kokoda Trail in Papua New Guinea, and almost all the classic walks in New Zealand's South Island are among my personal favourites – the Himalaya will always hold their honorary place as the spiritual home of trekking.

The make-up of a trekking party depends on the geographical location and the season. Most of the more popular treks follow traditional trading routes where teahouses and 'hotels' are plentiful. These days on many of the more established routes, you can strike out quite safely on your own or in small groups with no assistance from porters or guides on what have become well-trodden trails. Sadly, however, political uncertainty in Nepal during the last few years means the country is not as safe as it once was, so you should always research the situation on the ground before heading off alone into remote areas.

The season for trekking in the Himalaya varies with the area's geographical location and height. In Nepal the best trekking falls into two short bursts of activity, in March and April and from September to November. During the summer, the rivers are in flood from the monsoon which spreads north from the Bay of Bengal and hits eastern Nepal at the end of April. Between May and October the upper reaches of the trans-Himalayan regions of India are passable. These include areas such as Ladakh, Zanskar and the magnificent Spiti valley. After

November, anywhere in Nepal above the snow line (around 3,500 metres) is effectively cut off.

Anyone who has never experienced life on trek would be forgiven for imagining a daily slog through inhospitable terrain. Discomforts there are from time to time, and matters of hygiene can sometimes leave a little to be desired, but the compensations of the simplified routines of life pared down to the bare necessities can be powerfully therapeutic. Group psychology is the anvil on which the success or failure of a trekking holiday is forged or broken. When it works, few dinner parties back home can ever compete with the night-time camaraderie experienced in remote camps far from the trappings of civilization.

A typical trekking day with one of the more up-market trekking agencies begins with 'bed tea' at around 6 am, a welcome source of warmth when overnight temperatures can fall to −15 °C. All water used for cooking and drinking is boiled and filtered by the Sherpas so that stomach upsets are kept to a minimum. Hot 'pinkie pani', a solution of potassium permanganate, is left outside the mess tent for washing hands before every meal. A hole is dug and a 'loo' tent put up each evening and filled in again the next morning. Camp cooks show remarkable ingenuity in providing three appetizing and generous meals a day under the most arduous conditions.

One of my personal trekking highlights was a journey I made to the kingdom of Mustang in northern Nepal in the early 1990s, shortly after it had been opened to outsiders for the first time since WWII. On previous trips I had only been able to walk as far as Jomosom at the foot of the Kali Kandaki valley, but now we were able to cross the 3,600-metre foot pass which led to Lo Manthang, the fourteenth-century walled 'city' of Mustang.

Here we were granted an audience with King Jigme Palbar Bista, the twenty-fifth direct descendant of the kingdom's original founder. On our return journey we stumbled on the fresh prints of a snow leopard deep in a remote mountain chasm. It was considered a sign of great good luck and in this magical country we had certainly been treated to more than our fair share. But it was typical of the type of unforgettable experience you can expect to encounter on a trekking adventure in the more remote corners of the globe.

The Natural World

Many of us only ever encounter wild animals in a zoo or on TV and are often overwhelmed by the raw emotional power of encountering animals in the wild or experiencing at first hand rare natural phenomena. Whether it be tracking down the 'Big Five' on a safari drive in the African savannah or witnessing one of nature's set-piece masterpieces like the wildebeest migration in the Serengeti, the northern lights or a total eclipse of the sun, each has the power to awe and humble.

Some of my most treasured travelling moments have revolved around encounters with animals: standing rooted to the spot as an emperor penguin in Antarctica pecked inquisitively at my boots; being awoken in my sleeping bag in sub-zero temperatures by the warm breath of a husky dog nuzzling my face under a full moon in the Yukon; watching a family of bears at play in Yellowstone Park; watching dolphins dance around the bows of our boat in the Caribbean Sea. But nothing can quite compare with the thrill of a first glimpse of gorillas in the wild. On my first trip to Africa I caught a fleeting glimpse of one as we drove through a remote mountain forest in the south of Uganda and I made a pact with myself that I would one day return for a closer encounter.

Like millions of others, my imagination was later fuelled by David Attenborough's legendary TV romp with a mountain gorilla. Until that moment, nearly a century of King Kong demonizations had brought the species to the brink of extinction. But from the moment that baby gorilla started playfully undoing Attenborough's shoelace as its parents looked on unconcerned, the penny finally dropped. It was us, not them, who were the real demonic apes. As the anthropologist Konrad Lorenz once wrote: 'I've found the link between apes and civilized men – it's us.'

Today, there are only about 650 mountain gorillas left on the planet and their ability to avoid extinction is by no means certain. Around 350 live in the war-ravaged Virunga Forest which straddles the borders of Uganda, Rwanda and the Congo. The rest live in Bwindi Impenetrable National Park in Uganda where, nearly 30 years after my first brief encounter, I finally came face to face with a giant silverback gorilla called Mubare, the 'one who likes sleeping'. Human contact with gorillas is strictly controlled to avoid them contracting disease or compromising their ability to survive in the wild, but those precious 60 minutes watching Mubare's babies riding around on their mother's back and chasing each other up and down trees will remain with me forever.

This experience was the climax to a wildlife spectacular which included a mesmerizing two weeks in the Kibale Forest in Western Uganda as a volunteer on an 'habituation' project set up by the Jane Goodall Institute. The project's primary aim is to acclimatize the forest's community of over 70 chimps to short visits by small groups of tourists. The money raised is used to create a safe natural environment, free from the threat of human predators. Although there are estimated to be over 150,000 chimpanzees left in the wild, 30,000 of which live in Uganda, their long-term fate is far from assured. Every year hundreds are killed for meat or die from snare wounds and disease. Many are sold abroad as circus acts by unscrupulous dealers.

The Kibale Forest was like a looking-glass world in which us naked apes were able to study our furry cousins over the chasm of the six million years since our common ancestor walked the Earth. Observing chimp behaviour in the wild gives a fascinating insight into the complexities of the behaviour of our own species, especially in light of the fact that it is now thought we may share as much as 99.4 per cent of our DNA.

On one occasion I was lucky enough to see a mother tenderly suckling her baby less than 24 hours after its birth – a very rare sighting in the wild. Less heart-warming, but just as memorable, was the day the group of chimps we were following embarked on a 'border patrol', a highly aggressive territorial display worthy of the famous bone-hurling scene in *2001, A Space Odyssey*. All around us chimps were 'buttress-banging', screeching demonically and leaping in the air before charging the huge forest trees and smacking their hands repeatedly against the buttress roots. This produced a sound like a tom-tom drum and in the distance we could hear the answering cries and the eerie drumming of the neighbouring group of chimps. Researchers in the field have recorded actions like these resulting in the deliberate genocide of one group by another.

Observed within 24 hours of each other, these dramatically contrasting behaviours seemed to go some way to explaining how our own species is simultaneously capable of rising to the sublime heights of a Shakespeare or a Leonardo while at the same time plumbing the genocidal depths of Hitler or Pol Pot. Not for the first time during that magical interlude with the Kibale chimps, I realized that our encounters with the natural world can sometimes teach us as much about ourselves as the animals we travel so far to see in their natural habitat.

Indigenous Cultures

Initiation rituals, creation myths, witch doctors, spirit houses, divination ceremonies, fertility cults. Given the long list of mystical and magical experiences largely extinct from our modern, secular societies, it is hardly surprising that the lives of the surviving tribal peoples of our planet have taken such a hold on our collective imagination. Whether it be the Dream Time of the Aboriginal peoples of Australia, the myths and legends of the

Inuit of northern Canada, or the shamanic trance rituals of South America, implicit in contact with indigenous peoples is the tantalizing possibility of the revelation of a wisdom we in the West have either forgotten or ignored.

When in armchair traveller mode back home, poring over books full of glossy pictures of exotically clothed tribal warriors, it is hard not to be seduced by this image. Sadly, however, Western contact with indigenous cultures has always been fraught with problems. From the original genocide of the Spanish conquistadors during the first voyages of discovery in the sixteenth century to the destruction of the habitat of the Marsh Arabs by Saddam Hussein's Ba'athists, the centuries-old cultures of tribal peoples rarely survive contact with the outside world.

The rapacious search for precious metals, minerals, oil and wood has led to the destruction of many tribal homelands. Forced exposure to an alien, materialist culture has done the rest. Adventure tourism, or so the argument goes, can be a balm for this sorry state of affairs. If we benign travelling souls can make contact with remote tribal societies around the world, bringing our money and patronage, there can be a mutually beneficial exchange of material well-being and wisdom.

Sadly, it rarely works out this way. To begin with, native environments often cannot sustain the influx of large numbers of Westerners playing at 'going bush' but actually demanding modern amenities and causing a drain on scarce resources. The disparity of wealth, where a pocketful of change to us can equal a monthly income to them, all too often leads to a culture of dependency which rapidly erodes tribal communities. On the other hand, it is easy to forget that many indigenous peoples do not want to be preserved in aspic, indulging the nostalgic whims of a post-colonial era. They, too, want improved housing and medical facilities while at the same time developing in a way that preserves their cultural beliefs.

Guy Marks, who with his wife Amanda set up Tribes Travel, has extensive experience of bringing small groups of tourists into contact with indigenous peoples. Guy stresses that fair trade and sustainability should be at the heart of the exchange.

> If we can harness even a small percentage of the tourist pound for the good of developing communities then we have a real chance of helping the alleviation of poverty in some of the world's most fragile societies. There is also an environmental advantage to tourism in these areas. When communities receive income from people coming to experience their environment, they also realize there's a positive value in conservation. This allows conservation to take its place alongside destructive options like logging, hunting, or mineral and oil extraction as a viable option for making ends meet.

Personally, whenever I have come into contact with native peoples, I have always been painfully aware of the moral complexity of the interchange. Like Guy Marks, I prefer the rare occasions when I have been lucky enough to be invited into a tribal community either alone or in a small group. These include a magical chance encounter with the Kogis of the Sierra Nevada of Colombia and a visit to the Naga people of northeast India.

The former group, the Kogi Indians, were one of the only indigenous civilizations to survive the Spanish Conquest unconquered and may be the only native people in the world who have succeeded in keeping their culture and complex shamanistic beliefs almost entirely intact. They refer to themselves as the 'Elder Brother' and believe that they are the guardians of life on Earth, a force that we, the prodigal 'Younger Brother', are in imminent danger of destroying. We encountered a small group of Kogi on a trek to the 'Cuidad Perdida', or Lost City, the sacred city of their ancestors which was abandoned during the Spanish Conquest. Their quiet dignity, striking features and the message they have tried to communicate to the outside world made a profound impression.

The Nagas were infamous during the British colonial era for their centuries-old tradition of hunting human heads, part of their animist beliefs in which fertility from the world of the spirits is channelled into the realm of the living. Nagaland, one of the Seven Sisters of states in India's remote north-east sandwiched between Tibet and Burma, has been isolated from the outside world since Indian Independence in 1947. After decades of persecution, many Nagas now believe that small-scale responsible tourism may be the solution to their problems and will bring their plight to the attention of the outside world and help regenerate a region of breathtaking natural beauty.

But while encounters with tribal peoples like the Kogis and the Nagas can be among the most rewarding of travel experiences, it is up to all of us who are curious about the lives of indigenous peoples to learn the lessons of the past and ensure a fairer exchange that will genuinely enhance the lives and environment of some of the world's most fragile communities.

Expeditions

These days the word 'expedition' is used so widely that its true meaning is in danger of being forgotten. For most of us, it conjures images of the great feats of leadership, courage and endurance demonstrated during voyages of exploration like the 1914 Antarctic Expedition when, against all odds, Shackleton and his men lived to tell the tale after the destruction of their ship, The *Endurance*, in the pack ice. But all too often in our celebrity-obsessed age, the word is applied to headline-grabbing stunts which achieve little of any real worth.

Dictionaries define 'purpose' as the key element of an expeditionary journey, be it scientific, military or exploratory. Exploration was certainly at the heart of the most famous expeditions to leave these shores during the Victorian era. But as the last of the world's wildernesses, 'lost worlds' and 'forgotten peoples' have one by one been mapped, explored and often exploited, the old-style explorers of the Victorian era have become an endangered species. Today, many of the 'expeditions' which hit the headlines do not fulfil that primary prerequisite of 'purpose'. No doubt someone, somewhere, will one day reach the South Pole naked in a supermarket trolley, but our knowledge of Antarctica will not have been enhanced in the process.

Although they often go unreported, by far the most important expeditions being mounted today are scientific in nature and aimed at adding to our knowledge of the planet's most fragile ecosystems. As Nick Crane, twice winner of the *Daily Telegraph*/Thomas Cook Award, believes:

> The really worthwhile expeditions these days are composed of biologists, anthropologists, meteorologists and their ilk. Today's explorers are not Scotts or Shackletons and Amundsens but scientists exploring global warming and disappearing species.

In 2002, research by a team of 200 international scientists and researchers for the campaigning group Conservation International revealed that despite population growth, agriculture and resource extraction, almost half of the Earth's land surface is still wilderness, occupied by just 2.4 per cent of the world's population. So the scope for expeditions which build on our knowledge of these wilderness areas is far greater than many of us imagine. While the globe may indeed have been well and truly mapped, it has still not been entirely explored.

the Royal Geographical Society (RGS) is the principal organization in the UK concerned with helping people with scientific and exploratory expeditions overseas. Twenty years ago it supported fifty expeditions a year, now it helps between 500 and 600. The Expedition Advisory Centre of the RGS – and its sister organization The Institute of British Explorers (IBG) – provides information, advice and training to 500 or so groups a year with an annual seminar every September.

'The RGS is the spiritual home of exploration,' says Olly Steeds whose 1999 Xanadu Expedition researched the Silk Road that once stretched from Genghis Khan's capital Karakorum in Central Mongolia 1,400 miles to Yuan Shangdu (Xanadu) in north-east China.

It's a place where reality meets fantasy. I had a dream of making an expedition into the unknown and I knew the RGS was where all the great explorers had gone to plan their expeditions, but I wasn't sure whether it was open to Joe Bloggs! How wrong I was. Without them, my expedition could never have happened.

Shane Winser, Expeditions Adviser at the RGS says:

The key to our supporting expeditions these days is that they are meticulously researched and actually contribute to scientific or exploratory knowledge in some key way. Also it must be of benefit to the host country. We need expeditions which provide a better understanding of our world.

Shane is also increasingly sceptical of a growing trend towards ill-planned stunts posing as expeditions mounted in the full glare of the media spotlight to satisfy commercial sponsors anxious to squeeze every last piece of publicity from the enterprise.

Artificial barriers like walking across a desert when you can go by camel only mimics the achievements of the true explorers who were taking on hardships not just for their own sake but for the purpose of extending mankind's knowledge. Indeed the term expedition is so loosely applied that it is hard to distinguish from an 'adventure journey'. Where there is still purpose it is generally for the enjoyment or growth of the individual or individuals concerned and not for the benefit of either the host country or mankind's knowledge in general.

Alongside the work of scientific and exploratory expeditions supported by the RGS, a number of conservation and community projects are sponsored by youth organizations like Trekforce and Raleigh International. Raleigh runs around 11 expeditions a year working on projects ranging from building schools in Namibia to tracking endangered species in Chile. The projects are all supported by host country government ministries and international development organizations and are designed to continue long after Raleigh's involvement has ceased.

Alongside these organizations are environmental conservation charities whose work is carried out by a mixture of qualified experts and paying volunteers. Among these are Greenforce and Earthwatch who work at the invitation of the host country to assist wildlife conservation schemes and produce survey data for areas of conservation significance. For an increasingly large number of people, paying to make an active contribution to these projects provides an invaluable way of combining a thirst for adventure with the knowledge that something important has been achieved.

Space. The Final Frontier

Few photographs have made such a powerful emotional impact on our lives as the first global image of the Earth from space. Known affectionately as The Blue Marble, it was taken by the crew of Apollo 17 on 17 December 1972 and captures our planet floating like a luminous jewel framed against the inky blackness of space. This iconic image, still NASA's most reproduced photograph, soon came to symbolize a new awareness of our fragile place in the universe.

Since that photograph was taken, more than 400 astronauts have seen for themselves this ultimate view of our home and many have testified to the life-changing qualities of the experience. So far, however, there have been just two space tourists:

the American Denis Tito and the South African Mark Shuttleworth, both of whom spent over £14 million for the privilege of spending five days aboard the International Space Station. But, tantalizingly, holidays in orbit may not be restricted to the super-rich for much longer. Despite setbacks like the Columbia disaster of February 2003, some scientists believe that holidays of a few days spent in orbital hotels may be within the financial reach of as many as a million of us a year by 2020.

So what would the ultimate adventure traveller expect to experience during a holiday in space? Current thinking goes something like this. After take off from a conventional airport in a plane, probably looking a bit like Concorde and powered by conventional jet engines, they would climb into low Earth orbit, around 60 miles high. At this point, rockets would propel the plane into full orbit where it would dock with a space hotel accommodating around 100 guests. Here our space tourists would enjoy mind-blowing views of both the Earth and the planets while dining on hydroponically grown food, playing zero-gravity games, swimming in zero-gravity swimming pools and taking spacewalks.

Not only is the technology for holidays in space well within our grasp, but consumer research from around the world also suggests that there is considerable demand for them. Experts predict that if the cost of a few days in a space hotel could be made available for around £6,000 at today's rates, demand could be as high as 15 million people a year. If these figures are accurate, it could well be that the industry's working model of one million is conservative by comparison.

In an effort to inspire competition and help provide funds to make these dreams a reality, the St Louis-based X-Prize Foundation is offering a $10 million reward for the first privately funded team to develop a craft capable of taking three people to an altitude of 100 km and returning them safely to Earth. To win, the craft must be capable of repeating the feat within two weeks. At the time of writing, 24 teams from five countries have entered.

One of the two British contenders for the X-Prize, Bristol Spaceplanes, is currently developing a sub-orbital spaceplane, the Ascender, which will take two crew and two passengers on a 30-minute flight with two minutes of weightlessness and views of the UK and the curvature of the Earth. Fitted with both conventional jet engines and rockets, Ascender will climb to 9,000 metres (30,000 feet) before firing its rockets and climbing to a maximum height of 100 km. It will then fall back to Earth under the pull of gravity, re-enter the atmosphere, and fly back to the airfield from which it took off.

Already the market for space tourism is being softened up. The leader in the field, the American company Space Adventures, offers tourists the chance to visit the Yuri Gagarin Cosmonaut Training Centre in Star City outside Moscow and take a zero-gravity flight in an adapted Iluyshin-76. The plane climbs to around 10,500 metres (35,000 feet) where it performs a series of climbs and dives to give passengers in a padded cabin about ten episodes of weightlessness lasting 30 seconds each. Alternatively, for around £8,000, you can fly at faster than twice the speed of sound in a MiG-25 climbing to the edge of space and high enough to clearly see the curvature of the Earth.

While holidays in space may be technologically well within our grasp, the huge investment required from private investors and the rigorous demands and potentially massive costs of safety certification make the future uncertain. There is also a battle for hearts and minds to be won with environmentalists who believe that the conventional airline industry is already doing enough damage to the planet without an even more destructive tourist industry in space.

Nonetheless, the dream of holidays in space is unlikely to die. As David Ashdown, leader of the Bristol Spaceplanes bid for the X-Prize, predicts:

The relative number of space flights versus commercial airline flights would be small and on the plus side the cost of environmental studies in space would be cut by a factor of ten to one. Some people argue the massive cost of the Apollo programme was worth it simply for that one photograph of Earth from space that became a symbol for the environmental movement. With a million people a year going into space, that feeling would spread. The environmental balance sheet will be a net benefit.

3
The Adventure Sports Phenomenon

The last two decades have seen a phenomenal growth in the popularity of adventure sports of all kinds: on land, on water and in the air. Advances in technology have pushed forward the boundaries to such a degree that what was impossible only a generation ago is now within the reach of most of us – of either sex and of almost any age – both physically and financially. Magical experiences like exploring a wreck deep under the Indian Ocean, 'mushing' with a team of husky dogs in the Arctic or flying like a bird over the Alps in a paraglider are all options that are today commercially available through adventure tour operators to anyone who is reasonably fit.

While almost all adventure sports can be enjoyed without leaving the country, many are also dependent on the right geographic conditions – diving and climbing being the most obvious examples – and many of the best locations around the world for a favourite activity may well be beyond home shores. Often these are desirable destinations in themselves –

adventure sport Meccas like the Alps or New Zealand's South Island for example – and these days more and more people combine the enjoyment of a favourite sport, or learning a new one, with a holiday exploring the rest of the country or region in question.

Air Sports

Of all the elusive dreams of the human species, few have been so frustratingly long-lived before their ultimate attainment as the dream of flight. And yet in little more than a century, that dream has become commonplace. But while flight itself is no longer the mystery it once was, the desire to fly like the birds using only rising currents of air is as strong as ever. During the last few decades a revolution in non-motorized gliding or 'free flight' has led to a surge of popularity in air sports like hang gliding and paragliding alongside adrenalin-pumping sister sports like skydiving and bungee jumping.

While the age-old dream of flying like the birds found expression in mythical characters from Icarus to Peter Pan and Superman, turning it into reality proved considerably more difficult. Leonardo da Vinci was the first person to understand the principles of the flight of birds and among his many sketches of flying machines are designs for both gliders and parachutes. 'If a man is provided with a length of gummed linen cloth with a length of 12 yards on each side and 12 yards high,' he scribbled in a notebook in 1485 next to a diagram of a primitive parachute, 'he can jump from any great height whatsoever without any injury.'

It would be over 400 years before Leonardo's ideas were put into practice. The first successful glide, on bat-like wings, was made in 1889 by the German, Otto Lillienthal – a flight which ultimately led to the Wright Brothers' historic first flight in December 1903. But with the initial focus on motorized flight, it wasn't until after WWII that gliding and parachuting were taken up as sports in their own right. By the 1970s, the invention of the hang glider meant there was now a portable craft that could be foot-launched from a hill or tow-launched from flat ground. And during the 1980s, research into new types of acrobatic parachute canopies evolved into paragliders which could be inflated by pulling them up into the wind, allowing pilots to soar on rising currents of air. Soaring like a bird over some of the most sublime landscapes on Earth from the Alps to the Andes is an intoxicating thought for many people and has restored much of the sense of excitement of those first pioneering aviators.

The dawn of the age of the paraglider meant that for the cost of a second-hand car, you could be the proud owner of a flying machine that fitted into a rucksack and could be taken anywhere in the world. In flight, it resembled a magical flying armchair suspended from a spider's web of gossamer cords. One of the best ways to get a taste of the thrill of free flying is to sign up for a tandem paragliding flight. Many of the world's most dramatic mountain and coastal locations have commercial operations and allow the complete novice to enjoy the sensations of free flight without needing to worry about the technicalities.

It was in just such a way that my own passion for free flying began. After a maiden flight over the spectacular Lake Wanaka near Queenstown in New Zealand's South Island, I was hooked. Back home again I realized how lucky I was to be living near one of the best flying sites in the UK, the South Downs. Signing up with my local club, I had soon invested in a 'wing' and was itching to fly. My first flight as a newly-qualified Club Pilot, looking down over the South Downs from Chanctonbury Ring in one direction and to the south coast in the other, was a euphoric and memorable experience. At 500 metres high, the only sound disturbing the silence was the soothing hum of the breeze through the Kevlar lines attaching my harness to my paraglider. Only a few months later I was to find myself at 2,500 metres soaring for more than two hours watching the sun set over Lake Annecy in the French Alps.

Free flight sports are among the most awe-inspiring adventure activities yet invented. The knowledge that they are within the grasp of almost everyone, so long as you have the desire and the right mental attitude, will inspire anyone whose gaze has ever drifted up towards to the clouds and wondered what it would be like to be up there all on your own.

As a source for the growing demand for adrenalin, however, few adventure activities can rival bungee jumping for a short, sharp shot of the hard stuff. The pioneering of the sport by the New Zealanders A.J Hackett and Henry Van Asch in the 1980s is a paradigm for the growth of adventure sports travel itself and caught the imagination of the times. The duo had been inspired by the exploits of the tribal farmers of Pentecost Island, Vanuatu, in the South Pacific who throw themselves off wooden towers with vines round their ankles to celebrate a successful yam harvest. Hackett and Van Asch conducted some extensive testing of latex rubber cords which eventually led to a series of extreme jumps from a ski gondola nearly 100 metres above the snow in the ski resort of Tignes in France.

When 'A.J' himself later jumped from the Eiffel Tower and into the international spotlight, the bungee legend was born. The world's first commercial jump site opened on the banks of the Kawarau River near Queenstown, New Zealand – a site which is still seen as the spiritual home of bungee and which is currently being redeveloped to house a museum of the history of the sport. Bungee jumping has since spread all over the world with commercially run jumps taking place from bridges, cranes, cable cars, hot air balloons and even helicopters.

As a veteran of both the Victoria Falls jump and Queenstown's Nevis High Wire showpiece, both with around a 140-metre drop, I can testify to the fact that the location – 'quality jump space' as Hackett calls it – significantly adds to the sense of ritual and drama surrounding the sport. The sense of anticipation, not to say the rising sense of panic, walking on to the bridge at the Victoria Falls and looking down into the chasm of the Zambezi Gorge or taking the glass-bottomed gondola on to the jump platform suspended in the middle of the Nevis Gorge, is guaranteed to turbo-charge the heart.

Steeling yourself for the inevitable is the worst bit. The legs being tied together, the undignified shuffle to the jump platform, the weak pretence at bravado before the big drop. Ask someone who has just made their first bungee jump what it was like and you will find the answer not in their stream of superlatives but in the pupils of their eyes. Thought is banished from the brain as every nerve in the body stands on end. A whirlpool of sensations assaults the stomach. Your eyeballs feel as if they are about to burst out of your skull. It's like a rocket-fuelled combination of sex'n'drugs 'n' rock'n'roll. In fact for those few seconds of pure, terrifying pleasure, it probably beats the lot.

Air Sports – Favourite Worldwide Destinations

Ballooning: Albuquerque, New Mexico, USA; Serengeti National Park, Tanzania; Andalucia, Spain.

Bungee jumping: Queenstown, New Zealand; Bloukrans Bridge, Garden Route, South Africa; Victoria Falls, Zimbabwe.

Gliding: Victoria, New South Wales, Australia; Utah, USA; Andes, South America.

Hang gliding: Kossen, Austria; Owens Valley, California, USA; St André, French Alps.

Paragliding: Olu Deniz, Turkey; Lake Annecy, French Alps; Western Cape, South Africa.

Skydiving: Empuriabrava, Spain; DeLand, Florida, USA; Chinigue, Santiago, Chile.

Water Sports

If humans have finally learnt to fly like the birds, so too have we discovered the key to Davy Jones's locker. After centuries of experimentation with diving bells and primitive diving suits fed with air from the surface, the invention of the aqualung in 1943 by Emile Gagnan and Jacques Cousteau opened the door to a world that had previously existed only in the imagination. Cousteau's pioneering underwater documentaries revealed a world teeming with life and colour. Courtesy of a cylinder of pressurized air and a regulator that delivered air to the diver on demand, scuba diving was born.

Today it has been estimated that as many as a million people a year learn to dive worldwide. A certificate from internationally recognized bodies like PADI (Professional Association of Diving Instructors) or BSAC (British Sub Aqua Club) qualifies the holder to dive anywhere in the world. The sport can be enjoyed everywhere from the warm waters of the Caribbean and the Red Sea – where the colours are intense, the sea life exotic and there are cocktails on hand in the bar afterwards – to more challenging locations like the colder, temperate waters of the UK. Magical underwater environments from wrecks to coral reefs, walls, cave systems, lakes, rivers and even the freezing waters under the Polar ice caps are all now a possibility.

Often the most memorable diving experiences are encounters with sea creatures: watching the dark shadow of an approaching manta ray like an underwater caped crusader; turning somersaults with fur seals; that first heart-stopping encounter with the unblinking stare of a shark. Underwater caverns and caves can also be a revelation. On one dive in a cavern under sea cliffs off the coast of Australia, I felt as if I was flying down the nave of a cathedral on a level with the stained glass windows as shafts of coloured light speared the depths below. Instead of a congregation, strange, ungodly beasts flitted by – a porcupine puffer fish, a feather duster worm and schools of bullseye fish.

These days the range of water-based adventure activity sports has grown exponentially and includes everything from resort sports like windsurfing, water skiing and jet boating to that original classic, surfing. The genesis of the current boom in British surfing can be traced back to the early 1960s when two travelling Aussie lifeguards arrived in Newquay on the shores of north Cornwall with surfboards strapped to the top of an MG. As the sport took off in a big way, the first major international contest was held there in 1984, an event which later developed into the Rip Curl Newquay Boardmasters held annually on Fistral Beach. The Rip Curl has since earned a reputation as a proving ground for hot young talent breaking into the higher echelons of world surfing.

These days you can also rediscover the maritime skills of a bygone era as a deckhand on a new generation of traditional tall ships. The sight of a tall ship under full sail is probably more likely at the beginning of the twenty-first century than at any time since their heyday in the nineteenth century. Many either restored originals or faithful replicas earn their keep in film roles and as adventure training ships. The *Soren Larsen*, on which the famous *Onedin Line* series of the 1970s was filmed, is now based in New Zealand's Auckland Harbour taking passengers on trips around the South Pacific. Helping to crew a tall ship complete with creaking deck, yardarms and moonrakers amid a working laboratory of pulleys, blocks and ropes vividly brings alive the true meaning of the phrase 'learning the ropes' and inspires a profound sense of respect for the men who sailed these ships in the days of fighting sail.

An even older type of vessel has also enjoyed a recent surge in popularity. Kayaks, originally made of sealskin stretched over a wooden frame, started life as Inuit hunting craft in the Arctic, maybe as much as 5,000 years ago. The modern sport was pioneered in the UK and has gained worldwide popularity as modern materials like fibreglass and, more recently, roto-moulded plastic have brought with them the benefits of low cost and durability. The basic skills, enough to ensure safe passage in calm seas, are easy to learn. Kayaks are silent, graceful craft that don't pollute and have a minimal impact on wildlife. Depending on the mood of the sea, lake or river, kayaking can vary from one day feeling as if you are being tossed violently around in the drum of a washing machine to on the next being a sublimely peaceful experience listening to the call of sea birds in the morning mist.

White-water rafting is one of the most popular of group adventure activities. Many travellers have discovered the joys of the sport on the Lower Zambezi River, downriver from the Victoria Falls, being tossed around like rag dolls on rapids dubbed 'The Wall of Death' and 'The Terminator', but of the longer white-water river journeys, the Franklin River in Tasmania – which flows through some of the most dramatic wilderness areas in the southern hemisphere – is one of my favourites. During medium or low water, most of the rapids fall into the category Grade 2 to 4, providing adrenalin-pumping but safe rafting. But during heavy rains the mood of the river can change with alarming speed as water cascades off the saturated buttongrass plains above the gorge. At these times the level can rise by as much as three feet in one hour. When this occurs, some of the rapids in the central section of the Great Ravine are transformed into snarling Grade 6 death-traps with all rafts and equipment having to be carried along the river bank.

Every corner of the 50-odd miles, from the put-in point on the Collingwood River to where the Franklin joins the Gordon River and flows into Macquarie Sound on Tasmania's west coast, reveals some new natural wonder. One of the most memo-rable is a campsite at the bottom of the Great Ravine. 'Rafter's Basin' is the perfect location for a rest day during the ten days it takes to raft the Franklin. It is a boulder-strewn bend in the river which in summer is carpeted with the white buds of flowering tea-tree shrubs. On the far bank, the bleached trunks of fallen trees have been tossed aside by the flood and look like the fossilized skeleton of a mammoth. Overhead, sea eagles often circle in the evening sunshine hitching a lift on a passing thermal. Not for nothing has the Franklin gained a reputation as one of the world's great wilderness destinations.

Water Sports – Favourite Worldwide Destinations

Diving: Cairns, Great Barrier Reef, Australia; Cayman Islands, Caribbean; Red Sea, Egypt.

Kayaking: Sea of Cortéz, Baja, California; Cyclades Islands, Greece; Marlborough Sounds, New Zealand.

Surfing: Queensland, Australia; Bali, Indonesia; California, USA.

White-water rafting: Zambezi River, Zambia; Sun Kosi River, Nepal; Franklin River, Tasmania.

Windsurfing: Maui Island, Hawaii; Canary Islands; Dingle Peninsula, Ireland.

Land Sports

While there has been a revolution in adventure sports on the seas and in the skies, on land the process has been more of an evolution of traditional pursuits like cycling, horse riding and climbing, all of which can now be enjoyed in increasingly remote and challenging terrain throughout the world.

Most dramatically, the evolution of the mountain bike from the traditional touring bike has changed cycling out of all recognition. In the process it has hugely increased the terrain available to the recreational cyclist. Off-road wildernesses from the Lake District to the Himalaya, once the sole domain of the walker and climber, have now been colonized by an alien species on two wheels kitted out in day-glo colours and space-age clothing.

Legendary mountain bike Meccas, from the Slickrock Trail near Moab, Utah – arguably the most famous mountain bike trail in the world – to trails in Africa, the Bolivian Andes and the Kathmandu valley in Nepal, offer sublime and vastly contrasting landscapes. Along with these new classic trails have come a new lexicon of technical terms from 'bunny-hopping' (the art of jumping a bike over bumps or ditches), to 'gnarly' (the type of rough, obstacle-ridden terrain beloved by mountain bikers the world over).

My own love affair with the bicycle started in my early teens when I enthusiastically explored the vast network of rural lanes and byways in my native Cornwall. In my 20s I graduated to a marathon 5,500-km journey across America, followed by a string of shorter journeys across Europe. But it wasn't until the 1990s that I discovered the joys of mountain biking when I joined the inaugural tour of CycleActive, one of a new generation of adventure tour operators which has sprung up to cater for the huge popularity of adventure bike touring.

Our journey across Zimbabwe took us from the capital, Harare, to the Victoria Falls via the jagged quartz lanscapes of the Chimanimani Mountains in the Eastern Highlands to Matopos National Park, the ancient tribal lands of the Matabele people. While political instability means that Zimbabwe is temporarily off-limits, Africa in general is an excellent choice for mountain bike touring. Well-researched routes and a back-up vehicle to ferry you across the less interesting sections mean you can enjoy some of the most remote and beautiful parts of a country without enduring the monotony that sometimes goes with long-distance cycling.

A sense of connection to the land is central to many adventure activities and in no other sport is this more true than horse riding. In many ways it is the original adventure sport, enjoyed millennia before the concept had been thought of, and there's surely no better vantage point than the back of a horse for peeking, both literally and metaphorically, into the back yard of other people's lives. It's also a great way of establishing a bond with the people who live in the more remote corners of our planet, particularly those who still depend on the horse in their day-to-day lives. Never was this more true than on a journey I made into the mountains of the Hindu Kush in the remote North-west Frontier Province of Pakistan. The sound of hooves was the perfect accompaniment to scenes of timeless beauty: women in saris winnowing maize by the river's edge; men guiding ploughs still pulled by oxen; sheaves of corn being harvested with a scythe and gathered by hand.

The challenge of experiencing the extreme environments of wilderness locations through adventure sports of all kinds has also led to a resurgence in the arcane art of 'mushing'. Few sights in nature are as hauntingly beautiful as that look of the frozen midnight in the unblinking gaze of a team of husky dogs. Half dog, half wolf, they stalk the borderlands of the imagination somewhere between cuddly toys and Rottweilers of the ice floes. It was Jack London's 1903 bestseller *The Call of the Wild*, a tale of life in Canada's remote Yukon territory, which first brought husky sledding to the attention of the public. In Jack London's day, mushing was the only means of travel during the winter months. The tale of Buck, a kidnapped ranch pet forced to fight for survival in a team of sled huskies during the Klondike gold rush, still carries enormous power over a century after it was written.

In the 1980s, in an effort to revive the spirit of the early gold seekers, trappers and mail carriers, a race was devised along the isolated backwood trails and mountain passes of the Yukon territory. The Yukon Quest is an epic 1,600-km race run each February between Whitehorse, Yukon, and Fairbanks, Alaska, and is one of the world's most demanding dog-sled races. The emphasis is less on all-out speed, as in the better-known Alaskan Iditarod, but more on bush survival skills and the mutual dependence of man and dog in temperatures that sometimes reach an unimaginable −60 °C.

Surviving the intense cold and the hazardous terrain are not the only problems on a mushing expedition. Irate grizzly bears woken from hibernation are not known for their charm and the cartoon-strip stereotype of the moose is not quite so humorous when the real-life variety has just eviscerated your lead dog. An average of only three hours of sleep every 24 hours also has some strange effects on the mind. It's called being 'in the zone'. Veteran musher hallucinations vary from a dog turning into a musher's naked girlfriend to a stranger sitting cross-legged in a sled basket blowing smoke rings and sipping a can of Coke.

After helping out during the Quest one year as one of the support team to veteran musher Frank Turner, I was rewarded with my own team of dogs on a journey into the wilderness area surrounding Turner's kennels near the town of Whitehorse. Each of our group of five mushers was equipped with a team of six dogs hitched in pairs to a central tug rope. Grappling with skills that were second nature to a trained musher. I gradually discovered how to use the skidoo pad, a foot-operated brake that looked like a doormat with spikes in it. Then there was the all-important snow hook, the only sure way to stop the team leaving you to your fate during pit stops in the wilderness.

Frank had taught me the commands for left (gee) and right (haw) but although for me this was the outer reaches of the known universe, for the dogs it was merely darkness on the edge of the town and it was questionable who was in control of whom. On one occasion, before I discovered that leaning back on the runners made the sled glide better, a corner taken at top speed almost resulted in a catastrophic wipe out. But out of sight of the other teams, I was often alone in the wilderness, the shush of the sled and the panting of the dogs the only sound track to a memorable experience.

One night, alone with my team, I was given a grandstand view of the northern lights, like the live performance of a celestial graffiti artist. First a tulip opened its petals before a genie burst from its lair, swirling and twirling in the freezing night air. The scientific explanation of solar wind striking the outer atmosphere hardly compares with the native Inuit's belief that the lights are their tribal ancestors playing football with walrus skulls. Either way, it sure beat watching TV.

Land Sports - Favourite Worldwide Destinations

Canyonning: French and Italian Alps; Arizona, USA; Blue Mountains, Australia.

Caving: Jura, French Alps; Belize, Central America; Waitomo, New Zealand.

Cycle touring: Garden Route, South Africa; North and South Island, New Zealand; Swiss Alps.

Dog sledding: Okavango Delta, Botswana; Torres del Paine National Park, Chile; Karakoram and Hindu Kush, Pakistan.

Mountain biking: Moab, Utah, USA; Haute Savoie, France; Kathmandu Valley, Nepal.

Rock climbing: Chamonix, France; Yosemite Park, California, USA; Romsdal, Norway.

Ski touring: Haute Route, Chamonix-Zermatt; Canadian Rockies; Mount Cook, New Zealand.

4

The Five Ages of Adventure Travel

The Short-break Traveller

While some may argue that only 'independent' travel can be described as genuinely adventurous, many more of us are delighted that travel destinations from the Sahara to Alaska are now a possibility for a two- or three-week break away from the pressures of office life. In the not-so-distant past, the organization and planning required to travel to remote locations like the Amazon or Mongolia would not have been possible, or desirable, in so short a time frame. Cheaper airfares, combined with an increasingly knowledgeable and adventurous travelling public, has resulted in a huge growth of short-break group travel to a wide range of countries well beyond the traditional list of tourist destinations.

The logistical organization of journeys into rainforests, up rivers or over mountain ranges can now all be pre-arranged, pre-booked and pre-paid. A glance through the AITO (Association of Independent Tour Operators) Holiday Directory reveals around 100 companies whose offerings could broadly be described as 'adventure travel', all cross-referenced by destination and activity. You can now choose between a range of activities and destinations as well as more luxurious alternatives when, at a price, you can rough it during the day in the knowledge that your creature comforts will be well taken care of at night.

The Daily Telegraph Adventure Travel & Sports Show every January at London's Olympia is an annual litmus test of the state of the adventure travel market. The show has grown from 30 exhibitors with 5,000 visitors in 1995 when it was first launched to more than 250 exhibitors and 30,000 visitors today and has recently launched a second annual venue in Manchester.

The shows's organizer and creator, Martin Anslow, says:

> I had become increasingly frustrated at trying to find information on the type of holidays I was interested in and there was clearly a growing demand for adventure holidays so I decided to solve the problem myself and bring everyone in the industry together under one roof. Many of the visitors who come to the show are simply looking for adventurous holiday ideas but people are also inspired by adventure in general and what may be possible for them during time off of any duration. That's why our programme of talks is always so popular. I also think that in the past this sort of travel was largely restricted to young people with well-off parents but adventure travel is open to everyone these days.

The number of people taking short-break adventure holidays each year is notoriously hard to estimate, largely due to the difficulty of defining exactly which types of holiday fall into the category of 'adventure travel'. Industry estimates, however, suggest that around 150,000 people in the UK take an adventure holiday each year. Simon Tobin, chairman of Explore Worldwide, the largest adventure travel operator in the UK, says that before the 11 September attack, the number of people taking adventure breaks was growing by around 15 per cent a year. But even though this figure may have dropped in the short term, the market has demonstrated great resilience and is still growing by around 5 per cent.

The type of people who want to go on an adventure holiday is also changing, says Tobin:

> As well as many more women who don't want to travel alone but are happy to travel solo as part of an organized group, we are also seeing many more people over 50 who are curious about a world which up until now they have been unable to explore due to either work or family commitments.

Paul Goldstein of Exodus Travel emphasizes the importance of operators demonstrating ethical environmental credentials.

> People are increasingly concerned that the holidays they choose fall under the 'sustainable tourism' banner. Many of the 78 countries Exodus travels to are in the developing world and low-impact tourism where the hosts benefit rather than international hotel chains is the style they are after. If it is not sustainable, be it in Nepal, Peru, Tanzania or Tibet, it is not viable for either us or them. There is an old African proverb that says: 'This country was not given to you by your parents, it was loaned to you by your children.'

Even with only a few precious weeks off a year, it seems that more and more of us are happy to rough it on holiday experimenting with life outside our usual 'comfort zone' in the search for a genuinely challenging and exciting experience. On one such occasion I found myself kayaking down a crocodile-infested river in Australia's Northern Territory. Our guide Martin Wohling, aka Snowy, runs a river safari operation in the town of Katherine close to some of Australia's most dramatic wilderness areas including Kakadu and Arnhem Land.

'I get all types', Snowy confided one evening as we sat mesmerized by the flames of our 'bush TV':

> Everyone from highly stressed couples trying to put their marriages back together to day-trippers who only want to party. For me it's fine either way, but I prefer to take people where they've never been before both physically and mentally. People usually respond to the challenge and often tell me their lives have changed after a few days on the river. No longer being number one in the food chain does extraordinary things to people's heads.

If an adventure holiday can be said to achieve anything, doing 'extraordinary things to people's heads' is probably as good a description as any I've yet heard.

The Charity Challenger

'Why exactly am I doing this?' It's a thought that passes through many an adventurer's mind at some time or another. The knowledge that many potentially dangerous situations are self-inflicted only serves to heighten the sense of exasperation. The last time I was afflicted with similar misgivings, however, my resolve was strengthened by the knowledge that, this time at least, altruism was at the root of my predicament. Expertly trussed in a climbing harness with ropes, clasps and caribiners attached, I was about to attempt my first ever abseil.

The location was a cliff face in Wadi Rum, Jordan's spectacular desert wilderness, and the event was part of a three-day fundraising charity challenge in aid of young people from the UK's most deprived inner cities. Competitors, who each had to raise £2,000 in sponsorship, were grouped in teams of four. During the previous 48 hours we had completed a gruelling 30-mile mountain bike ride, a treasure hunt through the ancient cave city of Petra, a 4WD desert drive and a night-orienteering exercise crossing 200-foot sand dunes. Not to mention expert tuition in the ancient Bedu art of goat slaughtering.

Charity fundraising by means of adventure challenges is big business these days. As many as 15,000 people a year from the UK take part and the charities themselves see them as a reliable, if not spectacular, form of fundraising. They are also seen as a useful form of PR and galvanize efforts from a younger sector of the population than is traditionally involved in fundraising.

While some people pay for the cost of the travel themselves – plane ticket, food, accommodation, etc. – this is usually deducted from the sponsorship money raised. If you fail to raise the sponsorship target (typically £2,000 with a £200 registration fee), you will usually be asked to make up the difference out of your own pocket. When the bottom line is finally calculated, only around 50 per cent of the original sponsorship money donated will have made it into the coffers of the charity concerned.

Charity challenges often favour exotic, long-haul locations, their destinations reading like a 'Where's Where?' of adventure travel. On the day I am writing this, for example, a national newspaper has an ad for a children's charity splashed across the front page urging readers to: 'Make a Difference. Trek the Great Wall or the Inca Trail. Bike across Cuba or Iceland. Climb Mount Kilimanjaro or the Himalayas. Kayak the Costa Rican Coast or ride on horseback across Mongolia.'

The choice of locations and activities such as these testifies as much to the lure of an exotic location as to the particular charitable cause itself. Few would argue that this matters if the final result is the same. In the past, however, the main complaint of critics has been that sponsors did not realize that 50 per cent of their contribution to a charitable cause was being spent on sending the challenger on what many would describe as a holiday. After all, adventure travellers pay good money to ride bicycles across Cuba, so why shouldn't the charity challenger?

More recently, these criticisms have been diluted by a general familiarity with the concept and most people are now fully aware that they are also paying for their challenger's exotic foreign trip but are still happy to go ahead with their sponsorship. The charities themselves are keen to emphasize that their challenges are no push-over, often requiring considerable training – and volunteering of free time – beforehand.

A more potent criticism, perhaps, is the charge that the host country itself often reaps little benefit from the challenge. In response, some charities now make donations to causes within the host country and the Institute of Charity Fundraising Managers (ICFM) has introduced guidelines of maximum group sizes and desired objectives while in the host country.

Charity challenges do not end when the challengers arrive home, however. Having reached terra firma in one piece after my abseiling adventure, my last evening was spent with my fellow competitors sipping cocktails next to a swimming pool at a local restaurant. 'You mustn't let on we had such a great time,' pleaded one. 'After all we did sweat blood and raising the sponsorship pledges was hard work. Actually squeezing the money out of the b****** is going to be harder still.'

The Gap Year

For the 40,000 or so school leavers who every year go on to higher education, the gap year has become an unmissable rite of passage. A well-spent gap year has become a certificate of admission to adult life bringing with it not only the exhilaration of freedom from parental control but also the sense of self-reliance necessary to look after yourself in a sometimes dangerous world.

For the vast majority, the very act of travelling abroad, solo or with friends, is an adventure in itself. There is certainly no shortage of possibilities. These days a whole sub-sector of the travel industry has grown up around the gap year. The options available to school leavers that both want, and need, to work as well as travel during their year off are also huge. The choice of voluntary placements from conservation to teaching or helping in the building and running of schools and hospitals in the Third World has now expanded to more than 900 volunteer organizations operating in more than 200 countries.

Lucy Scott, who went on to study at Liverpool University, started her gap year working for Raleigh International in Costa Rica and Nicaragua for three months.

I particularly valued staying and working among an indigenous tribe in Costa Rica. The simplest and most basic needs that we would take for granted are so gratefully received and you can gain so much more from each situation if you can learn to relate to each other as equals.

Afterwards I was keen to visit neighbouring countries and similar hospitable people. So I decided to travel throughout Central America for two months starting in Costa Rica and travelling up to Mexico via Nicaragua, Honduras, Guatemala and Belize. Central America is incredibly cheap and easy to travel around using public buses – the so-called 'chicken buses' – and it's a perfect spot to learn to scuba dive as Honduras has the cheapest diving in the world. From Mexico I flew to Peru and spent two months travelling around Peru and Bolivia.

I interpret adventure travel as unusual, perhaps rather bizarre, maybe even scary experiences that are incredibly exciting. Although skydiving was both exciting and scary, I personally wouldn't say it was adventurous. I trekked in Nicaragua's jungle for a month which was physically, and mentally, incredibly challenging. I found this particularly adventurous as it was unchartered territory and a unique experience and there was always the uncertainty of not knowing what was coming next.

I also spent the night in a Mayan temple at Tikal in Guatemala surrounded by howler monkeys and a jungle full of rebel soldiers so I could watch the sun rise over the jungle. The scariest moment was probably riding for seven hours on a mountain bike 3,500 metres down 'the most dangerous road in the world' in Bolivia with a sheer drop all the way down. We started just outside La Paz speeding in snow and ice and saw where two cars had plummeted off the edge only hours earlier.

My motivation for these sort of adventurous experiences is the knowledge that however gruelling or tiresome it can be at times, you always know that in the long run you'll be pleased you did it and it will have been worth it. The great moments will always outweigh the bad and will be the ones that are remembered forever. To know that you accomplished what seemed a mere impossibility will give you such strength and belief in the future to try similar things again.

Lucy Macfadyen, who later studied at Edinburgh University, also remembers her gap year for its many adventures:

I didn't do any sort of work while I was abroad but I certainly had a lot of fun. I was travelling with a friend and we bought a round-the-world ticket and left in January and were away for five months travelling via Hong Kong, Bali, Australia, New Zealand, San Francisco and New York.

Our primary aim was to get to Australia where we spent three months and the other places seemed like good places to stop off en route. I like adrenalin and we did a lot of adventurous things including skydiving, bungee jumping, white-water rafting, sailing round the Whitsunday Islands and driving jeeps on Fraser Island, the largest sand island in the world off the east coast. In Australia these kinds of adventure sports are advertised everywhere, everyone was doing them and they were a lot of fun.

Although most of the time we were pretty much on the usual gap year trail, we did stay with some relatives of mine who live on an enormous sheep farm in Victoria in the middle of nowhere. This was just as exciting as doing the whole skydiving thing as we were doing things that were part of their everyday life but totally alien to us. For example when we arrived, they challenged the two of us to round up 500 sheep and take them six miles across the property on motorbikes. It appeals to me to try out things like that which are just so far away from my normal way of life and you don't always get that on the tourist trail.

The Career Break

These days more of us than ever before are taking extended breaks at some time in our careers. These range from a few months to a year or more and usually involve negotiating time off – or even leaving a job for good – and go well beyond, both in terms of time and scope, a traditional annual holiday. While the reason for wanting to take time off ranges from a desire to see more of the world to a need to reassess the direction in which your life is going, the ingredient of adventure is an increasingly important component.

Tom Griffiths – editor of the website www.gapyear.com – believes that the career break is in fact just another form of gap year, albeit at a different stage of the life cycle.

Young people are now heading into a life of portfolio careers and taking time out is seen as a positive, not a negative thing. Life is a series of gaps. Pre-university gaps, during- and post-university gaps, career gaps (the fastest-growing gap year market), pre- and post-baby gaps, stag and hen gaps, post-wedding gaps, pre-retirement gaps, the list goes on. The result will be a change in the mentality of society, away from the 'live to work, work to live' routine of a slow climb up a career ladder and forward to a more exciting life path which simply involves doing what you enjoy in life and achieving that dream. Life is short. Why waste your time doing things you don't enjoy?

Rosie Walford, who studied experimental psychology at university and has worked as a business consultant in creative problem-solving and creative leadership, believes a break from a career in which there is a significant element of adventure can help bring fresh perspectives to your personal life as well as clarifying the future direction of a career.

Being in a big landscape or involved in an adventure activity is deeply beneficial to people who are at a turning point. I know from the breaks I have taken in my own career that setting aside established patterns and challenging oneself both mentally and physically can be enormously productive.

Rosie's experiences inspired her to set up The Big Stretch (www.thebigstretch.com), a travel company which helps people to reassess their lives holistically and come up with their own new creative solutions in the context of an adventure break.

Getting out into nature while focussing on a repetitive activity like walking or kayaking can trigger the brain into what is known as an alpha state. This is when the subconscious becomes more available to the conscious mind and throws up innovative solutions to problems. Being physically on the edge can also put you more in tune with your emotional signals that in turn help you access your intuition back in everyday life. All this can be combined with some big-picture thinking so the whole process can be lastingly creative.

After herself gaining important new perspectives from Rosie's methods, Marina Royles, who had worked for 20 years for a graphic art and stationery retailer in London's Covent Garden, decided that it was time to take a break from her normal routine and negotiated a three-month sabbatical with her fellow directors.

I chose to concentrate on SE Asia. In Borneo I climbed Mount Kinabalu and then spent some time helping the local village people of Kiao with their English to help them keep their jobs as mountain guides. In southern Thailand I discovered a new-found passion in diving before heading on to Vietnam. I went from Hanoi in the north up to the hill tribes in Sapa and then followed the Mekong south to Saigon. I then started a trip in conjunction with Oxfam to Laos. We visited lots of local NGOs [Non-Government Organisations] and saw the work of one group trying to clear undetonated bombs and the effect they have had on the local community. We also spent time with an elephant charity and visited the local hospital for sick, abused and distressed elephants along with those that have been victims of land mines.

The adventure part was very much the reason I chose this style of trip and the places I visited. I purposely visited countries where there would be language barriers and the culture was totally different to my own. It was an important learning curve for me to be able to feel and live like this, one of those rare moments when you understand for yourself what it must have been like in medieval times. I went back to my old job with a fresh pair of eyes and with a very different outlook on the world. The whole experience enriched my life and I now know what hardship is about and it certainly made me appreciate how easy my life back home is in comparison.

Inclusive Adventure

There are few more potent barriers to travel than physical inca-
pacity. Able-bodied readers need only recall the last time they
were sea sick or badly twisted an ankle on holiday to realize
the truth of this statement. But few travellers' tales are more
inspirational than those of severely disabled adventurers – para-
plegics and tetraplegics with no use of their limbs – who have
achieved the seemingly impossible. Proof positive of the power
of the mind over matter.

Take Erik Weihenmayer, for example. Despite losing his sight
at the age of 13, Erik has become one of the most celebrated
and accomplished athletes in the world and in the process rede-
fined what it means to be blind. He was the first blind climber
in history to reach the summit of Mount Everest and later
became one of fewer than 100 people to climb the Seven
Summits – the highest peaks on each of the seven continents.
Then there is Trevor Jones. Trevor was paralysed from the neck
down in a skiing accident but, with adventure in his blood, he
was determined to learn to sail and fly independently. After first
converting a microlight, he then built the first yacht ever for
tetraplegic control and completed a circumnavigation of the UK
and Ireland in the Around Britain Challenge.

Just as remarkable are the disabled adventurers who decided
to take up the challenge of Robin Dunseath, a modern-day
Phileas Fogg. Robin suffers from a heart condition but nonetheless devised an 'Around the World in 80 Ways' challenge in
which 80 different forms of transport were used to circum-
navigate the globe in three months. The intention of the challenge
was to demonstrate the power of disabled adventurers to make
light of their physical challenges and lead full lives despite their
disabilities.

Miles Hilton-Barber, Mike Mackenzie and Caroline Casey
took up the challenge and decided to join Robin on his journey.
Miles, who is blind, had previously competed in the 240 km

Sahara Ultra-Marathon and the Siberian Ice Marathon as well as man-hauling a sledge over 400 kilometres across Antarctica. Mike Mackenzie was injured during the war in Bosnia while working for an aid agency and is paralyzed from the waist down. He now counsels newly injured people and their families and formed the consortium of spinal charities known as SIT – Spinal Injuries Together. Caroline, who is also registered blind, had trekked 1,000 kilometres across southern India on the back of her elephant, Kanchi, raising £250,000 for charity in the process.

Their epic three months of travelling around the world resulted in some extraordinary situations, as Mike recalls:

> The most scary experience for me was riding camels in South Africa. As I have no use of my stomach muscles to help me balance, I didn't think I could stay on the camel's back for very long, but somehow I survived it. We also crash landed a hot air balloon in the desert outside of Las Vegas. The balloon was caught by the wind, bounced and dragged a long way along the ground and resulted in broken ribs and toes among some of our able-bodied team members.

And the most unusual experience?

> It has to be when Miles was pushing me in my wheel-chair along the bottom of the Red Sea, 12 metres under-water. I didn't fancy exposing the mechanics of my own wheelchair to the Red Sea and so managed to borrow one from a hotel – of course they didn't know we were going underwater. It was also quite bizarre riding a Santa's sleigh through the centre of Edinburgh with carols blaring out in early September. Not to mention paddling a cardboard boat down the River Liffey in Dublin.

For Robin, the adventure was a triumph.

> We actually used over 100 different methods of transport, made over 90 speeches to disabled and other challenged groups and raised some £500,000 for charities around the

world – and that included buying 500 artificial legs for the people of Thailand.

Miles, an inspirational public speaker, says the journey has a message for all of us, able and disabled:

You may not be able to change your circumstances in life but you certainly can change your response to your circumstances. Focus on your opportunities in life, not your limitations.

5
Five Classic Adventure Destinations

The Amazon

Matt Bannerman

An Amazon riverboat is a good place for a long argument. In a huge region whose rivers are its roads, these boats are the equivalent of Greyhound buses: on board it is stuffy and cramped; beyond the rail is an empty, unchanging panorama of brown water and green jungle. On the long, lonely reaches between sparse settlements, once you have finished your novel and written your postcards, there is little else to do but pick a fight with your neighbour.

On one such journey I slung my hammock next to a Brazilian biologist and disputed for 72 hours the proposition that the Amazon was an adventurous place to travel. He was from the south of the country and had travelled widely around his continent and beyond: the high Andes, Patagonia and the Australian outback. Debate was leisurely as the river slipped by, punctuated by long siestas and the occasional sighting of sloths.

My arguments were based on romance and history: what could be more daring than Francisco Orellana's 1539 descent of the river in two home-made boats, or Baron Alexander von Humboldt's discovery of the Casiquiare canal linking the Amazon and the Orinoco, or even Colonel Fawcett's mysterious disappearance in the far south of the basin, hunting for lost cities?

'I'm not impressed by dead Europeans,' said my new friend and fell asleep. The next morning it was raining, the near bank barely visible through the grey curtain of falling water, and the biologist had marshalled some arguments of his own. 'Look, the country is as flat as a billiard table for hundreds of miles. It's never cold or really hot like the desert. If you eat fish you'll never be hungry, and there's really very little out there inclined to eat you. I just don't see what the fuss is about.' For an hour we watched the rain hosing down, dimpling the surface of the river like beaten bronze. 'Oh yes,' he added at last, 'and you are never, ever short of water.'

I had to concede that he had a point. For those eager to test themselves against extremes of climate or topography, other parts of the world, many of them covered in these pages, offer a stiffer examination. Yet ever since the early explorers reported a 'sweetwater sea' in the newly discovered continent of South America, the river and its forests have fired the imaginations of travellers from around the world, and every day the new clutch of backpacks circling the carousel at Manaus airport, the hub city of the Amazon, shows that its magnetic pull is undiminished. If the biologist was right, then why is it that, in the twenty-first as in the sixteenth century, in New Zealand as much as Norway, the Amazon remains virtually synonymous with adventurous travel?

As with much in Amazonia, the answer has to do with all that water. At this point it is traditional to parade the statistics, the vast quantities of rainfall and discharge that crown the Amazon as the greatest of the world's rivers: the figures are impressive and everyone has their favourite example. But in truth, you cannot appreciate just how much water is in the Amazon until you are on it. Until you have been fired through a gorge by the power of a tiny tributary; or drifted imperceptibly down the middle of a reach so broad that you cannot see either bank; or seen massive tree trunks floating in freshwater a hundred miles out to sea.

Sooner or later every traveller to the Amazon realizes that here the balance of the elements has shifted, that they have entered a world of water. For me it was when passing through a village during the annual flood. I met a man taking grass from a floating meadow to the floating raft on which he kept his floating cattle. His vegetables grew in a floating garden, his family waved from a floating house, his dog barked from a floating kennel. There was no dry land, he blithely informed me, for 30 miles.

For the adventurous traveller, all this water has several important implications. High up on the edge of the basin, in Peru and Bolivia, Amazon tributaries offer some of the best high category white-water rafting in the world. Inspired by Orellana, a handful of eccentrics continue downstream, 'running the Amazon' from source to mouth in a variety of unusual conveyances including a giant inflatable sausage and a surfboard. Below the rapids, the risks change. There, as Paul Cripps of Amazonas Explorer, a leading rafting operator, puts it: 'they either die of boredom or are run over by a cargo ship.'

The Amazon and the flooded forests that adjoin it are a fantastically productive fishery and the main source of protein for the urban centres of the region. But beyond the reach of the commerical boats, to the far north or south of the basin, some superb sport fishing can be found. Hiking to a remote stream, stumbling after an Amerindian ghillie, to cast a line for the spectacular peacock bass or a man-sized catfish, is a different order of experience from watching a float in a canal back home.

Most of all, however, it is the water that makes the wilderness. Apart from the disastrous Trans-Amazonica highway, whose cavernous ruts are the preserve of Camel Trophy Land Rovers and the occasional courageous cyclist, the Amazon, its rains and its rivers, have defeated the road-builders. Once the tarmac gives out at the edge of the cities, you walk or you float. The hammock-hung riverboats are a popular option for travelling from town to town, but the real workhorse of the Amazon is the canoe. Planked or dug-out, high-powered outboard or tear-drop paddle; they are used for anything and everything, especially during the wet season. Then, for the people of the flood plain at least, any activity that takes place outside the house, be it fishing, gardening, bathing or visiting, takes place in the canoe.

Rising early one morning during a stay at a flooded community on the Upper Amazon, I followed two men as they paddled their dugout away from the houses and into the mist-hung forest. Hoping for a sacred ritual or some traditional food gathering, I was taken aback when in perfect harmony they dropped their paddles and their shorts, shifted their behinds over opposite gunwales and took their ease with a companionable and synchronized grunt.

Such feats of balance are not for the beginner: even for experienced kayakers the Amazon canoe demands practice. Not least amongst the rewards is the superb platform being afloat offers for viewing wildlife. As with the Amazon water cycle, the reality of its flora and fauna can seem very different to the hype. I knew when I arrived that this is by far the largest and least disturbed area of tropical rainforest on Earth; I knew that this is the planet's most biodiverse ecosystem. What I learnt on my first walk in the forest, a sweaty, uncomfortable and frustrating few hours near the mouth of the Japurá, was that diverse does not mean abundant, and that the only animals present in any quantity were blood-sucking insects.

You are not immune from mosquitoes in a canoe, but you can move silently, approach more closely, and, in the areas where the river enters the forest in the flood season, float along barely beneath the canopy. Amazon wildlife often becomes more visible and demonstrative near to water. On our way back to camp after that first disappointing trek, a dozen pairs of scarlet macaws crossed the river from feeding grounds to roosting trees. Later, in the last of the light, a series of plosive 'huffs' betrayed a family of lipstick-pink river dolphins hunting close by. In the chilly dawn we woke to two rival groups of howler monkeys wailing at each other across the river that marked the frontier of their respective territories, like a hundred children swinging on a hundred rusty gates.

But what of the dangers? The vampire bat, the anaconda, the voracious piranha and that little fish that swims up your wee? The truth is that in the rainforest a mild discomfort rather than imminent death is the order of the day. You will be extremely lucky to glimpse a jaguar, let alone be despatched by one in the traditional head-bite. If an anaconda allows you to see it, it is probably digesting its weekly meal and seeking only peace for its siesta. Piranha are ever-present and rarely a concern: bored children pull in dozens of them with tiny hooks and chicken skin, and then dive in themselves with howls of delight. Vampire bats prefer cattle, giant catfish prefer the depths of the river, electric eels prefer not to waste their charge.

There are, of course, exceptions. The stingray likes to bury itself in shallow water just off sandy river beaches and is often trodden on, with spectacularly painful results: if you must wade, use boots or follow someone else. And whilst the vast majority of Amazon snakes are harmless and beautiful, two in particular are highly venomous. Any expedition travelling far from medical help should be appropriately equipped. But most of the Amazon fauna is far less fearsome than its reputation. In an absent-minded moment I have driven a canoe over a large black cayman, much to both of our surprise but to no one's especial danger. There is a fish called a candiru which lives a parasitic life under the gill covers of the larger catfish: if it is inclined to leap salmon-like up the weir of your urine then the local people have never been told of it, as they pee in the river with impunity.

Emerging from the jungle at the end of an arduous trek, it is as well to remind yourself that someone has doubtless been there before you, and probably without the benefit of insect repellent. People have survived in the Amazon forests for the best part of 15,000 years: not the fierce female warriors of the original Amazon myth but a rich variety of indigenous cultures that the first ethnologists began to appreciate only as they were disappearing, driven back by disease, slavery and waves of settlers. Despite some level of protection, the process continues today in the form of wildcat mining, military expansionism and land speculation. If any uncontacted tribes remain in the most inaccessible comers of the Amazon, we can only hope they keep their heads down.

The situation is not entirely gloomy, however. The people of mixed ancestry who now populate the main rivers and tributaries have a fascinating and vibrant culture of their own, and make exceptional guides, their intuitive understanding of the forest and its inhabitants overlaid with a lively mythology in which dolphins come ashore to seduce unwary girls and wild ape-men roam the woods with backward pointing feet.

And there are even signs of rapprochement between newly confident indigenous peoples and the authorities. Three years ago I stood on the beach at São Gabriel of the Waterfalls, far up the Rio Negro, listening to the roar of the rapids and watching two groups of young men from the Tukano tribe and the Brazilian Army contest the inaugural World Blowpipe Championships. Competition was intense but good-humoured, the Tukano won in a sudden death 'puff-off', and everyone had a good laugh when the gringo's dart plopped feebly into the sand.

I can hear my friend the biologist scoff, and indeed for the true adrenalin addict many of the Amazon's pleasures can seem a little esoteric. True, you can dive in the inky water of the Rio Negro, you can BASE jump from Venezuelan *tepuis*, you can even surf the Pororóca tide-race at the river's mouth, but then you can do all of this cheaper, safer and better elsewhere. Those like me who return to Amazonia are drawn by its wild water, its wildlife, its irrepressible people and most of all by its endless capacity to surprise us. Incidentally, after protracted negotiations I brought that blowpipe home in a 12-foot length of plastic drainpipe and am currently training for a surprise challenge in the next Championships by skewering my partner's soft toys with curare-tipped darts when she's not looking. *Hasta la vista*, Piglet!

Matt Bannerman is a freelance travel writer and photographer who has worked in Africa, Latin America and the Middle East.

African Safaris
Brian Jackman

When Calvin Cottar meets his guests in Kenya's Masai Mara game reserve, he still conveys them to his safari camp in a wooden-bodied 1920s Rolls Royce hunting car. Cottar is a fourth-generation Kenyan whose great-grandfather, Charles Cottar, came out from Iowa in 1911 to become Kenya's first professional white hunter. He died aged 67, killed by a rhino, but not before he had set up the oldest-established safari outfitters in Africa.

The Cottars were also the first to use vehicles on safari – hence the continued presence of the vintage Rolls at their 1920s-style luxury camp. Here Calvin and Louise, his wife, set out to recreate the glamour of that bygone era with candlelight dinners at which waiters dressed in full-length Swahili kanzus offer a silver service of curried guinea fowl and roast eland.

But with the mess tent and its zebra-skin rugs and wind-up gramophone, all resemblance with the 1920s ends. In those far-off days when it took forever to reach the bush, clients came to hunt the 'Big Five' – elephant, buffalo, rhino, lion and leopard. Nowadays you shoot them with a camcorder and can fly from London to Nairobi in under eight hours and be in camp before lunch. And although the Cottars still keep their beloved old Roller for fun, their other safari vehicles are state-of-the-art, go-anywhere Land Rovers.

Africa, too, has changed utterly. Everywhere, from Kenya to the Cape, its people have won their independence and the hunting grounds where privileged colonials once bagged their buffalo-head trophies are now protected parks and sanctuaries. Most people, hooked by cult movies such as *Out of Africa* or by TV wildlife documentaries like the BBC's long-running *Big Cat Diary* series, go on safari to see wild animals in safety and experience wilderness in comfort – with perhaps just enough of the frisson that comes from close encounters with such charismatic creatures as lions and elephants.

So where do you go? Which countries? Which parks? Which safari lodges or tented camps? The choices, like Africa itself, are endless. But when planning a safari, as when buying a house, one consideration overrides all others: location, location. The problem is not so much knowing which are the best locations: it's choosing between them.

Recently I set off on a mobile camping safari across the Serengeti Plains in northern Tanzania. No road lay before us; not so much as a tyre track; a boundless steppe in which lions rose from the grass to stare at us and herds of wildebeest shrank aside to let us pass, then closed behind us like a tide. On we drove, among sweeping cloud shadows in which giraffe stood out like markers, measuring the distance between us and the horizon. Surely, I thought, these rolling grasslands must be the most beautiful place on Earth?

And yet, only a couple of summers ago, paddling through the Linyanti Swamps in a fibreglass canoe, I had felt just the same about Botswana. All along the Linyanti River the night lilies were closing to conserve their scent, and the day lilies just opening. Bee-eaters balanced on swaying reed stems. From the ebony trees on the bank rose the chanting of Cape turtle doves. 'Work-harder, work-harder,' they sang, over and over in the clear dawn light. And in a cove among the trees, a solitary bull elephant with broken tusks was drinking at the water's edge. This, too, was as good as it gets.

Accommodation is a more subjective choice. Safari chic or no-frills bush camp? Both have their devotees. Over the years, responding to the demands of American clients, tented camps have become increasingly more luxurious. It's a trend that began in Botswana and has now spread north all the way to Kenya, where private lodges such as Loisaba and Ol Malo on the Laikipia Plateau provide all the comforts of a five-star hotel.

Someone once said that to go on safari you must sleep under canvas, and that if you stayed in a lodge you were only on holiday. This is no longer true, especially at places like Elsa's Kopje in Meru National Park, whose individual cottage rooms are open to the four winds. But it emphasizes the magic of getting closer to the wild. And sleeping under canvas enables you to hear the lions when they roar before dawn – the most thrilling sound in Africa – without ever compromising your safety.

Camping doesn't come much swankier than at Mombo, Wilderness Safaris' flagship property in the Okavango Delta, where the tents are on decks raised on solid wooden pillars. Did I say tents? Mine was more like a full-blown marquee, with a four-poster bed and air-conditioning and an outdoor shower under which I could cool off in total privacy – except for the disinterested gaze of wandering antelope and buffalo herds. But the point about Mombo is that its biggest luxury has nothing to do with air-conditioning or his-and-her wash-basins. What counts most is the quality of its game-viewing, with more than eighty lions within a morning's drive, and almost daily leopard sightings.

But if you are looking for a more authentic, down-to-earth safari experience, then look no further than Zambia, where Norman Carr, the legendary Luangwa Valley game warden, reinvented walking safaris in the 1970s. The idea caught on and can now be enjoyed in many other parts of Africa, notably in the vast Selous game reserve in southern Tanzania. But the

Luangwa is still the finest place in which to travel on foot and brush up your bushcraft with an armed scout and an experienced guide such as Robin Pope, whose tented camp, Tena Tena, is generally acknowledged as the best in the South Luangwa national park.

Alternatively, for a true back-to-nature experience, you could fly to Kutandala, Rod and Guz Tether's remote bush camp in the North Luangwa national park. Kutandala means 'to make a journey', and is owned by Rod and has just three grass huts on the banks of the crystal-clear Mwaleshi River. The dining room is simply a shady Natal mahogany tree; and yet even here amidst such simplicity there's no escaping the essential comforts of safari life, since Guz is a brilliant chef trained in the arts of haute cuisine.

Remoteness is a quality that is everywhere becoming harder to find but there are still a few boltholes like Kutandala where it feels as if you have the whole of Africa to yourself. Kitich is such a place, hidden deep in the Matthews Mountains of northern Kenya. So is Serra Cafema Camp on the Kunene River in Namibia, with Angola on the opposite bank and nothing behind you but the stony thirstlands of the Hartmann's Mountains. Combined with a fly-in safari up the Skeleton Coast, it is hard to imagine a more away-from-it-all experience. Unless, that is, you head for Katavi national park in Western Tanzania which clocks up fewer than 250 visitors a year and yet is heaving with lions, elephants and buffalo herds up to 3,000 strong. Chada camp is almost the only place at which to stay, a four-hour flight from Dar es Salaam; but it's run by Roland Purcell, one of Tanzania's top guides.

Choosing a knowledgeable guide can make all the difference to your safari. Usually this means booking a mobile safari on an individual basis – perhaps two couples or enough people to comfortably fill a Toyota Land Cruiser – and is therefore an expensive option. But with it comes the freedom to go where you wish and spend as long as you want watching birds or big cats to your heart's content.

At the more rugged end of the safari spectrum are adventures with a single purpose, such as climbing Mount Kilimanjaro. At 5,896 metres, Kilimanjaro's Uhuru Peak is the highest point in Africa, and getting there usually involves a three-day endurance test with the risk of mountain sickness thrown in. But the reward – apart from the sheer sense of achievement – is the view across the plains of Amboseli National Park, thousands of metres below, to infinity and beyond.

On other safaris, no less adventurous in their own right, the journey itself takes precedence over the wildlife. Travelling on horseback through the Okavango is an exhilarating way to encounter wild Africa but you must be an experienced rider. On the other hand, no lessons are required for a camel safari. The camels are led by a man with a rope and never move faster than walking pace, eating up the miles with an effortless soft-shoe shuffle. All you have to do is clamber aboard and cling on to the saddle as the animal lurches to its feet with an alarming fore-and-aft heave. A private lodge called Sabuk on Kenya's Laikipia Plateau is the place to go, and from here on it becomes pure fantasy – Lawrence of Arabia meets East Africa – as your caravanserai files through the bush to the accompaniment of wooden camel bells.

Three times I have made camel safaris across northern Kenya and every one has been a magical experience. The north is a harsh and unforgiving land, yet its beauty is undeniable and as soon as you leave the beaten track, following the sand rivers and elephant paths that weave their way through the orchard-like commiphora thickets, the years fall away and you can imagine yourself back in the Africa of a century ago when there were no vehicles to ease your way through the bush.

By contrast it is hard to imagine a more different habitat than the Okavango with its reedbeds, water lilies and green-gold floodplains. And what better way to explore these dreamy waterlands than on elephant back from Abu's Camp? This is where an American, Randall Jay Moore, stood conventional wisdom on its head and proved that you can train African elephants to carry people. A five-day stay at Abu's Camp is possibly the most expensive safari you can buy. But there is no greater privilege than to be allowed to ride on the broad back of a ten-foot, five-tonne tusker, swaying and splashing on a slow march through paradise.

From end to end, Africa is one huge adventure, filled with enough excitement to satisfy the most addicted adrenalin junkies. Savagery there is, and sudden violence, as when lions erupt around a kill, brawling and threatening each other with lips laid back in ferocious snarls. But in the end it is not the head-high threat of an angry elephant that gets to you, or the sight of hyenas dismantling a zebra carcass. It is the smell of the grass and the echoing cries of doves at dawn, the big skies and immense horizons. Above all it is the taste of freedom; the sense of all that emptiness and solitude on a scale unimaginable in Britain.

I remember discussing this with Ralph Bousfield, who runs Jack's Camp on the edge of the Makgadikgadi salt pans in northern Botswana. We were sitting in the shade of the Seven Sisters, a baobab tree as old as Stonehenge, where Livingstone and other early explorers had camped long ago. 'This century the world's greatest luxury will be space,' said Bousfield, staring out into the infinity of the pans. 'And out here there is still room to breathe, to count the stars and be yourself.'

Brian Jackman is a freelance journalist and author with a life-long passion for travel and wildlife and is Britain's foremost writer on safaris.

The Himalaya

Stephen Venables

'In a hundred ages of the gods,' wrote the ancient Hindu sage, 'I could not tell thee of the glories of the Himalaya.' That sense of limitless possibilities, of infinite wonder, is what inspires the modern traveller to return, time and time again, to the greatest mountain range on Earth. The word 'Himalaya' translates roughly as 'Abode of Snow' and it is the transforming power of snow, with all its reflective luminosity, which makes the Himalaya so holy to millions of Hindus and Buddhists. The mountains gleam and glitter, they seem to hang in the sky, almost detached from the Earth.

Everything about the Himalaya is vast. The main range stretches nearly 2,500 kilometres from Kashmir in the north-west to the jungle frontier of Tibet and Arunachel Pradesh in the east. At each end of the range a giant peak stands sentinel. In Kashmir the summit of Nanga Parbat rises to over 8,000 metres above sea level; the vertical elevation from the Indus River at its foot is over 7,000 metres. The eastern bastion, Namche Barwa, is not quite so high but still rises well over 6,000 metres from the bed of another immense river gorge – the Tsangpo.

These two rivers define the Indian subcontinent: the Indus flowing down into the Arabian Sea and the Tsangpo becoming the Brahmaputra before flowing into the Bay of Bengal. Defying geographical convention, both rivers begin their improbable journeys *north* of the Himalaya before cutting their way south through the mountains. And with divine symmetry, in this land where geography and religion are inseparable, each has its source close to the holy Tibetan mountain, Kailash. As if to reinforce that sense of holy design, the other two great rivers fed by the eternal snows, the Sutlej and Ganges, also rise close to Kailash.

When the Austrian mountaineer Herman Buhl stood alone on the elusive summit of Nanga Parbat, the first human being to do so in 1953, and looked out north over the Indus, he did not see a great plain beyond. No – an infinite sea of peaks stretched further beyond the river gorge – the Karakoram. Further west those mountains continue as the Hindu Kush into

Afghanistan. Further north still lie the Pamir, the Tien Shan, the Kun Lun. Likewise in the east, whole ranges extend far beyond Namche Barwa. So when we say 'Himalaya' we are usually talking expansively of a whole complex of ranges; or at the very least we are lumping together the Himalaya and Karakoram ranges.

For us, the modern adventure tourists, this immense tangle of mountains, rivers and glaciers represents a fantastic playground. For climbers there is every imaginable challenge, from the physiological extremes of trespassing into the deadly thin air above 8,000 metres to elegant rock climbing on fairytale granite spires. Botanists have, particularly in the eastern Himalaya, the world's finest treasury of temperate plants to explore. Geologists can marvel at the cataclysmic collision between the Indian and Tibetan tectonic plates which created the Himalaya about 50 million years ago. Paddlers and rafters can experience some of the wildest white-water on the planet. Cyclists have even pedalled to Everest Base Camp.

But for the great majority of visitors it is the pastime of 'trekking' which is the Himalaya's most compelling attraction. Jimmy Roberts, the British expatriate Gurkha officer who really invented the modern trekking industry, once commented that a Himalayan trek offered all the delights of an expedition approach march without the blood, sweat and tears of actually having to climb a mountain at the end. It is travel for travel's sake. There is a simple, primal satisfaction in arriving each evening at a new campsite, then moving on the next day, adopting the nomad's rhythm, seeing the landscape unfold before your eyes. And because this is mountain country, there are always climactic moments such as the crossing of a high pass alongside the ongoing thrill of rapidly changing terrain.

Take, for instance, the popular trek to the Goeche La in the Indian principality of Sikkim. In one week you progress through semi-tropical forest, then through rhododendron and magnolia forest, to pine forest, to alpine meadowland, eventually climbing to a level where only a few hardy plants and lichens survive in a wasteland of rock, snow and ice. And, to put this all in perspective, from the highpoint of the trek, you gaze up at the summit of Kangchenjunga, the world's third highest peak, still 3,000 metres above your head.

The great charm of the Himalaya is that so few roads penetrate into the high valleys and the only way to travel is on foot. As most of us are not able or prepared to carry food and supplies for up to a month, we employ local people to do the hard graft. It is a luxurious style of travel, dependent on an economic imbalance whereby even moderately well-off Westerners can afford to pay the wages of local Himalayan porters. So, while staff carry the luggage, pitch the tents and cook the meals, we, the pampered trekkers, can travel light and enjoy the scenery, with hardly a care in the world.

One of my most enjoyable treks in this vein was the famous Everest approach march in Nepal. From the roadhead at Jiri, we walked for nine days, crossing a series of high passes leading into the area of Khumbu, where our 'sirdar' or headman, Sherpa Pasang Norbu, lives. The long climbs and descents were hard work but, with no significant load to carry, they just left one pleasantly tired, rather than exhausted. And, on arrival in camp, all one had to do was read or swim in a river or go exploring while the staff prepared a large evening meal.

However, about 20 miles south of Everest, all this changed. We had come here not just to trek but also to climb a difficult peak – the 6,343-metres-high Kusum Kanguru. No one had ever set foot on its south-west face and as soon as we left the main trail to Everest it became apparent that no one had ever even reached the foot of the face. Pasang and his staff were brilliant, agreeing to continue up a densely forested, trackless gorge. But the initiative had to come from us – the crazy mountaineers. Suddenly our gentle trek turned into a real adventure, as Gurkha kukri knives came out to hack through thickets of bamboo and we took three days to travel three horizontal miles.

Base camp was a terrace cut into a steep grassy bank. Above that, the mountain itself presented several thousand metres of unknown, uncharted ice and granite. Three weeks after reaching base camp we succeeded on our new route and took turns to stand on Kusum Kanguru's deliciously pointed summit.

I mention that adventure because, even on the celebrated Everest trek, you only had to stray a few yards from the trail and you could find yourself in uncharted wilderness. For all sorts of reasons, not least shortage of time, the vast majority of Himalayan trekkers stick to well-known 'classic' treks. And many of these classics, such as the Annapurna circuit or the more austere trek to K2 base camp in the Karakoram, offer almost unparalleled splendour and diversity. However, with a little effort, the more adventurous trekker can strike off into the unknown – or the nearly unknown.

Perhaps most satisfying of all is to shoulder a big rucksack, say goodbye to all those camp staff, and set off on your own. One summer three of us did just that in the Karakoram. The plan was to explore the area around a high glacial basin called Snow Lake. To get within striking distance, we employed eight local Balti men to carry supplies for a week. Then we paid them off and were on our own. We visited various passes and we nearly made the first ascent of a peak just under 6,000 metres – I returned to finish the job a month later – then, with snowshoes on our feet and monster sacks on our backs, we headed across Snow Lake and up on to a high saddle called the Khurdopin Pass. Our map could best be described as sketchy and our knowledge of what lay on the far side of the pass distinctly vague. But we were experienced mountaineers; we had enough food to keep us going for several days, a stove and a tent: and that uncertainty was what made the journey compelling.

It is the same with climbs as with treks. Many excellent companies organize climbs of such peaks as Mera in Nepal or Stok Kangri in Ladakh. It is a chance to put on a pair of crampons and reach a Himalayan summit, not painfully high but still far higher than anything in Europe, amongst some of the greatest peaks on Earth. It takes you into a slightly different dimension from a mere 'trek'. But, again, with a little effort and hard graft, provided you are well grounded in basic alpine technique, there are thousands of rarely climbed peaks to attempt, not to mention hundreds which have never been climbed at all, particularly in the eastern marches of Tibet.

And, if you are a seriously committed extreme mountaineer, the scope is limitless. Ninety per cent of mountaineers visiting Pakistan and Nepal concentrate on the prestigious 'eight-thousanders' – the world's 14 highest peaks – with ever greater numbers crowded on to the two 'normal' routes up the highest of all, Everest. Yet, even today, many of the 'seven-thousanders' – in Afghanistan, Pakistan, India, Nepal, Tibet and Bhutan – have only had one ascent; some are still unclimbed. As recently as 1985, attempting the unclimbed peak of Rimo I in northern Kashmir, we found ourselves heading up the approach valley without any knowledge of what the mountain would be like when we got there; only one party had been there before, in 1929, and it had failed to take a photograph! And as for extreme rock climbing: we have barely scratched the surface.

All this talk of virgin summits may conjure up images of pristine wilderness. Yes, the high summits have an unearthly, ethereal quality and in the valleys there are still tracts of dense forest, but the Himalaya is not, generally, a wilderness like Antarctica or much of Alaska and Greenland. Its charm lies in the jostling of man and mountain. Although ostensibly a barrier between the Indo-Gangetic plain and the high plateau of Sinkiang and Tibet, the ranges are criss-crossed by ancient tracks. Muslim pilgrims from Sinkiang still cross the mighty barrier of the Karakoram on their way south to Mecca. Tibetan salt is still carried across high passes to India and Nepal and, now that China has slightly relaxed its occupying grip on Tibet, Hindu pilgrims are allowed to visit the sacred mountain of Kailash.

Although, as a mountaineer, I am always conscious of the Western visitors who have created their own legends over the last hundred years or so, I am usually following – at least on the way to base camp – in much more ancient footsteps. And almost every valley has its villages, farms and high pastures. Some of my most precious memories are of meetings with the people who live in these mountains: a shepherd playing his flute beside a glacier in northern Pakistan; two Buddhist monks passing the time of day on the way over a 5,000-metre pass; a family in Kashmir giving us a meal of fresh new potatoes flavoured with rock salt; a Balti porter singing joyfully with a pink rose stuck behind each ear.

Of course, our interactions are usually of a business nature, buying goods and services from local people. And of course you meet the occasional rogue who tries to pull a fast one. That is the nature of tourism. But my overwhelming experience has been of generosity and welcome. At times, in our rush to excel and achieve and flex our exploring muscles – or in our anxious impatience to make the flight home – we can all too easily become brusque and forget that we are here as guests in a foreign land. The other thing to remember is that, for all its immensity, the Himalaya is not, actually, infinite. Mountain landscapes are precious and fragile and we always need to retain that sense of respect and wonder, like the Sanskrit poet of the Skanda Purana who concludes his description of the Himalaya by telling us that this is 'where Shiva lived and where the Ganges falls from the foot of Vishnu like the slender thread of the Lotus flower.'

Stephen Venables is a mountaineer and writer and was the first Briton to climb Everest without oxygen.

The Polar Regions
David Hempleman-Adams
There had been ten days of storm in a too-small yacht in the Southern Ocean, the worst ocean in the world. Waves breaking

right over us had carried our life raft away in the night despite two chains holding it down to the cabin roof. In the rush and the noise and the spray none of us had even noticed its going. Not that it mattered. As our skipper pointed out, if the boat had gone down we would not have survived ten minutes in the raft, and there was no one to come and fetch us. We had passed icebergs, great flat-topped platforms, island-sized things that put aircraft carriers to shame. We had hit a small, all-but-melted one, a 'growler' that barely broke the surface but bashed a dent in our bows.

But now sun broke through the cloud, land was ahead, and that land was Antarctica. The coast was sheer cliffs of ice, far, far above our mast. Just one cove of black rock broke the white line where the wind was so strong it blasted the ice away. It is called Commonwealth Bay and the winds there can blow at 300 kilometres an hour. It was a hairy anchorage, dodging between a rock and a towering grounded iceberg, with only metres to spare either side. It was the first and last time I saw our skipper turn pale.

Heading for shore in an inflatable zodiac we saw three large rocks ahead and landed by the middle one. The one at the end rolled over, opened an eye and lazily flapped a flipper. It was an elephant seal, a vast mass of blubber, shapeless, sunning itself; even on its side it was higher than we were. It looked at us incuriously, and decided that we just did not matter. Then it closed its eye, briefly wobbled a bit of flesh that might have been midriff or quadruple chin or a bit of quadruple belly, and went back to sleep. We were quite irrelevant to its life. We were interlopers. In all that huge emptiness, we did not matter. Antarctica makes you feel not just small, but tiny. If this place does not teach you to respect the world, nowhere will.

The same is true at the other end of the world – the northern Polar regions. The first time I went to the Arctic was to climb Mount McKinley in Alaska. It was summer but I remember the fresh air and a vast wilderness and I could not stay away. I returned to try for the North Pole in 1983, a solo push. Getting out of the plane – an old, shuddering DC3 – it was pitch dark: this was in February, with 24 hours of darkness. Making a base in −40°C is so cold that the hairs on your nose start to freeze. But walking on the frozen sea into emptiness; dragging your possessions behind you like an overloaded demented snail; there is still nothing quite like it on Earth. I failed: a fall and cracked ribs meant that that time I had to give up. But that wasn't the point – the place had got to me. I have been coming back more or less ever since.

These are the last true wildernesses, the last places on Earth where man does not properly belong. And they are to be found away from the airstrips, the research stations, the strange Moon-base-like science colony of the South Pole itself, and the metal shacks and portacabins like Eureka and Resolute Bay that are the northernmost settlements of Arctic Canada. Leave those behind, and what is left is the food and the shelter that you have dragged with you: there is the wind, and the ice, and the cold; there is yourself and your companions, and whatever is in you and in them: and there is nothing else. If you are going to survive, it is on your own resources, mental and physical; and on nothing but that.

In Antarctica you can still feel just a little of what those early explorers and their men must have felt. Amundsen, Scott, my own – and so many other people's – hero, Shackleton: their courage and their endurance are beyond expression. There is huge interest today in these men: and for a reason. What they went through, we can never go through. They faced the unknown. They knew at the outset that they would be away for years; they were leaving not just their homes, but all news of their homes. The challenges they faced were far, far greater than anything that we confront; but we can feel something of it, just in part, just a fraction, all the same.

On our yacht trip to the Southern Ocean, our goal was the South Magnetic Pole which moves about a bit: about a mile or so each year. At present it lies a few miles off the Antarctic coast which accounts for why we needed the boat. But the first man to reach the South Magnetic Pole, in 1911, when it was still on the landmass of Antarctica, was Sir Douglas Mawson; and our black rock cove, Commonwealth Bay, was home to Mawson's Hut. Mawson is an unjustly neglected figure in Britain; but a hero, and justly, in his own country, Australia.

His story is one of the greatest epics of survival in a continent that spawns epics. He had set out with two companions. A crevasse swallowed one of them and most of their dogs and almost all their food. Struggling back, he and his Swiss companion fell ill, poisoned through eating the only food they had to eat, the livers of their remaining dogs. His companion died. Mawson himself, so weak that he had to cut his sledge in half to be able to pull it, fell down yet another crevasse and only his last reserves of strength and of will enabled him to haul himself out of it. As he said later, it seemed so much easier just to give up and to die there.

He struggled, ill, exhausted, starving back to that hut; and as he crested the last rise to see the hut and the bay below him, he saw also his rescue ship, the *Aurora*, sailing away. It had waited as long as it could for him, to the very last agreed day and beyond; and now it had to leave, to avoid being iced in. And Douglas Mawson knew another winter must pass before it could come back to look for him again but, somehow, he survived that winter in his hut. We saw, outside it, a boot left by him or by his eventual rescuers. We saw a seal he had killed and dragged to the door, the hemp rope around its neck still perfectly preserved by the cold for 80-odd years. It is a cliché to call Antarctica a deep-freeze; but it is one.

We had got to his hut after what seemed to us a wild adventure. But, in comparison, our trip was nothing. These men were so admirable, their achievements so stirring; small wonder that we should want, in our small way, to emulate them. We are not those men. Our times are different and things change. On the other side of the continent luxury cruise ships stop off at Scott's Hut now and after almost a century of perfect preservation it is being destroyed by the moisture in the breath of tourists.

But there are still challenges, still adventure in the Polar regions; and still people face up to them. Care is needed with everything. My first time in the Antarctic was to climb a mountain, Mount Vinson. I wanted to climb it because it is Antarctica's highest, and therefore one of the Seven Summits, the highest mountain in each of the seven continents. We flew in a Hercules plane to a place called Patriot Hills and came to a slow, bumpy stop. The ramp went down; we were on a runway made of blue ice. An American got off first, stood on the ice, went head over heels – and flew back out again on the same plane with a suspected broken elbow.

The Polar regions set challenges for everyone, and everyone meets them in their own way. After the yacht trip to the Magnetic South Pole I organized a sledging trip for complete beginners to the North Magnetic Pole. We called it the Ultimate Challenge and the idea was to sledge from the coast of Arctic Canada across the sea ice with ten young people, none of whom had ever done anything remotely like that before.

The most amazing thing about the Ultimate Challenge is how people changed. When we left, we had a good idea of how most people in the group would react but I remember in particular a guy called Andy Higgs. He was very quiet and sat at the back of the tent: he had Arctic shock. Each day he was slow, worried about frostbite. Three days out of Resolute Bay he asked if he could go home at the only sign of civilization that we would pass, the Polaris Uranium mine, a week's sledging out of Resolute.

I said 'OK, but if you are leaving us in four days you can at least help with the navigation before you go.' So every hour I would ask him where we were. Each night I would get him to mark out the route. I showed him how to navigate with the sun and wind. Each day he became more and more confident, with his navigation, and also within himself. When we reached the mine I said 'Why don't you stick with us till the re-supply plane, which is only six more days, and go out on that?' Each day he grew in stature. The re-supply came but there was no question of Andy going. By the time he got to the magnetic Pole he was the strongest member mentally and physically on the team. That was the most satisfying trip I have had, and for that one reason alone.

We are not Scotts, we are not Amundsens, we are not Shackletons. But what we are, we are: and the Poles find it out in us. My own time came in 1996. It was nearing the end of what was the first unsupported solo trek to the South Pole by a Briton; I had fallen and damaged myself and strapped up my back with duck tape and cardboard which, with Ibuprofen, had meant I could carry on. I was tired, and I had been out there it seemed forever, and I was 13 miles from the South Pole. Then I saw the steam from the South Pole station, rising on the horizon. The tears welled up in my eyes and froze on my cheeks and I knelt down and cried. I was glad that I was alone. By the time I reached the Pole the next day I had had my private moment. They don't get much better.

David Hempleman-Adams was the first person to complete a solo expedition to the Magnetic North Pole and the first Britan to walk solo and unsupported to the South Pole.

New Zealand

Richard Madden

Like many an adventure writer who ideally prefers to be in the great outdoors rather than writing about it, I confess to being guilty of the odd diversionary activity. My current vice when confronted with a blank screen is to flick through a pack of playing cards I was given by a kayaker friend during my last trip to New Zealand. Each card is illustrated with a different photograph of adventure activities taken in locations around the country, all superbly shot by the Kiwi adventure photographer, Chris McLennan. They instantly take me on a fantasy journey to one of the world's great adventure travel destinations and remind me of how much I still want to do and see there the next time I am lucky enough to return in the flesh, rather than just a daydream.

The six of diamonds, for example, is a paraglider flying high over jagged mountain peaks. Where, I wonder, was that taken? In the Mount Aspiring Range near Wanaka in the Southern Alps, perhaps? Or on second thoughts, I suppose it could be over the volcanic peaks on the Tongariro Crossing in the North Island. The eight of clubs shows an impossibly perfect scene of sea kayakers paddling across a deserted bay through lime-green waters bordered by a twist of golden sand. Well, that's easy. It has to be the Abel Tasman Peninsula in the north of the South Island. The king of hearts is of a mountaineer abseiling on a snow-covered peak. But wait, he's got a mountain bike slung over his back. So where on Earth is that? And so the game goes on.

Some of the locations and activities I have been to and tried myself. Not all by any means are the preserve of death-defying adrenalin junkies. Many depict favourite Kiwi pastimes like 'tramping' – trekking or walking to a non-Kiwi – as well as sailing, horse riding, white-water rafting and whale-watching. Others like 'bungee canoeing' or skydiving from a microlight seem, well, just plain mad. But, as a whole, the pack neatly encapsulates how New Zealand has in the past two decades transformed its image from the old cliché of a remote sheep-farming outpost on the edges of the known universe to the adventure Mecca it is seen as today.

Many of McLennan's photographs were taken in and around Queenstown in the South Island. Starting out as a gold boom town in the 1860s, Queenstown in recent decades has pioneered the whole concept of adventure sports reinventing itself in the process as an adventure Mecca. Today the town attracts over a million visitors a year, more than half coming from overseas, the town's permanent population of only 16,000 being swamped by a factor of three to one during the peak season from December to mid-February.

Much of Queenstown's success can be put down to its location. It undoubtedly has one of the most inspiring settings in the world, backed by the Remarkables mountain range and looking out over the cobalt blue of Lake Wakatipu, the second largest of the southern glacial lakes – enough in itself to set the heart racing. But when, in the 1980s, A.J Hackett and Henry Van Asch set up the world's first commercial bungee jumping operation at the nearby Kawarau River, a phenomenon was born. Queenstown had found its modern incarnation and rapidly developed into a centre for adventure sports of all kinds from the perennially popular thrill rides like jet boating on the Shotover and Dart Rivers to extreme sports like sky surfing and BASE jumping. Today Queenstown is adventure central for adrenalin junkies, the place where extreme sports fanatics congregate to enjoy their near-death experiences and invent new sports. At the last count there were over twenty world champions or record-breakers living in the town.

But while Queenstown pulls in a healthy percentage of the younger adventurers visiting New Zealand, for others the town is somewhere to avoid. There is, they argue, so much more to the country than mere thrill-seeking. Statistics usually bore more than they illuminate, but in the case of New Zealand they vividly illustrate this argument. A country similar in size to the British Isles has a population of fewer than four million souls compared to over 58 million in Britain. Its 13 national parks, 20 conservation parks and over 3,500 reserves cover over 30 per cent of New Zealand's land area. More than 70 per cent of the landmass of the South Island is mountainous. The Southern Alps are longer than the French, Austrian and Swiss Alps combined. And so the list goes on.

ll this means in practice is scenic diversity on an epic
he South Island it means the towering, tree-covered
surrounding Milford and Doubtful Sounds that rise verti-
cally from the sea to heights of over a kilometre high and where,
when the winds blows, waterfalls flow upwards like some
gravity-defying drawing by Michael Escher. It means dense rainforests, coastal lagoons, glaciers and lakes and the soaring peaks
of the Southern Alps crowned by Aoraki, Mount Cook, at 3,764
metres Australasia's highest peak. Further north there are the
hundreds of kilometres of protected bays, inlets, coves and
golden sand beaches of Marlborough Sounds and the Abel
Tasman Peninsula. In the North Island it means everything from
the 'winterless' Bay of Islands stretching languidly towards the
warmer waters of the South Pacific to the surreal geothermal
landscapes around the volcanic heartland of Mount Ruapehu
surrounded and softened in turn by a land of lush, rolling dairy
pastures, the traditional image of a sheep-rearing New Zealand.

These are landscapes that have a primeval, almost mythical,
quality as if the land was created for a race of gods as well as
humans. It is a quality first noted, celebrated and made sacred
in the creation myths of the first colonizers of New Zealand,
the Maori. Chief among them is the legend of the half-god,
half-man, Maui, who created New Zealand by fishing the North
Island in the form of a fish out of the ocean from his canoe,
the South Island. Stare at any map of New Zealand for hours
as I did, and with the best will in the world it will make no
sense at all. Until, that is, you meet a Maori yourself who will
explain to you that the fish is in fact a stingray when suddenly,
magically, everything slots into place. The east and west coast
are its fins; Wellington its eye; Lake Taupo its stomach; and
the Northland its whipping, stinging tail.

Modern myth makers have also recognized the primeval
quality of New Zealand's landscape. Films like *The Piano*, shot
on the wild, untamed shores of Karekare, west of Auckland, have
created an aura around the country that rarely disappoints, even

in real life. Chief of the modern myth makers, of course, is Peter Jackson, director of *The Lord of the Rings* trilogy and himself a New Zealander. Jackson bought the screen rights to the film long before anyone else believed a 'real-life' version was possible. But as a Kiwi, he knew from experience that if anywhere in the world was an incarnation of Tolkien's Middle Earth with every-thing from its rolling Shire-like downland to enchanted wood-land and Mordor-like mountain ranges, it was New Zealand.

These days Orcs – as opposed to Aucklanders – seem to populate much of the country. I met my first on a heli-hiking trip in the Southern Alps. Dave Williams is a mountain guide based at the Hermitage, the modernized complex of the old hut where climbers including Sir Edmund Hillary set out to climb Mount Cook. Dave was an Orc extra in one of the battle scenes filmed near Twizel on Lake Pukaki in the third film in the trilogy. 'It was incredible,' he told me. 'Every single Orc suit was hand-made and all were slightly different from each other. Those films cost about $NZ350 million to make and have been the best single advertisement for New Zealand ever. But I suppose it's the ultimate fantasy adventure movie which could hardly be more appropriate for a country like ours.'

No one can say they have experienced the true spirit of New Zealand without first having acquainted themselves with at least some of the hundreds of kilometres of marked and well-maintained track which snake through the remote mountain and coastal areas of both islands. Eight of these trails have been designated as 'Great Walks' taking between two-and-a half and six days to walk and including the world-famous Milford and Routeburn Tracks in Fiordland National Park. All the designated trails are punctuated with well-equipped tramping huts which means tough wilderness areas can be negotiated without the need for a heavy pack laden down with a tent and camping equipment. In fact, on most trails, camping is not allowed.

The huts, often located with superb views over dramatic scenery, vary from the more spartan variety used by independent walkers to the well-maintained lodges used by organized groups and manned by a warden with cooking facilities, mattresses and hot water bottles at the end of a long day's hike. Along the more difficult, steep, or plain muddy sections of the trails, board walks have been built which makes life easier for the walker but, more importantly, protect fragile environments from being eroded away by the tens of thousands of pairs of boots that come through every year.

On my most recent visit, I tramped the Hump Ridge Track, a newly designated trail in the far south of the South Island. It's a tough but exhilarating three-day walk which climbs from the coast up into the borders of Fiordland with sweeping views over the Foveaux Strait to remote Stewart Island – in Maori legend the anchor of Maui's canoe. Waitutu Forest, through which we tramped, is a virgin forest of podocarp trees dating back to the Jurassic Period and has been described by the conservationist Dr David Bellamy as 'perhaps the most important forest of its kind in the world'.

It was easy to see why. Not only did it feel as if we were in the presence of the 'Ancient of Days' as we walked under those wizened trunks and gnarled branches smothered by giant, beard-like mosses but clearly visible from the highest ridge were the layers of its long history as it was forced up stage by stage out of the sea, each level 100,000 years older than the last. Peter Jackson clearly hasn't walked the Hump Ridge quite yet. For when he does, he'll realise that this was one location he missed out on. For if ever there was a real-life Fangorn Forest, home of the Ents, this must surely be it.

Whale-watching – the ace of hearts an idle flick through my pack of cards reveals – is an experience I have so far missed out on. Seeing at close quarters a whale breaching or their huge tails breaking the surface of the sea has an almost iconic attraction. The place I shall be heading for on my next visit is

Kaikoura, north of Christchurch in the South Island. Sperm, minke, blue, fin, sei, killer, beaked and pilot whales are attracted here by the warm and cold currents which converge off the coast bringing copious quantities of nutrients to the surface which in turn attract huge shoals of feeding fish with whales in their wake. Humpbacks also pass through on their annual pilgrimage to Antarctic waters to feed. During the winter months you are virtually certain to see one species or another.

But, living on the other side of the planet, visits to Aotearoa, the Land of the Long White Cloud as Kupe the legendary Polynesian who first discovered New Zealand dubbed it, is not something that happens as often as I would like. Until it does, the ace of hearts is a marked card.

Richard Madden is a writer and the Adventure Travel Editor of The Daily Telegraph.

PART II
MAKING THE DREAM REALITY

Nigel Gifford

6
Adventure Travel Agencies

The choice of how to arrange and prepare for your adventures gets wider by the day. Besides the more recent option of direct booking on the Internet, in the last 30 years the number of companies, organizations and operators worldwide has grown from a handful of enthusiasts and small specialist lifestyle businesses, to large corporations who take thousands of bookings each year. Where do you begin or, as they would say in Sikkim, '*Kay Gurnay?*,' 'What to do?'

Arranging an adventure has been likened to buying 'futures' on the commodities market. You think you know what you have bought, you certainly won't have seen it, you have committed funds in advance, and you have made an assessment that the risk will pay off and you will be satisfied with the rewards. You have made an educated gamble, for which you have had to commit your irrevocable credit or pay up front.

It is vital that you make the right decision. If you are not taking sole charge of all the arrangements yourself, you need to pick the right tour operator or agency to suit what you want to achieve. You will be deciding on the delegation of much of what is described in these pages, and paying someone else to address each of these topics for you.

What Do You Want?

Before you decide what kind of company or organization to approach, or even whether to approach one at all, there are a few questions you will need to ask yourself. Try to have some idea of the time of year you want to travel, the amount of time you have to do so, and the type of adventure you are after.

Is it quite a straightforward experience, like visiting somewhere you have never been? A physical challenge requiring stamina and 'true grit' with an element of risk or the facing of specific dangers where you will have to negotiate unforeseen hazards? A personal feat of endurance that takes you right to the edge of your 'comfort zone', or perhaps a 'yardstick adventure' where you can measure various aspects of yourself against other people? Something inspired by others who have set out before you to achieve an amazing personal 'best or first'? A quest for knowledge? An insight into different cultures? Or a spiritual journey to search out fabled legends and religious myths? A journey back in time to discover family history? An enterprise or escapade to find, 'something lost' – buried artefacts, hidden treasures or something 'rumoured to be' but as yet unfound, like Jimmy Angel's gold secreted on the vast rock plug tepuis and mountain tops of the Venezuelan forests?

If you are still unable to decide, then the adventure travel company will be happy to make suggestions for you to consider, based on your interests and what you tell them about yourself and your ambitions.

Available Preparation Time?

Next, look at the time you have available for planning. This is the most vital part of the pre-departure stage. How much time do you have to devote to arranging your adventure? If the answer is plenty, plan it yourself, if you want to. If you are limited to weekends, perhaps you could do with some professional help.

Do you even want to make the time available for planning? Perhaps you would prefer to allocate your free time to something else. You may feel that you do not have the confidence at this stage to plan on your own. If this is the case, make this adventure an 'off-the-shelf' escapade or one with 'bought-in' services.

Today (at the very simplest level) it is possible to make a telephone call, make a booking, pay in advance for all services and arrive in the country with everything ready for you. All you have to do is turn up on time at the correct airport with the right clothing and equipment. For those people with limited time for preparation due to busy lives and work schedules, using the services of full-time specialists is a very sound option.

The following section looks at the types of companies that can help you. Many of them are noted by name in the Gazetteer section at the end of this book.

Conventional Travel Agencies

National chains of travel agents

Wandering down the high street, just about anywhere, it is impossible to miss the national, branded travel agents. The core of their business comes from conventional holidays and travel. The shop will be full of racks of seasonal brochures and the staff will have been taught how to sell off the page. Some of the more senior staff are likely to have visited some summer and winter resorts on familiarization trips with the intention of giving them the ability to sell from 'first-hand' experience. However, it was realized some time ago that bespoke planning for FITs (free independent travellers) is not a viable profit centre to the mainstream business of the nationals, and most of them have stopped giving this type of service. Basically with the national chains, if it is on the shelf, you can buy it, subject to availability.

Independent travel agents

Independent travel agents are also found on the high street, but often not in such a prime location, and they may need a little 'scouting out'. These are commonly partnerships or family businesses whose owners learnt their trade in travel with one of the national chains. A good many of them are more versatile than the national chains and give good customer service. Some have not discarded the old skills of independent planning and can offer adventures that involve skilled activities or specialist knowledge (in wildlife or culture, for example). They are very good at providing the 'in-country' travel facilities, accommodation and other straightforward logistics.

Some of them hold agencies for adventure tour operators, but do not have the in-house knowledge to answer any but superficial questions. For example, it is unlikely that they could provide an answer to the various problems a trekker might encounter at altitude. While they would be happy to take a booking, they would be nothing more than an interface between you and the tour operator.

Adventure Travel Organizers

Adventure travel agents

Adventure travel agents are a new breed to the trade, usually comprising a sole trader or a partnership with no interest in conventional aspects of package travel. They only hold agencies for adventure tour operators and they are a very good starting point for the first-time adventurer. They should offer impartial advice on the different tour operators' products. Some of the staff may have first-hand experience of packaged adventure travel, and may even have worked as a group leader in Africa South America or parts of Asia. The general knowledge will be good solid stuff, and they should be able to offer advice and tips which are practical and down to earth. Remember that they will be passing you to a tour operator to manage your day-to-day itinerary, and will not be acting or making arrangements directly on your behalf.

Getting the best out of agencies

Whatever you decide, it is important that you start with the mindset that you want to build a good professional working relationship with the individuals in the company you eventually pick. You want the relationship to be one that is financially fair to both parties, and you especially want their knowledge to be pertinent to your plan, up to date and based, if possible, on personal experience of the country and terrain. If you begin with this mindset, adventure travel planners and providers will react to you in a generous spirited, open, informative manner.

Using a tour operator leaves you free to make the most of your time prior to departure, to perhaps spend time with family and friends or organize extended time off with your employer. The services of operators that offer bespoke planning and preparation might also give you a better chance of completing your adventure in good style with a higher chance of success. Many have a great understanding of local customs and situations, and an infrastructure in place to gather local news that will be of great value to you.

UK-based tour operators

Tour operators based in the UK plan and operate their own programmes abroad. They are usually privately owned and the principals generally have many years' experience of the countries in which they operate, and first-class contact at all levels of commerce and local government pertinent to travel, general trading and society.

They generally fall into two categories. The first category includes those that promote and sell a more general adventure providing insights into a wide aspect of cultures and landscapes, but keep to a very well-trodden and established path and routine with very formalized and structured itineraries. There is usually little or no flexibility in what they provide. Let there be no mistake, however, these companies have some really great programmes with well-trained managers, and they are well handled and organized in the main. Often they cater for sizeable groups of all abilities and ages and the structure of the daily plan is tailored to suit the widest range of needs or limitations. Such operators' programmes are ideal for those 'putting a toe in to test the water' on their route to more individual adventures in the future. They provide a great starting point for a first experience and a not-too-steep learning curve.

The second category of operators often provide experienced leaders for their groups who know the country well and have an in-depth knowledge of unusual topics (the ornithology of Central Ethiopia, marsh lilies of Dhal Lake, the salt trading route of Nepal and Sikkim, etc.) Their programmes are invariably imaginative and off the beaten track, can sometimes be more demanding physically, and require clients to be flexible in attitude as well as having an easy-going outlook. Quite often their clients have had some previous travel experience of a similar, but milder, form with the first type of operator and will be looking for a particular, specific adventure that takes them deeper into the aspects of a country that is their real interest.

Operators of this type might also have fixed departures, usually for between around six and ten people. Very occasionally, they do not fill the places to the required minimum level to cover the costs and viability, and will consolidate people on to other programmes or departure dates in an attempt to prevent disappointment and to ensure the venture remains a commercial proposition. This is not always their fault – bookings get cancelled, often for very understandable reasons such as ill health, a change in working circumstances or unforeseen family matters. Sometimes operators do not make the decision to cancel or consolidate until ten weeks or so before the departure date. If it happens, and it is very rare, it should not happen less than eight weeks before departure, as by then all the clients will have paid for their adventure in full. If it is you that is forced for medical reasons to cancel at this point, you should be covered by any travel insurance, so should not be out of pocket.

If you wish to avoid such pitfalls, bear in mind that these specialist operators also excel at individual planning and bespoke itineraries, which, contrary to most people's belief, seldom cost more than a fixed departure. Indeed some operators in this category only deal with planning individual itineraries to your request. These operators are arguably the core of the UK adventure industry in terms of real involvement, concern and sensible understanding and commitment to ecological and sustainable tourism issues.

Overseas operators

Operators based abroad usually began as 'in-country' ground agents for Western tour operators and are probably still providing such services. Today, they effectively have dual roles. They facilitate group needs for the clients of Western adventure travel companies under a contract and fixed price. This will include all the logistics, client support and staffing. In addition they promote their own 'parallel adventures' via the Internet under the same or a different trading name.

It is advisable to remember that such operators use the best facilities and staff for their contracts with the Western based operators who send them their clients, which are their main source of their regular income, their own programmes next, and casual FITs,

Internet bookings and 'walk ins' get whatever is left over, or what can be hired at short notice or is available – and that usually means only sub-standard facilities or unskilled staff are left.

Websites

There are some very good referral-only websites that set specific criteria for the companies they list on their sites to meet, ranging from the operators' involvement with responsible tourism, their commitment to ecological projects and the way in which they interact with their clients. They carry out regular audits on the companies and request feedback from those who have used the site to select an adventure or a bespoke planning service. These sites are financed by a fixed annual fee, or by a commission paid to them by the tour operators if clients book through the website introduction.

Internet-only operators

Getting speedy and regular replies to your emails does not necessarily mean that you are dealing with anything more than one person connected to the net who has a website. Only make your enquiries and bookings if you are completely convinced that the company you are making your arrangements with exists, or that you actually know the people. A telephone call does not count. Have you met them and seen their offices? Do you know other people who have successfully dealt with them? Phantom services are out there. People have booked all sorts of non-existent car hire, hotels and other services and paid in advance. Do not leave yourself open to joining the list.

Charitable Adventure Organizations

When it comes to planning or selecting a fundraising adventure, contact with charity/adventure organizations can sometimes prove very confusing. Some organizations have their enquiries and even bookings managed by their fundraising departments, which may be staffed by volunteers who give their time to a different aspect of the charity each week. Often these people, while trying to be helpful, can only repeat to you what you already know, i.e. the description of the charitable adventure that you have enquired about. As this market has mushroomed, charity adventure programmes have sprung up which are poorly thought out and badly managed. These fundraising adventures are designed to appeal to your good nature, and seem to want to provide a type of 'righteous purpose' for your efforts.

Do not be bamboozled. Look for those charities that have a three-way integrity for their fundraising adventures – a great adventure for you, sensible fundraising targets and well-established and respectful working relationships in the countries in which the adventures are based. There is a very good book called *Green Volunteers* that will help you see what you can do in various parts of the world. It will be of very real benefit in this type of work and provide you with a great adventure.

7
Fix Your Aim and Objectives

As the saying goes, if you don't know where you're going, you'll end up somewhere else. Whether or not you are going to rely on an adventure travel agency to make your plans and arrangements, you will want to be clear on what it is that you are setting out to achieve on your adventure.

Sometimes the proposals that adventure travel staff and consultants hear about make you believe that almost anything is possible. One recent idea was for someone to swim the Atlantic non-stop in a specially made heated swimming pool towed behind a suitable support ship. The adventurer was to be fed while swimming and stay in the water the whole time until firmly docked alongside the east coast of America. There was little doubt of this Herculean task finding a place in the *Guinness Book of Records*. The proposer hoped to have the whole project completed in a two-week summer holiday with a carefully managed budget of £1,500. This sum was to include the hire of the support ship and the construction of the towable swimming pool.

While such plans keep one's faith alive – and no one would want to stifle creative thinking – most people are content with more realistic ideas, and that is the assumption made here.

Decide on Your Aim

The Atlantic swimmer's proposal does at least generate a clear message for all who set out on adventures, whether you intend to plan for yourself or book a package. You need to have a focus to base your plans upon and it should be the specific reason for your undertaking. In the adventurous world this is called the 'aim'. The Atlantic swimmer did have a specific intention, and it is easy to see what it was. Your intention needs to be singular, clear, concise and simple for you, and everyone else, to understand. Yet that is not all that an aim must be. It can be ambitious in terms of your own personal challenge as long as it has one more key ingredient – it has to be realistic. It seems that the swimmer only managed to convince himself of how realistic his aim was.

To help you determine the aim of your adventure, here are some suggestions as to the adventurer you might be or want to set out to be: first timer; lone traveller; with family; with friends; alone, but with children; teenager; honeymooner; older/retired; want to be professionally accompanied/guided or escorted; spiritual; artistic; cultural; ethical; charity/fundraiser; vegetarian; hitchhiker; trekker; polar; desert; rainforest; wildlife; mild adventure journey; mild adventure activity; packaged holiday adventure activity; independent activist; extreme adventure; expedition; aid worker; writer; researcher; photographer; camper; ethical; green traveller.

Considering what type of adventurer you are going to be is not an exercise in stereotyping but rather a useful means of identifying what you want. For example, you could decide that you intend to be a first-time lone traveller with the aim of making a trek. If this is so, you've just established your aim.

Supporting Objectives

It is also important to know what you want to achieve. You must decide on an objective, or several of them, that works in support of your aim. Planners will tell you that you can only have one aim, but you can certainly have more than one objective. Perhaps you could add to your aim something like the following . . . with the objectives of trekking to over 6,000 metres, to experience a different culture and to make a photographic record. Combining the two now gives you your aim and your objectives. You are a first-time lone traveller with the aim of making a trek, with the following supporting objectives:

1   to trek to over 6,000 metres
2   to experience a different culture
3   to make a photographic record.

If nothing else, this exercise will start a clear thinking process for you, and from here you will begin to visualize the various aspects that need to be attended to in your overall planning (or even what you might delegate to someone else). A list of pre-departure tasks will emerge with an obvious order of priority.

Using the example, you would want to find out more about the countries in which it is possible to trek to 6,000 metres, research how to get there and work out the best climatic conditions for the trek. This would lead you on to the logistics (discussed in the next chapter), the safety aspects and the culture of the countries before you make your decision about where your destination will be.

This may have stimulated other thoughts in your mind about much more detailed research such as specific route planning, or it might have made you realize that now you have your adventure in mind, the next step is to talk to an adventure specialist.

It is important to bear in mind that the greatest threat to the whole adventure can be overenthusiasm, trying to do too much and having too many objectives. This is something bespoke adventure planners see very often.

At High & Wild a colleague recently advised a young couple who wished to go to Canada for eight days. They wanted to track grizzlies in the wild, see moose and canoe in the Algonquin National Park, visit relatives in Vancouver, make a tandem skydive and pan for gold in the Yukon. They had set their hearts on all these objectives as part of this adventure. The impracticalities of achieving all this in eight days had to be pointed out to them – the long-haul flights, the distances to be travelled in country, the reliance on weather and avail-ability of guides and instructors. Do remember that you have a human frame, so try not to make your adventures unneces-sary trials by ordeal. Too many objectives, like miracles, can never be guaranteed, and such unrealistic aspirations lead to the inevitable road of disappointment and a much higher poten-tial for overall failure and real-time disasters.

All modern-day adventure travellers and professionals, whether they are pursuing physical, cerebral or spiritual goals, start by defining their aim and objectives. It is not difficult, but it is logical and requires common sense and allocation of time to get each aspect in place prior to departing.

Fix That Aim

It is suggested that you write the aim and objectives down and re-read them occasionally just to make sure that you have not headed off on a tangent. In modern business terms, this is what companies call a mission statement. It becomes the focus of the business and stops people putting their energy into developing areas that are not relevant and would waste time and resources. For adventurers, this is exactly the same.

Using such simple criteria will allow you to stay focused and be logical in what you set out to do, and your efforts and time will be used effectively. Most importantly, you will quite quickly be able to see what proportions of your budget you might need to allocate in support of the aim and the individual objectives. This could mean that you decide to drop some of the objectives before you set out if the costs are too great. You might also drop an objective when you have started on the adventure due to time constraints, difficulty of travel conditions or lack of funds as a result of some unexpected expense.

Aim and objectives

- You can only have one aim. It should be focused, clear, concise, stated, simple, ambitious but not unreasonably so – and realistic.
- You can have several objectives, but once again, be realistic. They should not be false or untenable.
- Assess your motivation and commitment honestly.
- Look seriously and honestly at your ambitions.
- Do you have the stamina for your plans?

Motivation

So now you have your aim and your objectives, but there is something else that binds these two together – motivation. Ask yourself what your motivation is for adventure. The strength of your motivation, resolve and your reasons for travelling make up your commitment and without having these questions fairly and honestly answered within yourself, you would be better to stay at home and save yourself the effort and the cost. Really think through and test your resolve in any way you can, and be careful not to be talked into something by peer-group pressure, rather than peer-group suggestion.

Where do motivation and ambition come from? Sometimes, they are part of a logical sequence of events that happen, sometimes they take a hold for no identifiable reason, but eat away and won't give up on us. The film *Close Encounters of the Third Kind* was the motivation for a mountaineer some years ago, as one sequence of the film filled the screen with the most awe-inspiring rock mountain they had ever seen. They just knew that wherever that mountain was in the world, they would find it, climb it and reach the top. There was no question of them not achieving this – the motivation and ambition was total and the commitment never wavered. Three months later, with American climber Vern Clevenger, they were standing on the dry, parched flat summit of Devil's Tower.

Those who undertake adventures professionally agree that motivation and ambition for adventure are never the same twice, and the depth of both varies from person to person. They also know that there can be a blurred line between ambition and obsession and the result is seldom healthy, usually creating tunnel vision and a disregard for safety and friendships. For an adventure to be a success in real terms, these aspects need to be well balanced. All agree that success in adventure is not worth too great a price.

8
Planning and Logistics

Attention to good logistics is at the very heart of any adventure's success. Any travel plan, whether it be solo backpacking or a group expedition to a remote location, needs diligent attention at the planning stage to reach the adventure's aim and objectives, particularly with regard to food, accommodation, transport or specialist equipment.

Too often logistics is made out to be some form of deep, mystical science that needs a double honours degree to be understood or applied. A science it may be, but it is easily summed up in one line: logistics is the movement of people and/or supplies from A to B. And all you have to do to be a successful logistical planner is to think through each stage and not make any assumptions or take great leaps of faith.

Although we do not consciously 'think logistics' out loud, we all carry out simple logistical programmes or projects daily. These can include negotiating our way to work each day or just planning a shopping trip to the supermarket.

Adventure logistics is no different as long as you think clearly and logically and do diligent research. Bill Tilman, one of the grand names of travel, adventure and exploration of the last century, is quoted as having said, 'If an expedition cannot be planned on the back of an envelope, it is too big.'

Snail Scenario

Galen Rowell, the American adventurer, used the term 'snail scenario' for the most minimal logistic plan that works for us Westerners. In essence, all the comforts and needs of home are carried on the back, or in effect in the backpack – a simple answer that provides versatility in any plan, and can very often be organized in the head or on the smallest scrap of paper. One does have to admire Tilman though – a tough, physically hardened man who was renowned for taking the equipment and supplies that we would use in a week and make it last for months.

In Galen's snail scenario you set out with the basic essentials, either as an individual or with a companion. Any personal items are individually packed and the commonly used items are shared in the individual loads with a fair distribution of weight and size. Shared load – shared logistics, giving the plan maximum flexibility and allowing you to head in any direction without further fuss or unacceptable impact in logistic terms – other than the unpredictable reliability of buses, trains and planes, food, fuel and water, along with your personal cash flow.

The snail scenario can also be the final part of a wider and more complex plan where the adventure has a static location or base camp, with smaller groups going to and fro on a regular timetable.

Logistics on a Larger Scale

For larger or more complex adventures, it is worth preparing a theoretical paper version or even using a computer spreadsheet package that incorporates estimated and actual costs. To start your own logistic plan, ask yourself, 'what do I need to get me there and back?' Keeping this in mind, put all the aspects you can see as being pertinent as building blocks underneath the aim and objective. Some of these blocks may eventually be discarded, but others that you did not include at first may take their place.

Most people visualize this part of the planning as a pyramid shape, with the aim at the top of the pyramid. It is simple to imagine, so you might like to keep this in mind from here on with the example below that includes some of the issues that will arise when considering the logistics. Even if you are using the services of an adventure company, this is exactly the type of plan they will have worked towards on your behalf.

Aim

Objectives

Terrain and weather. Leadership.

Route and locations. Travel plan. Tactics. Speed of deployment and rate of consumption and control of supplies. Water. Position of personnel, supplies and stores. Re-plenishment and repair. Medical requirements and evacuation. Local transport. Local food and fuel. Special diet. Local purchases. Packaging. Labelling. Movement of freight. Number of team members, their selection to support the aim and delegation of responsibilities. Audit of supplies and reassessment of needs. Funding.

This plan is pertinent to setting out on any adventure. The blocks from the pyramid will also be the main headings for any critical path plan (see page 104) that evolves to meet deadlines and the start and the finish of the adventure.

This paper exercise will be the proving ground of such key issues as the viability of the adventure, establishment of its organizational needs, the composition of the team, delegation of specific management tasks and responsibilities, reporting routines and the need for update on progress made on each subsection of the logistics. This undertaking should also highlight and define the potential weaknesses and strengths of the plan itself.

Think Everything Through

As one of the support group involved with Sir Richard Branson's first round-the-world balloon attempt based in Morocco, I used to attend the launch site daily. My responsibility was the provision of the nutritional requirements of the flight and the packing of the capsule with all foodstuffs twelve hours before take-off. It became apparent to me, because of questions being asked about payload and the potential reduction of water and food, that the engineers were looking at solving an unforeseen problem at the last minute – weight reduction.

Through discussion with one of the project managers, it emerged that during the building of the capsule and in working out the size of the balloon fabric required to lift it into the air and sustain the journey round the world, some erroneous assumptions had been made as to particular weights, including the crew's minimum requirement for water. It began to dawn on me that, even with the minimum payload, the capsule was never going to get off the ground.

In the end, the concerns that several of us held never manifested themselves, as during the launch countdown and preparations while inflating the balloon, the envelope became untethered and was badly damaged. The flight had to be abandoned until the following year and a new envelope was built. But I still have this overwhelming feeling that this piece of bad luck on the first launch saved some very shame-faced logistical planner from enormous professional embarrassment in front of the world's press as Sir Richard's Virgin Challenger capsule went absolutely nowhere.

Think Back and Laterally

It is said that the more adventures you take part in, the better a lateral thinker and problem solver you will become. People often reinvent the wheel when with a little sideways thought a problem is easily solved.

Soldiers who have served in the Special Forces use the expression 'the ground never changes'. By this they mean that no matter how sophisticated machines and weapon systems become, if you are in a particular environment and climate and ignore the lessons learnt through past tactics and logistics, you will end up relearning them at a heavy price. A good logistician will look back in history to see how people moved, lived and survived in a particular climate and environment. Do look back – it is surprising what you will learn that will help with your logistics. For example, how old and established is the rail system in the place you are going to? Similarly, how old is the postal system? Can you pre-position equipment and supplies if you need to in this way? It will invariably be more cost-effective.

Critical Path

A critical path allows you to estimate the time that each planning task will take and to check progress – particularly useful for larger or more time-sensitive ventures. It gives you a very visual appreciation of how fast or slow your plan is progressing in getting the adventure started.

This can be done by producing a simple graph with topics on the left-hand side and days or months along the top. By writing in the topics and leaving a double space underneath, you can use the first space to make your estimated time to get something completed and the second to note the actual time it took when it is complete.

Most importantly with a critical path, you can constantly check on the progress being made in your planning. If you have delegated some organizational tasks to others, it is important to have regular updates from all concerned. These people may be fellow travellers, suppliers, packaging companies or travel providers. The critical path will also demonstrate the success, or otherwise, of progress being made in funding if you are trying to raise cash from sponsors or elsewhere.

Planning tips for larger adventures

- Logistics is the movement of people and supplies from A to B.
- Ask yourself, 'what do I need to get me there and back?'
- Think laterally. What can I use that is already in place?
- Remember 'the ground never changes' – history will have some answers.
- A critical path will give you a visual progress chart.

9
Fact-finding Research

The Internet has opened up a vast resource of information for planning your adventures, but this does not mean that you should ignore newspapers and the magazines where operators promote and advertize specific opportunities and special projects. Also do not forget travel books – not only are they wonderfully relaxing to read, but they are often a first-class source of information.

Newspapers

If you are prepared to look beyond the obvious, newspapers can be a useful mine of ideas. David Browne, who loves to travel to unusual destinations, found inspiration buried deep in one national newspaper travel section's two-page article on Turkey. More than half the space was taken up with descriptions of coastal resorts and the possibilities of good value sunseeker holidays, but near the end of the article there was a small section on opportunities for adventure and some background on ancient Turkey. It provided some real gems of information. Did you know, for example, that Turkey's mountains are part of a chain that stretches all the way to the Himalayas? And that there's white-water rafting on the River Coruh which cuts through some spectacular gorges as it flows on its way to the Black Sea? May and June are the best times to go because the river rises with the snow-melt from higher in the mountains and this gives the wildest ride. The article also provided a clue for a future adventure for David: to walk Turkey's first long-distance footpath, the Lycian Way, which is 300 miles long and takes in views of the Turquoise Coast and dozens of little villages.

Now and again newspapers carry advertisements or promotions for less conventional travel opportunities, such as a cruise to explore the Antarctic and visit the Falkland Islands. The best time to go is towards the end of the year when it is spring and summer in the southern hemisphere and the region has come out of a long, dark winter. For those of us without heroic tendencies the idea of exploring a small section of the Antarctic Peninsula with an expedition leader and from the relative comfort of a well-equipped modern cruise ship has some appeal.

Cruises to the remote southern tip of the world do not come cheap, of course, but an informative article or even a descriptive advertisement in a newspaper can inspire you to think about a destination or project that might at first seem out of your range. That's the beauty of newspaper travel sections.

Magazines

There are numerous specialist travel magazines on the stands in larger branches of newsagents. *Adventure Travel Magazine*, or *AT*, is a British publication stuffed with ideas and helpful information; *National Geographic Traveler* is American and draws on the vast resources of the National Geographic Society for stunning pictures and reliable information. *Geographical* is the monthly magazine of the Royal Geographical Society in London and provides some very useful background material. Members of the RGS can elect to have some copies free as part of the membership subscription. Wexas also has a magazine which is free to members and which has well-illustrated articles about travel to some unusual places.

There is a list of travel magazines that feature adventure or expedition travel in the Gazetteer section at the back of this book. Many printed travel publications now also have online versions.

Libraries

Other resources for more detailed planning include public libraries and document archives. In the UK, the Royal Geographical Society has an enormous library collection of expedition reports, publications, pictures and other resources, which on request can be made available to members of the public, as well as those who are part of the society. There are over half a million items, including maps, photographs, books and manuscripts charting the history of exploration in the nineteenth and twentieth centuries.

The Limitless Internet

It is difficult to know where to start – the Internet is so full of possibilities. When travel companies first got to grips with the Internet, their websites were little more than advertisements for their travel and tour operator services, but now they include feature articles and helpful information beyond the sales pitch in addition to online booking facilities.

The Thomas Cook travel website is a good example of this development. It expanded from an advertising platform to become an informative and inspirational travel resource for a vast selection of locations. Their publishing house is famous for its international railway timetables and the website carries a series of articles on how to get the best value out of train travel using InterRail passes.

Government travel advisory sites

At a certain stage in your planning, the most significant Internet websites for research will be the country guides and advice provided by government departments. In the UK this means the Foreign and Commonwealth Office, in the United States, the State Department, and in Australia, the Department of Foreign Affairs and Trade. All these government websites are accessible on the Internet worldwide, and while they share much of the same information about each country, there are variations and specific details to suit their own citizens.

Most importantly, the government websites have the latest warnings or 'alerts' or 'advisories' about trouble in a country you may want to visit, and you can find the address, telephone and email details of every embassy and consulate in the world in case you need to contact them in an emergency.

In some of the more remote parts of the globe, you may be advised to contact the embassy ahead of your visit, especially if you are leading an expedition or adventure group. The appropriate consular staff should know that there is a group of British, Irish or American explorers or field-trippers coming to the country on an expedition. The embassy may have some up-to-date advice to give, or be able to put you in touch with a local contact who shares your interests.

It is important to remember, however, that the embassies are not to be used as a network of travel offices – they are there to promote trade and political relations but could be an essential line of help in an emergency. A growing number of British embassies have websites of their own, but the information about the host country is geared mainly to commercial companies who would be looking for investment opportunities or trade partnerships. The main thing is to look up the details of embassies and consulates in the regions you intend to visit and make a note of them.

Tourist office sites

A good place to search next is the vast selection of tourist office websites. These can give you an overview of the country or region you will be in and an insight into the history, climate and social conditions. Naturally, you will have to pick your way through pages of material promoting mass tourism and holiday resorts, but you will be rewarded with a better insight into the character of the country.

Some embassies promote their national tourist office on their website, but you can get to others very easily by putting the name of the country as a keyword in a search engine, such as Google or Yahoo. As an example, by carrying out a search on the name Mongolia using Google, you will be presented with its entry from the CIA World Fact Book, the UN official website on Mongolia and the website of the US Embassy in Ulaanbaatar among others. Take a closer look and you will find the website of the Mongolian Tourist Board which is packed with information in English about this fascinating country. Then there is *Mongolia Today*, an e-magazine promoting culture and the national custom of story-telling. One story sparked an idea for a travel project: a young man from northern Mongolia has embarked on an eight-year mission to walk around his own country and create a diary of what he sees and hears. He covered 8,000 km by tramping along the entire national frontier in his first two years, and is now looking for companions for his walk round towns and villages. Some day he hopes to publish his diaries and the account of his journey.

The tourist office websites can often give you links to more detailed information about regions, destinations and accommodation such as regular campsites or hostels or the location of mountain lodges which could be very valuable in the planning stage. Some will lead you to a language page which will enable you to learn a few basic phrases, and to a report on the latest weather which could be important if it is the season for hurricanes or flooding, for example.

A useful Internet tip

Store the web page locations that are relevant to your travel plans in your Favourites folder. You don't need to print out every page, but a file of selected pages or tables printed on paper would be useful for sharing with your travel companions when you meet.

Casting the net wider

It may well be that you have not yet decided upon one country, but with time on your hands and an inclination to do something more exciting than lounge around on a beach, you could try searching adventure travel companies. Try putting 'adventure' and 'travel' into Google or Yahoo and you will be surprised at the range of opportunities that come up. In among the thousands of websites could be something that sparks your imagination more than anything else. For example, if you are learning Spanish, why think only of Spain? What about making a trip to Havana, Cuba, taking a language course there and exploring the life and culture of an unusual part of the Caribbean at the same time?

A general search of the Internet using adventure and travel as keywords can lead on to ideas you would never have thought of, such as Green Tortoise bus tours of remote areas of North and Central America, including an expedition to Alaska; or to the Eco-resorts of Kenya whose website www.eco-resorts.com is a mine of useful information about the environmental issues surrounding tourism.

An Internet search could fire up ideas on which to build an aim or purpose for a trip. The well-known British explorer John Blashford-Snell crops up in various websites promoting the expeditions he has organized through the Scientific Exploration

Society. There are opportunities to join expeditions without any specialist knowledge and gain a lot of experience and confidence under the supervision of expert leaders. If you are not ready for a fully-grown expedition and would like to get some training in outdoor survival first, then there are numerous training centres promoting their services on the Internet.

Online booking and shopping

Another big advantage of the Internet is the range of things you can buy. If there's a book about the region you may be going to, you could order it online. Then there are items such as water filters that may not be in your nearest outdoor activities shop, but could be listed in an online catalogue. You can compare different versions of essential items and this can help you to get the right one for your needs.

Most airlines have websites with their schedules and destinations in view, and there are several well-known booking sites which could be very useful for long-distance travel planning. Don't be too hasty about buying a ticket online, however, because there could be better price deals if you shop around once you have gathered the information about the route you would like to take. The German Railway service Deutsche Bahn operates a train timetable website which is helpful for touring Europe and there are other websites that provide inspiration for great railway journeys such as the Trans-Siberian Railway and the Silk Route train journey from Moscow to Hong Kong.

Online retailers

If you are buying over the Internet, it's a good idea to try to locate a business in your own country, to avoid complications such as import taxes that you would have to pay at the post office when you collect a package. The button for 'contact details' will tell you where the supplier is based, and the end of the website address is a clue to the country – .co.uk indicates a company in the United Kingdom, .com is usually (but not exclusively) a trader in the USA, .ca is Canada, .za is South Africa, and so on.

Travellers' sites

Many travel websites have been established by individual travellers who want to share the sense of adventure. Some examples are the Turkey Travel Planner compiled by Tom Brosnahan, a writer and travel enthusiast, which you can find at www.infoexchange.com/Turkey, or the website of David Edwards who is the University Expedition Advisor to the Royal Geographical Society. He has put an expedition planning guide on his website at www.worldtalks.co.uk/expplanningtalk.htm, along with numerous photographs from expeditions that may whet your appetite for travel.

The Internet on the Internet

The Internet is so useful and global in its reach that you should also make a note of the location of Internet cafes in the countries you are visiting for updating your research as your adventure unfolds. There are websites that can help you to find them if you search on keywords like 'cyber cafe' or 'Internet cafe'. Public Internet access points are emerging all over the world, even in such peculiar locations as Everest Base Camp and a village beside the Mekong River in Vietnam. Sound research will assist you in your overall planning.

10
Fundraising and Sponsorship

One reason for asking for financial help with some of your adventurous travels and projects is that the market for tourism is governed by numbers and if fewer people are travelling to a popular destination, it makes it more expensive to provide flights and accommodation. It's called economy of scale. An adventure trip may be tailored to your particular aims and will as a consequence cost more than you may be able to manage on your own finances.

Sources of Funding

There are several ways of raising money. For a start, you can work for it. This is particularly relevant in a gap year where some months can be spent in a job to earn the money to put towards your expedition. Then there are your relatives who may be persuaded to help you.

There are a number of bodies, usually with charitable status or trust funds with money to be used for specific purposes, which could be approached for a cash grant to help with your costs. This is slightly different from commercial sponsorship, where a company will invest some money in your plan if it can get something back in terms of promoting its product on your gear or publicity photographs. These are all ways to raise money to support you and help you cover your costs.

There is another sort of sponsorship where you are responsible for raising the money for a charity or good cause. You may be familiar with this type of sponsorship through sponsored walks, bike rides, swims and other worthy activities. You may still need to find your own costs for carrying out the fundraising activity and it is important to be clear about whether you are raising money towards your own living costs or for donation to a good cause.

Getting Started

There is a comprehensive list of charities, foundations, trusts and other organizations that offer financial support for adventure travel in the final part of this book. Some are geared to scientific research in remote places overseas, such as the polar regions, mountains and wilderness areas. But there are numerous sources of finance to help with journeys of more personal benefit. I will mention a few in this chapter to illustrate how to go about asking for support from sponsors.

Anyone you approach for help will expect two things: a plan that clearly states your aim and a return on the investment, usually a record of your achievement such as an account of your trip or a talk to the people responsible for the money that helped you on your way. This should not be a problem if you have followed the advice given earlier in this book and defined your aim and objectives. These are also the key to deciding who to approach for funding.

Adventures Sponsored for Charity

Mencap is a leading British charity that supports people with learning disabilities and their families and carers. It has been organizing overseas adventure-style bike rides, treks and runs as fundraising events for some years. These events have the dual benefit of giving participants an experience of a lifetime and raising significant sums of money to help Mencap's work in campaigning and challenging attitudes of prejudice about mental disability.

For example, Mencap recently organized Project Renew, in which a group of thirty participants set to work on a school in Maputo in Mozambique that needed renovating. The classrooms, walls, flooring, plumbing and playground facilities were cleaned and fixed by volunteers using money raised through a sponsored trek at the end of the project. It created a safer, cleaner environment for children with learning disabilities and gave the volunteers an adventure to remember. One of the participants said it was a trip that surpassed all her expectations:

I have been on lots of adventure holidays before but none which has been quite so rewarding. The look on the children's faces will stay with me forever, coupled with the trekking and the unspoilt surroundings of Mozambique.

Mencap has also held sponsored trekking trips in Japan, bike rides in China from the Great Wall to Beijing, and expeditions in Brazil, Vietnam and along the Nile in Egypt. The method of raising funds is much the same. To take part in one of these adventures, you must register and pay a deposit of £300. Anyone who is physically fit and aged between 18 and 65 can take part. In the months before the expedition, you need to raise a minimum sponsorship pledge of £2,600. You must collect about 70 per cent of the money and send it to Mencap Promotions headquarters ten weeks before departure, to confirm your place. You then have time to raise the remaining 30 per cent.

Part of the money you raise covers your travel and accommodation costs and the rest goes towards Mencap's good cause fund. Additional costs such as travel insurance and airport taxes you must pay for yourself. You have the option to pay for all your own travel costs and give the whole of the money raised to Mencap, in which case you will get a long-haul adventure at the cheap rates negotiated by the charity's tour operator. All the details can be found on the Mencap website at www.mencap.org.uk.

Across The Divide (ATD) is a company that specializes in organizing adventure trips to raise funds for various charities and good causes. They have mounted sponsored treks in Peru, Namibia, Nepal and China, dog-sledding expeditions in the Arctic and voluntary work projects in Africa. The structure of fundraising is similar to that of Mencap. In the case of the sponsored treks they arrange for Cancer Research UK, you pay a personal deposit to register and set about raising 80 per cent of a minimum pledge of £3,000 to secure your place on the trip. The rest must be raised in the weeks after you return home. ATD organizes sponsored adventures for a number of charities including the Rainforest Foundation, Mines Action Group, Disabled Living Foundation. The Simon Community, Dublin, and the Children's Trust. The details are on the ATD website at www.atdexp.com.

Professional photographer Jim Kerr from Northern Ireland undertook a sponsored walk along the Great Wall of China with ATD. He not only raised money for charity but now exhibits and sells photographs from his trip and gives the proceeds to The Simon Community for homeless people in Dublin. You can see his pictures on the ATD website.

Charity Challenge also has a big range of sponsored adventures that include sailing, Mongolian horse riding and trekking in mountains, desert and jungle. The list of charities that have been supported by sponsored expeditions is enormous. Charity Challenge offers participants an Internet-based fundraising facility so donations can be collected from sponsors all over the world direct into the funds of your chosen charity. Your supporters can also follow your progress on a special personal web page.

A different kind of overseas charity adventure, the Assin Endwa Trust, was the brainchild of a group of gap-year students. The aim of the trust is to help the people of a village in Ghana to modernize their schools and health centre by organizing sponsored voluntary working holidays. In this case you pay for your own flight to get out there and a small sum to cover living costs, and pledge to raise at least £200 towards the cost of materials that will be shipped out to the project.

Securing Charity Sponsorship Pledges

These are just a few of the opportunities for combining an adventure with raising money for good causes. The challenge is more than the physical exertion in a strange land – the fundraising project can be hard work but enjoyable and fulfilling in itself. As with any sponsored event, people will want to know what you will be doing and who will benefit from the funds. You will need to plan well ahead and draw up lists of people you can approach. Don't feel that you have to do it all yourself: get friends and relations to help by collecting pledges from people they know.

Think up new things to do to draw attention to your project, such as holding a party or a family gathering and getting up and making a short speech about your plans and the cause you are supporting. Some people have raised funds through car-boot sales or garage sales of bits and pieces collected over the years.

There are a great many hints and tips for raising money on the charity expedition websites and while people will give more willingly for a charitable cause, the techniques are just as valuable if you are looking for support for your own adventure or expedition.

Mike and Fiona Thornewell from Nottingham undertook a North Pole Trek and raised money for two charities, Macmillan Cancer Relief and the NSPCC. They were supported by sponsorship from several local commercial companies, including Project Telecom who supplied them with satellite telephones, XMA Computer Products who provided a laptop for the trek, and the furniture retailer MultiYork who sponsored the trek and carried daily updates on its website. Over 100 individuals pledged support and BBC Nottingham devoted part of its community website to publicizing the adventure.

Help From Relatives

While you are thinking through your aims and making plans, talk them over with family and friends. You may have relatives with some money salted away which they could put towards your expedition if you present your idea with enthusiasm and charm.

Tell them about your plans well in advance and give them time to think it over; involve them in your planning by asking advice about their own travels in their youth. Don't just turn to them in desperation at a late stage because you are afraid you haven't raised enough earlier. Let them see that you are realistic about how much your adventure will cost and that you are going the right way about raising the funds. Let them offer to contribute as their way of sharing in your adventure.

Sources of Grants for Travel

Glenn Shaw is a remarkable adventurer and explorer who is confined to a wheelchair because of a brittle bone condition that has affected him since childhood. He applied for a grant from the Winston Churchill Memorial Trust under the category of Sport, Recreation and Adventure to carry out his dream adventure to go kayaking off the cost of Antarctica.

It was a very ambitious project and required a lot of planning and support but his successful application to the Trust for funding meant he could make his journey of a lifetime and he has become an inspiration to adventure travellers everywhere. He says he had wanted for years to kayak among the penguins and money from his Winston Churchill Fellowship enabled him to turn his dream into a reality.

The Winston Churchill Memorial Trust has a wide range of categories for overseas travel, and usually includes one covering adventure travel in most years. There is a grant specifically for canoeing called the Mike Jones Award. Clare Jones and Allison Inkster won a Mike Jones canoeing award to undertake a sea kayak expedition from Vancouver to Juneau in Alaska along the famous shipping route, the Inside Passage. Along with the aim of completing the journey of about 1,000 miles, the expedition was to promote sea kayaking and the participation of women in particular. The expedition also had a charitable side, to raise funds for the Jen Duncan Memorial Trust and enable other women to benefit from the experience of wilderness canoeing adventures.

Memorial trusts

The Mike Jones Award is typical of many awards set up in memory of an individual. Mike Jones was the instigator and inspiration of a small group of Britons who led the world in expedition canoeing. In his short life the succession of feats he achieved on white-water was more than the equivalent of an ascent of Everest. He also possessed a very real courage which, apart from earning him recognition as the world's premier expedition canoeist, eventually and tragically cost him his life, when he went to the help of a friend in trouble.

the Royal Geographical Society in the UK is an important supporter of expeditions, has several sources of grant aid and can give advice on raising money. The Journey of a Lifetime Award, for example, is a grant for a journey that will inspire interest in people and places by someone who can communicate their experience through a programme for BBC Radio 4.

The RGS grants also go towards the costs of expedition teams doing research and field work or small groups travelling abroad to help in conservation projects with local communities. The funds have clearly defined purposes, for example, the Ralph Brown Expedition Award is for a team on a research expedition in a marine environment such as coral reefs, while the Neville Shulman Challenge Award is open to individuals and groups to encourage exploration of cultures and environments anywhere on Earth while promoting personal development through physical or intellectual challenge.

Your plans may not stretch to a scientific expedition, but there is financial help available for more modest ambitions. People say travel broadens the mind and there is a wide range of funds to support travel projects for personal development. The Adventure Trust for Girls, for example, has a fund to help young people in their quest for adventure, but you must be female, aged between 11 and 18, and live or attend school within eight miles of Exmouth Town Hall, excluding the areas west of the Exe estuary. No doubt the founder of the Trust had a good reason for such a limited catchment area.

Connect Youth, a department of the British Council, runs programmes that give young people an experience of travelling and living abroad on activity-based projects. It also provides money to help those working with young people to develop their skills and establish contacts overseas. Connect Youth has a network of regional committees across the UK who can offer advice and support for the planning of an exchange.

Another source of funding for exchanges is the Commonwealth Youth Exchange Council. This is a UK-based educational charity which has money from sponsors to encourage exchange visits with young people in other countries in the British Commonwealth. Priority is given to youngsters who would not normally have the chance to travel to places as far away as Africa, Asia or the Caribbean and a grant could cover one-third of the travel costs. Your trip would have to be as part of a group aged between 16 and 25, and involve some joint activity and meaningful contact with young people of the overseas country. This includes staying in shared accommodation or in family homes, getting involved in some activity and hosting a group on a reciprocal visit to Britain.

Ethical Value

When you are applying for a grant or appealing for sponsorship it is important to be clear about your motivation for making your journey. Mass tourism to remote places has had destructive effects on the environment and the local communities. An adventure should be notable for its aim of helping people who live in the places where expeditions are undertaken. In part this is done through supporting them financially by providing them with business or employment.

The other side of this is to learn about threatened tribes, indigenous peoples of under-developed countries, understand their problems and represent their interests to the outside world on your return, by sharing your experience in talks, articles, reports, pictures and any other form of communication available to you such as websites. Local people in faraway wilderness areas are very generous to visitors and a responsible traveller will repay that generosity rather than just enjoy their company and exploit their help. The educational, social and environmental value of an adventure is a key criterion for grant aid or sponsorship for your project so your letters and application forms should reflect this.

Eligibility for Grants

All funding organizations have guidelines about the type of journey and activity that they will support, so make sure that you study them closely to ensure that your plans fit the requirements. The basic criteria for a travel grant are often quite strict because the money is coming from a fund that was set up for a specific purpose. Wilderness Lectures, for example, is a partnership of climbers and cavers which gives grants to support adventure travel and activities by people who can then come back and share their experience by giving a talk. These grants are purely for an adventure. The money is not for students doing research projects nor is it for people embarking on an organized or packaged tour or a sponsored activity for charity. It is important when applying for financial help that you read the conditions carefully, otherwise you could waste a lot of time.

The founders of the Wilderness Lectures Award, for example, say they want to give the money for a trip that makes them feel they wished they could do it themselves. They really want to give money to people who may be struggling to afford to go on an adventure to distant parts, rather than to the rich and famous of the expedition world. There is a website for the Wilderness Lectures Award that has more details and the guidelines for applications at www.wildernesslectures.com.

How to Apply for a Grant

There is no set pattern for writing a proposal for grant aid for a travel project, but there are some common rules that you should follow.

1   Read the guidelines set out by the organization offering the money.
2   Ensure that you and your project are eligible.
3   Make your application in the correct format. Some

organizations have a form, others require a letter outlining your aim and plan.

4   Make your application in good time. Some grant-awarding bodies meet only once or twice a year to select the projects they are going to support, and you need to know early on in your planning whether you are going to get financial support.

5   Frame your application to suit the particular organization offering the money and don't just send a standard appeal letter which could go into a local newspaper or in a mailshot to friends and supporters.

Once you have identified a grant-giving body that you think might be able to help, there are some points that need to be covered in your appeal, whether it is by letter or on a particular application form. These points can be summarized in a set of questions that you should ask yourself:

- What is your aim or purpose in making the journey?
- Where do you want to go and by what route?
- Who is going with you?
- How are you travelling? This will be crucial to planning the costs.
- What do you want to do when you get there?
- Will you need to buy any special gear?
- How will the trip help the people you meet and the environment in which you will live?

An adventure will have a better chance of success if it is well researched and you have plenty of background information about the area you are visiting before you leave home. The people you approach for support will want to know that you have done your homework and will be genuinely interested, so be prepared for their questions. Ask yourself, what is it that attracts you to this place?

This is an example of a well-prepared proposal which helped convince the panel of judges at *Outside* Magazine, an American outdoor adventure publication, to give a grant to pay a substantial part of the costs of a summer adventure:

Dear Outside Adventure,

I am writing in response to your Outside Adventure Grant. This is the adventure that I have in mind:

On April 1, 1999, Canada will return about 770,000 square miles of land, and the right to govern themselves, to the Inuit people. These people experienced great change in their lifestyle and culture due to the Anglo influence. Now they will have the opportunity to determine how they want to live in their land, to be called Nunavut.

This land is a hard land. I would like to visit these people and come to know a part of their heritage. To do this, I propose to fly into Pangnirtung on Baffin Island, on the eastern boundary of this newly created territory. From there we will explore the village, the nearby whaling stations, and remnants of an ancient past before beginning our walk across Auyuittuq National Park Reserve. A two-week hike across the park to Broughton Island will cover some 60 miles of Arctic terrain, giving enough time for side trips. These side trips may be to ascend nearby peaks, climb on rack cliffs or more fully explore Summit Lake. All of this takes place above the Arctic Circle.

The crew will be made up of my older brother Dylan, 17, my older brother Tristan, 15, and myself, 12. We have gone on adventures together all of my childhood, sailing, hiking, exploring and pirating. Growing up on a remote island off the coast of Maine, we have been each other's playmates and companions, always climbing trees or building forts. In the last two years, my brothers' adventures have been taking them far from our island home. When Tristan was 13, he went with a school-teacher friend and her family to raft down the Kayukuk River in Alaska. Dylan has participated in two Atlantic Challenge rowing competitions in Canada and Ireland, and has recently returned from a year as an exchange student in Thailand. Both of my brothers are experienced bird watchers and have conducted bird counts on the outer Maine islands for the Audubon Society. Last summer I went on my first bird count, banding puffin chicks on Matinicus Rock. We have each had rock climbing experience with Outward Bound instructors as guides, as the Hurricane Island Outward Bound School is very close to the island where we live.

As I mentioned, we live on a remote island off the coast of Maine. We have spent the last eight years living in a one-room dwelling, with 12-volt solar electricity, hauling water from a dug well, and harvesting our own firewood for heating. For the past five years we have been home schooled, and also have been the only year-round family on the island. We have been raised up to be self-sufficient and self-motivated. Since November of this past year, we rented a house on the neighbouring island of Vinalhaven. Like the Inuit of Baffin Island, we were immediately surrounded by conflicting value systems. For the first time in my life, I have been exposed to easy access of television, household convenineces, and merchandizing. Partly because of this sudden contrast, I am interested to see how the Inuit people view the return of their land and the chance to reinforce their traditional beliefs.

It is our hope that by interviewing, photographing and journalizing throughout our expedition, we could raise awareness of this land and its people; how they go about the transition and challenge that lies before them. My brothers and I are amateur photographers, and are willing and able to produce slide presentations and public talks. In addition we are interested in identifying and cataloguing birds and mammals both in the park and surrounding areas. We would also like to stretch our own physical and personal bounds with rock and mountain climbing.

Thank you for considering our proposal, we look forward to your response.

Very sincerely yours,
Louisa Hope Jackson

(Reproduced by permission of *Outside Online*)

Your first letter or application form will not need details of the costs. Your budget will only be needed if the sponsor likes your idea enough to be interested. That is why your first approach must be well thought out, even if it is brief. If your basic idea is sound, the sponsor will have some more detailed questions for you, arising out of your first statement, and that's when you will have to present an estimate of costs as far as you know them by then. A spreadsheet will help to present your budget clearly and you will be able to add to it as more things occur to you as your plans develop.

Your budget is an important tool for an appeal to sponsors for financial help. It does not need to be cast in stone and not every item needs to be costed down to the precise pounds and pennies or dollars and cents. Aim to keep your figures realistic, predict as many items as you can and then allow about 20 per cent extra to allow for such things as currency fluctuations in the period between planning and actually reaching your destination.

Also keep a record of pledges and offers of cash from all sources, because many grant-giving bodies will have a maximum that they can give – some set their maximum as a proportion of the total cost – and you need to be sure that you can cover your remaining costs elsewhere. The greatest mistake an expedition can make is to go into the field seriously under-funded. When money runs low, the first casualty is usually safety.

Commercial Sponsorship

Local businesses are worth approaching for support in the form of donations of cash or goods or clothing that you will need. This is a form of sponsorship. The benefit for a company is in the media coverage that they could get by being associated with an unusual project, as this can show the firm in a good light supporting an initiative in the local community.

There may be a way of displaying the firm's logo on your equipment or vehicle. If you have a website, there should be an acknowledgement of support there too. You may even feature in the company's in-house magazine which might attract more help from individual donors within the firm. Local newspapers or radio stations can be very helpful in giving you space and time to publicize your plan, and for a business supporter this could mean a free advertising plug.

Debbie Winton, from St Albans in Hertfordshire, was looking for commercial and other sponsorship to enable her to use part of her gap year to travel to Madagascar and Tanzania and she set up a website to publicize her plans and raise the money she needed. Her appeal was direct and succinct:

Like many sixth-form students. I am planning to take a year out before going to university. For my project I have decided to join the organization Frontier, part of the Society for Environmental Exploration, for six months on two expeditions. In January 2002 I will be departing for Madagascar where I will spend three months as a Research Assistant collecting information on the coral reefs which will aid conservation in the area. When the three months are up, I will travel to Tanzania where I will take part in a similar three-month project, this time studying a savannah ecosystem.

This is an amazing opportunity for me and will provide me with a sound basis for university where I am planning to study Marine Zoology.

This website contains information about Frontier, the expeditions I am joining and myself. I need to raise around £5,000 to pay the costs of the expedition and for equipment, flights, insurance, visa and other essentials before I am able to go. I will use this chance to appeal to your generosity. If you have any ideas for fundraising that may help me, or are in a position to sponsor me as a business or would like to make a donation, I would be extremely grateful. This is a huge task I have ahead of me and any support you are able to give would help me immensely.

It may be useful to approach people you already deal with in the local branch of national businesses, such as your bank manager. And you should look up business organizations such as the local Chamber of Commerce or the Round Table or Rotary Club because these are networks that could spread the word about your project and attract support that way.

The Raksha Urai expedition to Western Nepal is a good example of successful fundraising for a venture whose aim was to make the first ascent of the mountain and explore the surrounding valleys. The clothing company Helly Hansen runs an award scheme to support small, lightweight teams and provided a cash payment of £2,500 and a full set of clothing for each team member. The Mount Everest Foundation and the British Mountaineering Council also made cash grants. Lyon Equipment gave expedition gear worth about £1,000. The Canadian Himalayan Foundation gave a cash grant and loaned equipment in Kathmandu. Terra Nova Equipment lent the team specialist tents for the climb.

Metcalf and Eddy also gave some financial support and in exchange benefited from publicity for their environmental services worldwide such as drinking water schemes in developing countries. Back Country Cuisine, a New Zealand company, provided lightweight food packs at a big discount, and Pakistan International Airways agreed to a higher weight limit for the team's gear which saved them a lot on transportation costs. All together, collecting this amount of financial support and sponsorship in kind was a major undertaking and crucial to the success of the expedition.

Seven Deadly Sins of Fundraising

Not every grant or sponsorship application succeeds, of course, so it may be worthwhile examining some common errors of approach, known as the seven deadly sins of grant applications.

1   Placing too much emphasis on the end result of the project. For an organization to give you money there must

be something in it for them. Tailor your application to the needs and mission of your potential donor and show a connection with your project. If it is a commercial company, you may be able to show the value of publicity for their product associated with your achievement.

2   Creating a concept for which no funding is in sight. The time to talk to potential funders and supporters about an expedition is in the early planning stage, not after the leader has decided the goals, itinerary and personnel.

3   Developing a project that has already been done or could be done better elsewhere for less money. There may be support for an anniversary commemoration of a great expedition, but usually the 'been there, done that' approach does not appeal to funding bodies.

4   Lacking an appreciation of the marketing concepts of new, improved or free. An expedition needs to have elements of all these: a new location, perhaps use of new technology and a return in terms of public talks or an Internet site in which the funding body is featured as a financial supporter.

5   Misjudging the financial requirements. Expeditions and adventures cost money and funding bodies know that well. A bare-bones budget may look economical but could backfire on you if it is perceived as poor business planning. The donor's money and reputation are at stake. The best donors are entrepreneurs who understand risk and the fact that your project has the 'right stuff' to succeed. They will have experience of proposals being under-budgeted and know the pitfalls.

6   A project being too good to be true. It is important to keep your project's aim simple and attainable. Donors have to believe in your ability because they give money to people not ideas. They will want to know about your experience so far and about the leader and senior members of a group that you may be joining.

7   Having an inadequate plan. Expeditions that are successful begin with a strong plan both in terms of finance and in what is to be achieved. An expedition or wilderness adventure carries personal and financial risks and these must be manageable and appropriate to your level of endeavour.

Show Appreciation

Wherever you get pledges of support, do remember to say thanks to all who help and sponsor you, and provide them with news and pictures of your adventure. It helps to let them know that their money was appreciated and enabled you to do something worthwhile that you could not have managed without their help.

11
Travel by Conventional Means

Most adventure travel projects involve at least one return journey by air so some thought needs to go into planning for the best deal, not just in terms of price but also to plan the most appropriate destination and route with the best type of ticket to cover your needs. The airline industry has grown so much that the choices available can be bewildering.

Traditionally, most travellers make their arrangements through a travel agent and get the benefit of advice from trained staff who are familiar with the worldwide air travel network and the vast range of tickets and booking conditions. With the development of the Internet, much of this information is easily accessible by individual travellers or adventure-group planners.

With a bit of forward planning, you need never pay the top price. Leave that to business travellers with corporate business expense accounts. The range of discounts and special offers is huge, and a virtual industry of cut-price air ticketing has grown up as a result.

Booking Protection

Wherever you book your air travel, always look for evidence that you are protected by a scheme known as ATOL, or Air Travel Organisers' Licensing, devised by the UK airline regulator, the Civil Aviation Authority. A tour operator must pay a deposit, or bond, into a central fund which can be used to bring home passengers who would otherwise be stranded if something went wrong. ATOL protects your travel arrangements by air, such as flights and package tours booked through a tour operator, and is the UK's biggest travel protection scheme. The ATOL protection does not apply, however, if you book direct with an airline, rather than with a travel firm. The low-fares airlines, for example, do not have an air travel operator's licence and argue that fares would have to go up if they did, but there are new regulations in the pipeline to change this.

Many travel agents and tour operators are members of ABTA, the Association of British Travel Agents. Like the ATOL scheme, ABTA provides travellers with protection for the money they have paid for a trip and if the travel firm goes bust while you are away, you will be able to continue with your adventure and come home as planned. ABTA protection is not limited to flights and covers travel packages by coach and rail as well as by air. It works in a similar way to ATOL in that travel agents pay into a central fund from which the bills can be paid to hotel owners and coach firms throughout your journey if the tour operator has not already done so prior to going bust.

ABTA protection is not limited to cases of travel firms going completely bust. It has a compensation scheme for failures in any part of the arrangements that you have paid for. If you find the accommodation is not the type or standard that you had paid for, or if a service or facility such as a hired vehicle is not provided and you incur extra costs, then you may have a claim. But make sure that you complain at the time, do your best to get around the problems and deal with getting compensation when you get home.

Some companies prefer to belong to the Travel Trust Association (TTA) and protect clients through a travel trust account. The TTA are registered with the Office of Fair Trading. There are also some operators and agents who only provide ground arrangements, and while they need to have client fund protection in place, they are not required to be a part of any of the organizations mentioned here.

Most airlines also belong to the International Air Transport Association, IATA, which is an industry body representing around 280 airlines including the world's largest operators and covers 95 per cent of international scheduled air traffic. The organization's aim is to ensure that people and goods can move around the global air network as if they were on a single airline in a single country. IATA also helps to ensure that aircraft operate safely, securely and economically. It is through the cooperation of IATA member companies that travellers can reserve a ticket, pay for it in their own currency, use the ticket on several airlines in several countries, and even get a refund for unused portions of the journey anywhere in the world.

Getting Cheap Air Fares

Buying flight tickets at discount prices is not difficult and does not require inside knowledge of the industry. For the most part all you have to do is ask. There are numerous conditions, categories and deals which can bring down the cost of your air travel.

A travel agent would know about them but you may want to do your own booking, and as some of the best-priced deals involve several airlines along your route, booking direct with an airline may not be the cheapest option as they will not have access to the complex set of connections that are available. This information is the forte of ticketing agents and is the recommended route.

The general rule is that air tickets are cheapest if booked well in advance, though this is not always the case. Most discounted tickets have restrictions on them, so you must work out if the restrictions affect your plans. The main one to look for is the no-refund condition, which could lose you money if you cancel your trip or change your route. Your travel insurance should have cancellation protection but often the reasons for cancellation must be related to an emergency rather than to your change of mind. The restrictions may be in the form of a charge for changing the date of travel on a portion of your journey or an administration fee for the cancellation and rebooking of one leg or the whole of the trip.

Listed below are some ways in which you could save money on the flight portion of your adventure.

Be young

All airlines offer a big discount for youth fares and define youth as up to 26 years of age. Youth fares do not apply to every route or to every flight scheduled on a route, but asking about age concessions could be your first question. Travel agents that specialize in student travel such as STA, Travelbag and Wexas are fully up to speed on this and other special deals, but be aware that Internet reservation websites do not give you all the options.

Go in a group

Group travel has the advantage for airlines that they can plan ahead knowing that a block of seats will be occupied and paid for, and they will give a ten per cent discount for a group of ten or more travelling together. This is often expressed as 'the leader goes free' but that's just a marketing ploy to get the leader to book with them. It is really a percentage concession.

Look and book ahead

Most cheap fares are available for advance bookings so if your dates for joining an expedition or the time off for your own trip are known well ahead, book in advance. The cheap tickets may have cancellation restrictions on them, so your travel dates may have to be fixed at an early stage of planning. For most people planning a gap-year trip to join a project with fixed dates, or if you are fitting in an adventure in a summer holiday, this is not usually a problem.

Fly in low season

For many routes there is a high or peak season and a low or off-peak season and, in some cases, a shoulder period in between. Clearly, you can expect to get a cheaper ticket in low season because airlines don't want to fly with empty seats if they can help it. But you may be stuck with a limited period for your journey, such as the summer holidays between school and college or the end of the year when it's summer in the southern hemisphere.

Fly to another airport

Passenger routes are generally determined by hubs – central airports which are the home base of an airline – and on a map the airline's main routes radiate out from the hub across a continent or round the Earth. Generally most flights will be into a hub airport and there is more scope for cheap deals to fill seats. But there are other airports to consider. The low-fare airlines cut their costs by flying to small, often obscure, airports some distance away from the major cities they serve and this is not necessarily a problem for low-budget travellers.

Beauvais airport is north of Paris but is a lot less busy than either Charles de Gaulle or Orly airports which are closer to the city. Ryanair flies to Beauvais from Dublin because it costs them less in airport service charges. If you are heading to Scandinavia, then Skavsta airport takes in cheaper flights than Stockholm international, and Malmö in Sweden is just a short train ride away from Copenhagen in Denmark. It pays also to look around departure airports and see whether cheaper fares are available from a regional airport in the UK like East Midlands or Bristol when you take in the costs or savings in train or coach travel to reach them rather than one of the London airports. It doesn't stop there; there are special offers to places in South-east Asia if you fly from Amsterdam, or to the Indian Ocean from Paris, compared with flying direct from London.

Use a no-frills airline

The competition among airlines has increased rapidly since low-fare airlines like easyjet, Ryanair and others became fully established in the travel market. Their cheapest fares are for seats booked well in advance or on off-peak flights at awkward times of the day such as very early in the morning. But they are single-flight bookings and you can combine a cheap fare out with a cheap, medium- or top-fare flight back depending on how flexible you are about dates. The no-frills airline business has also taken off in the United States, with companies such as Southwest Airlines, JetBlue and AirTran Frontier, ATA Airlines and Spirit Airlines expanding their services into transcontinental routes across America.

Fly the Internet

Most major airlines now have an Internet reservation website and they are promoting this service by making online fares cheaper than tickets booked through a travel agent or direct with airline staff. But you must watch the additional charges. The advertized fare on a website promotion may not include airport taxes or administration fees which are an unavoidable part of the cost of a flight.

There are several Internet booking services that are not tied to a particular airline and will search for the best available deals on your selected route. A2B is operated by Travelocity and can identify cheap deals made up of legs or short-hop flights that work out cheaper than a direct flight with a national airline. Other websites worth looking at are Expedia, which is an international online travel agent, or Opodo, which is an online flight-booking service owned by a consortium of major airlines including British Airways, Aer Lingus, Air France, Lufthansa and Austrian, Italian and Finnish flag-carriers.

The Internet has opened up to the public the sort of search capability that was once reserved to travel agents and other travel industry professionals, through computerized reservation systems such as Galileo, Amadeus, Worldspan and Sabre. A public access website, however, is no guarantee that you will get the best fare available, only the ones that airlines are prepared to display. In the USA, the Orbitz reservation website is owned by United, American, Delta, Northwest and Continental airlines and was the subject of an enquiry by the Department of Justice in Washington into whether the website favoured the flights and deals of those airlines above others available to the public.

The advice, as always, is to shop around in the early planning stage and note that a travel agent may still be able to find a better deal for you, especially if your requirements are slightly off the regular tourist or business traveller routes.

Top tips for cheap flights

- Look out for youth discounts.
- Book as part of group.
- Reserve well in advance.
- Avoid high season.
- Be flexible in your choice of departure and arrival airports.
- Consider using budget airlines where possible.
- Try booking online.
- Find out about air pass options.

Open your jaw

Most journeys that people make on airlines are return or round-trip flights, starting and ending in the same city. This may not be the best arrangement for an expedition or adventure that involves an element of ground-level travel such as a trek or road, train or river trips. You may want to fly to one city but return from another because your ground journey may not bring you back to the starting point and you would want to avoid doubling back over a route already covered.

The ideal flight booking for this would be a deal known as an open-jaw reservation, and these are usually cheaper than two separate single tickets and can cost less than a point-to-point return ticket. You may need the help of a travel agent to fix these flights because they can be too complex for Internet-based reservation websites to cope with. An example of an open-jaw booking would be to fly from Miami to San José in Costa Rica and fly back from La Aurora in Guatemala, and perhaps explore the terrain of the two Central American countries using buses and trains.

A variation on the open-jaw deal is the closed-jaw or circular route booking. Here the flight out is to one airport and the next flight, which can be some days or weeks later, is from that airport to another location and staying there for some time before taking a third flight returning home. An example of a closed-jaw or circular trip would be to fly from London to Colombo and after spending some time exploring Sri Lanka, flying to Bangkok and enjoying Thailand before returning to London direct. Generally the fare will be similar in price to a return/round-trip ticket to Bangkok but you have the advantage of another venue for exploration or a project in addition to the furthest destination.

Go round the world

A variation on the circular route is the ultimate travel deal, the round-the-world itinerary or RTW for short. This could be advantageous if your main destination is on the other side of the globe, such as the Far East or the Pacific if you are travelling from Europe, and vice versa. Wexas regularly publishes RTW deals and most travel agents can construct a long-haul travel plan that allows you stop over in several places without doubling back on your journey. This would not necessarily be worthwhile, however, if your main destination was a popular holiday destination such as Australia or New Zealand because there is scope for discount fares to fill the seats on frequent flights to cities in those countries.

Buy air passes

For an expedition to multiple sites in a country or region of the world, you can save a lot of time and money with an air pass that gives you the freedom to fly without buying separate tickets for each leg of your journey. Some airlines provide a number of coupons that can be exchanged for flight tickets. In some cases they are not limited to one country or a single airline. An example is the Merco Sur airpass for Latin America. This allows you to travel between at least two countries among Argentina, Brazil, Chile, Paraguay and Uruguay, within 30 days and on any of four regional airlines, Lan Chile, Lapa Argentina, Tammeridional and Varig. Generally, airpasses or multiple-flight coupons must be bought outside the region as they are mainly designed to encourage visitors, not internal business trips.

Fly frequently

Another great way of saving money on air tickets is not to pay for them at all, but to use frequent-flier points or Air Miles. The schemes are known by various names, but are all the same in principle. People who travel by air on a regular basis, such as for business, are rewarded with loyalty points as an incentive to stick with one particular airline or alliance of several national airlines.

You may not have flown enough to have accumulated sufficient mileage points yourself, but you may have friends, relatives and other supporters who would be prepared to donate their points towards a free flight for you. This is an opportunity for a sort of personal sponsorship that is often overlooked in planning an adventure or expedition, and does not cost the donor anything in cash.

The Air Miles scheme started by British Airways has now been extended to other traders and you can save towards a flight ticket by using certain credit cards, shops and electricity suppliers and the range of airlines that will exchange Air Miles for flight tickets has expanded.

Go last minute

It is possible to get some good deals by booking at the last minute, but this is not recommended as a basis for planning an adventure or expedition. Last-minute discounts are not usually available direct from airlines. You would think that cutting out the middle-man would save money, but this is not always the case. Travel agents, consolidators and so-called bucket shops buy up seat reservations in advance to sell on to the public and are sometimes left with unsold units which they can sell at a price lower than the airline is offering because they would lose money if they remained unsold. Lastminute.com was famously founded on the idea of locating late deals, but there are now several Internet-based operators in competition.

Watch your baggage weight

Weight is an issue for an airliner so passengers are given a limit as to how much luggage or baggage they may take on board, typically 20 kg. If you must take more, you will have to pay extra. This allowance may not be enough for all the gear that would need to be taken on an expedition, so it is worth asking for some concession on the weight. Some expedition organizers have managed to negotiate good deals with airlines over the baggage charges and saved a lot of money as a result. This sort of gesture by the airline to support the expedition can be considered as sponsorship-in-kind and is definitely worth asking for.

Other Ways to Get Around the World

Adventure travel usually means travelling to a distant place overseas and involves airline flights for at least part of the journey. But flying is not the only way to go.

Rail travel

You should not ignore the possibilities of train travel all over the world. Thomas Cook Publishing (www.thomascooktimetables.com) produces two important railway guides, the European Timetable which is updated every three months and the Overseas Timetable covering railway networks in Africa, America, Asia and Australasia.

There are a number of epic rail journeys that are adventures in themselves. Most notable is the Trans-Siberian Railway from Moscow to Vladivostok, which has branch routes to Mongolia or China. The famous Orient Express is now a luxury premium-fare excursion train running from London to Venice, but it is possible to plan a journey using regional express trains covering the route of the original Orient Express from London to Istanbul. This is the kind of project that could be covered with an InterRail or Eurail pass. There is a list of special-deal railway freedom passes in the Gazetteer section at the back of the book.

By coach

Coach travel used to have a bad name as the cheap and not-so-cheerful alternative to trains. Now coaches are more comfortable and motorways provide a speedy route between cities not only in one country but across frontiers. National Express coaches in the UK (www.nationalexpress.com) are linked into a European network called Eurolines, so it is possible to travel intercity very cheaply and make further connections on the continent. You will see more of the country you are in and, like airlines and trains, it is possible to buy multi-journey passes. The whole of North

America is criss-crossed with Greyhound bus routes and Australia has an extensive bus network that can be covered with a pass.

High seas

It can be quite an adventure to travel by ship – not just on ferries or cruise liners but on cargo ships. Many freighters have a small number of passenger cabins and you can enjoy a no-frills voyage or even a round-the-world trip at a fraction of the cost of a luxury liner. In some cases, you are guests who dine with the master or captain of the ship and in others, you muck in with the crew. There are contact details for agencies specializing in cargo ships in the Gazetteer Section.

If you are more adventurous and feel like actually being a member of a ship's crew, then you might like to try sailing in a tall ship. It can be hard work but an enormous thrill to cross the oceans in the style of explorers from long ago. It's also very good for sail training experience and self-discovery because you are part of a ship's company and must do your best to get on with everyone at close quarters. The Jubilee Sailing Trust is the first port of call for information about the possibilities of adventure sailing in British-registered tall ships. Their website is at www.jst.org.uk.

12
Travel by Unconventional Means

Any form of unconventional travel adds an extra dimension to an adventure. They can be divided into two kinds: those that may seem unconventional to us, but which are quite normal in the country you are visiting; and those that you might take with you to assist in pursuing the adventure.

No adventure involves being static for long and once you are 'in country' you need to be on the move to get things up and running and to get the adventure underway and see it through. You will certainly want to be underway after a couple of days, at least, when you have had time to adjust to new time zones, culture, foods and temperatures.

Existing Local Transport

These are many forms of unusual transportation that might be available for you to consider as long as they are viable to your plan and reasonably reliable. You do need to move efficiently if you can and, whenever possible, at a time that suits your aim and objectives. All of your travel needs to be cost effective, readily available and, where possible, fit with the road and track systems, the local geography, environment, seasonal variations and the needs of the local people.

For example, in Asia, why not consider hiring or even buying an auto-rickshaw and reselling it when your adventure is complete? These very robust three-wheelers are versatile, inexpensive to run and have plenty of room for people, luggage or equipment. They run on unleaded petrol these days and have catalytic converters. Some of them are fuelled by compressed natural gas and in southern India, they have developed a herbal fuel that substitutes for petrol.

You pre-departure research, or even a prior reconnaissance, should include the searching out of such potential 'short cuts'.

Remote Locations

In many remote locations, rivers are more than a source of water and food – they are the main highways. You may find that using dug-out canoes, with either paddles or an outboard motor, provides a simple and cost-effective way of getting to and from your various locations. Crossing large expanses of water by 'flat ferry', as is common in the north-eastern parts of India, might provide a way of moving vehicles, motorbikes and scooters in a cost-effective manner.

In some really remote parts of the world, you may find people using high-wire 'death-slide' style pulley systems to get around their locality. Sometimes local people even send their children to school across vast voids or ravines in this way. The children are literally stuffed inside locally-made hessian sacks which may be attached to the contraptions with little more than a hook. This is certainly unconventional to us, but is a potential form of transportation that you might be able to either use directly or adapt to a specific regular or short-term need in your plan. Moving people and supplies in such a way might save days in what could otherwise be a circuitous route by local bus or truck.

Pack Animals and Porters

Pack animals could provide the ideal answer in hilly or mountainous terrain. Ponies, mules, yaks, camels and donkeys have moved people and their supplies in the most inhospitable environments for hundreds of years. Could elephants be the answer to an 'HGV-type' transport problem for you? Or could a llama or even a pack dog, in countries where this is permitted, solve a lighter weight-carrying problem?

In Ladakh a few years ago a friend and I learnt a hilarious, but well-deserved, lesson. We were making a reconnaissance for a group of young adventurers to trek under their own management in the Stok Valley area, and we needed to pre-position a small amount of safety equipment. Advised by a Kashmiri trader in Leh that ponies would be available, we set off to look for the pony man and to negotiate a daily rate of hire.

Unfortunately, we had been beaten by a day to the hire of the ponies by a local trader, and none were available. But all was not lost to us, we were told. There were some small donkeys available (much smaller than Shetland ponies) and four of them would be able to carry our loads. We strapped the loads to them and set off to negotiate our first natural obstacle, a river crossing.

No one had mentioned that the river was in spate, and the shallow crossing point was now waist deep, with the current so powerful it was grinding vast boulders along the riverbed. Naturally it was impossible for the donkeys to cross, unless of course we carried them, one by one, having first carried over the equipment they had been hired to carry! There were no other options, and it took us nearly a day to move across the river. In all the little donkeys, while wonderful companions, added more time to the completion of the task than if we had not hired them at all!

Thinking laterally can be valuable here too. Can you use the services of the local people? In Nepal, people can be hired to carry loads of up to 30 kilos in dokos, on pack frames, or in back packs. This is fuel-efficient, provides local people with an income and has no adverse impact if negotiated fairly and with good spirit.

Self Build

In river regions, you might consider having a raft built from local timber or driftwood or even building one yourself. Some years ago a group of friends from Leicester flew by light aircraft deep into the Nahanni territories of the Yukon, with nothing more than saws and axes. Using driftwood and discarded timbers from the beaver dams on the great Diamond Lake they built a raft and navigated the awesome Nahanni River back to the road head. It took 17 days and they saw no other people, but moose and grizzly bears kept them company from time to time.

In thick forest would it be feasible to make a canopy walkway to get about, rather than force a path through the forest? In fact it might be advantageous to have accommodation and all your living requirements in the treetops by fixing netting with a fine mesh and making a whole area that will support a conventional type of camp set up. Once the adventure was over, the walkway could be removed leaving no trace at all.

Bringing Your Own Transport

What vehicles could you bring with you that might make the adventure easier to manage in terms of movement of people, their personal requirements and all the supporting aspects?

Recently a miniature one-man airship was used to get around in the Indonesian rainforests. This fuel-efficient form of transport used solar panels to generate part of the power for the near silent electric engine.

In another instance of imaginative planning, there was a successful attempt some years ago to windsurf the Bering Straits. The windsurfer built a board that he could literally live on (sleep, cook and rest) and there was some protection from the elements that he could erect in bad weather. This adventurer showed great lateral thinking in adapting his transport in pursuit of adventure.

On a river, would a seaside-type pedalo prove a successful vehicle? Minimum maintenance, self-powering, environmentally friendly and it might even be available to hire rather than buy or build!

Skidoos have been to the North Pole and jet skis have been driven against the flow from sea to source along the navigable course of the Amazon. There have been microlights on snow skis and with floats to land on lakes, rivers and the open sea, and there are powered parachutes that will inflate and fly out of a small forest clearing. Such vehicles have a range of hundreds of miles. Ice kites can make an arctic journey in a third of the conventional time on skis alone, and land kites cross vast open spaces as fast as most four-wheel drive petrol-driven vehicles – assuming there is the wind to propel them.

The Other Dimension

There is a further dimension to consider here. Is the means of transport being used the adventure in itself? This applies to both 'in-country' available transports and those that you might import. Several people have made journeys by purchasing a locally-made motorbike, a pedal rickshaw, even an elephant, like Mark Shand and his lovely Tara, or Tom Fremantle who made a 2,700-mile journey through America following an ancestor's footsteps 140 years later with a cantankerous old mule called Browny. Such escapades have a real eccentricity about them, but why not?

Adventures by their very nature are going to be unconventional, so why shouldn't the transport be the same? There is no need for you to constrain your plan to fit what is normal, usual, available or 'been done before'. Most transport problems have been limited by people's vision of what is possible, so always question the view 'Oh, that has never been done before in this country or in this type of terrain' by asking yourself 'Why not?' and 'Is it feasible?' Pursue the possibility until convinced one way or the other.

The obvious thing to avoid is taking or using forms of transport that are simply unsuitable for the country you are travelling in. They will become more of a hindrance and a burden than you can ever imagine, and you do not want them to detract from the aim of the adventure to such an extent that you have to abandon the plan, or they have cost a disproportionate part of the funds you had available.

Impacts and implications

The limiting factor for any form of unconventional transport will be reliability and cost. You should never lose sight of these two factors and they should always be firmly balanced against ecological and conservation implications and the impact on local communities.

You certainly would not want your various vehicles and their need for fuel to have an untoward impact on villagers or local people and, for example, stopping farmers being able to get their produce to market. Conversely you would want to bring your cash and the income flow it could generate into the community so that the local people benefit from your presence, and feel the benefit from your time and goodwill in their community.

Fuel

All transportation needs fuel – even people- or animal-powered transport needs to eat. Remember to check that the areas you will travel through will be able to sustain their need for fuel and foodstuffs and that there is ample and adequate protection from the elements or accommodation.

Try to use locally-available fuels that are not harmful to the environment. Common fuels in remote areas are still diesel, kerosene and petrol, and it will take time for this to change, so you are likely to have to rely on these fossil fuels. Do try to ensure that they are used efficiently and sparingly, and if you can try to have a 'linear fuel system' – where one fuel will fill a variety of energy-providing functions such as Tilley lamps, cooking and generators – it can save on costs, space and overall weight.

Look towards the use of solar power in battery replenishment (some countries have rickshaw vans fully powered this way).

If using pack animals at altitude where acclimatization might be required, has enough time been allocated for this, so that it does not manifest itself as a problem? Remember that yaks and zoggs (yaks crossed with a cow) do not fare well at altitudes below 10,000 feet. Those that live at higher levels such as Tibetans and sherpas have to adjust too – the thicker air can make them feel sick and sluggish for the first few days.

Making Arrangements

Using transport that is already 'in country' requires little more than making a booking or reserving the vehicles for the time you need them. If you are working through a local representing agency, they will help you with this, and they will also ensure that you get vehicles that are in good repair (or, in the case of pack animals, in good health) and are reliable with a driver that can do 'on the move' repairs, who also either has the spare parts on board or can get them easily.

In many cases, if you intervene and become personally involved in the making of such arrangements, this will be seen as intrusive and may cause a 'lack of face' for your representative. You will be expected to trust the judgement of the local agency to work for your best interests, and they invariably do so well.

Sometimes such interference can have a payback several days into the adventure, where the porters, drivers or pony men will 'down tools' on some spurious pretext for more pay having seen that you are not used to how these types of deals are handled. This is all part of the game in such circumstances, and you are better off not being involved.

Where you have imported a form of transport to a developing country, there will be customs clearances for you to undertake and government departments may need to be satisfied before their use. This can also be a requirement of crossing a border, especially if the diplomatic relations are poor between neighbouring countries. There may be duty to be paid, and even punitive (yet refundable) deposits to ensure that you do not sell off the vehicle before you leave. There will also be freighting costs such as carriage, insurance and freight, called CIF to get the vehicle positioned for you at a seaport or an airport freight terminal.

If the use of such transport is key to the adventure, then these requirements will need to be faced up to, perhaps with the assistance of a freight forwarder in the UK and clearance company on arrival. Any spare parts, special lubricants, fuels or any aspects that are unusual have the potential to make even getting out of the warehouse a nightmare, and you may find that a 'dash' or tip may make the difference to the right officials. Once again, this should fall to your representative to manage.

Greatest Asset

Sometimes your presence may be required to help with any questions, and if this is so, politeness and civility, even in the face of incompetence, overbearing arrogance and rudeness, is the only true course open. In any such circumstances, your best, fastest and greatest assets will be a smile, and a gracious thank you for the interest, help and assistance given to you and your adventure. Your politeness costs you nothing, and will hopefully make way for others who follow to be treated a little more kindly.

13
Equipping Yourself

Wherever you choose to adventure on your travels, preparing for the differing environments and terrain is as vital as setting your aim and objectives, and arranging your travel plan. This means setting yourself up with the right clothing, equipment and skills. Your comfort, safety and day-to-day well-being depend on your preparations.

If you are travelling through an independent operator, particularly if they are a specialist, they should have first-hand knowledge of your needs and be able to advise you, besides providing you with a list of recommended items. Some, like High & Wild, go even further and give thorough pre-departure briefings face to face at no extra cost to clients. This covers every aspect of the journey from the quality of drinking water to the type of head torch that will suit you best. They will even arrange the hire of specialist clothing when you arrive to help keep down costs.

Special Skills

In most cases, it would be unwise to set out on an active adventure without the proper skills. There are many associations, unions and sports-council-approved bodies that can provide information for you on affiliated clubs and courses where you can learn the skills you need for your adventures before you set off.

Some of the clubs not only have people of all levels of ability who are happy to pass on their knowledge, but they have a great social calendar as well. Do make sure that those giving the instruction are fully qualified and have a depth of experience. Many instructors have pursued their own adventures – they may have been part of some at an international level – and also have a wide variety of contacts that they may be prepared to share with you, if they can see that you are committed to learning. You may also find that they are prepared to act as referees for your skills when you do go abroad and this might be necessary to get a special permit or to join a group with one of the active adventure tour operators.

There are exceptions, of course, and instances where learning the skills is a planned part of the adventure. Some basic skills cannot be learnt in the classroom or indoors, and there is only one way to learn and that's 'in at the deep end' with a qualified guide – bungee jumping, river rafting, dog sledding, survival training and travelling with camels, for example. Here the best you can do to prepare yourself is to have researched and brought with you appropriate clothing and equipment to suit the terrain, the temperature and the weather conditions that will keep you in relative comfort.

Buying Equipment

Selecting clothing and personal equipment for your adventures is not easy – the choice is vast. So where do you begin, and whose recommendations do you believe? Are the magazine reviewers in the pay of the manufacturers? Do the outdoor shops care only about their profit margin, and not the customer or the quality of what they sell?

The magazine equipment reviewers may know the equipment suppliers, but they are not in their pay. Reviewers pride themselves on their independence, and take very seriously the responsibilities they have towards you. They are well aware that an 'over recommendation' could put you in jeopardy, besides destroying their reputation. Look out for the reviewers that have tried out clothing and equipment for sustained periods of time and perhaps travelled with items into different environments all over the world.

Of course the outdoor shops care about profit margins, but they also care about customer loyalty and satisfaction. There is no advantage to them in selling you items that are below par or unnecessary to your needs. Always look out for a store where the assistant can give advice based on personal experience. Many of them, especially in the smaller stores, are outdoor enthusiasts themselves. The large chainstores can be very good, but invariably the small independent outdoor retailers have come into the business through the interest of the owners in outdoor activity or adventures. You may have to search them out, as they are seldom in the prime high street locations. The recent National Outdoor Retailer of the Year award went to a small specialist retailer with a shop in Bath and one in London. The owners Nancy and John Coppock have a wealth of personal experience and have just returned from trekking in Costa Rica. They live up to the company name of Itchy Feet, as does the small sales team.

Clothing Considerations

No matter what the terrain or environment, there are some basics that always apply. If you have sore feet and a sore crotch, you are not going anywhere. All other comfort is secondary to these particular bits. So make sure that your footwear is suitable and that your underwear is free flowing, allowing your skin to breathe. In all environments loose-fitting clothing will give you the most comfort – adventure travel (despite the sunglasses) is not a place for fashion. Durability of your clothes is the next most important thing, and their ability to be washed in just about anything from a bucket to a bathtub follows close behind. Jeans are not advisable for adventure travel. In the outdoors they may be tough, but they soak up and hold rainwater, take a long time to dry and have no resistance to wind-chill.

High-tech fabrics do work, but you need to research what makes them work to get the best out of them. You need to understand these fabrics from the layer of clothing that goes next to your skin to the final outer shell that is your immediate protection from the elements, whether extreme heat or static cold. They work on a compatible layering principle, and if you mix natural fibres with synthetics you will create a situation that does not let either fabric work to your benefit and comfort.

Recent innovations are chameleon fabrics that blend into the environment, and thermo-sensitives that automatically regulate the temperature next to your skin. These have not yet reached the open market for production into outdoor clothing, but it will only be a matter of time before they do.

Clothes to avoid include military-style trousers and jackets in camouflage colours. While travelling alone some years ago, Russell Brice was shot at on the Tibetan/Chinese border by a military patrol when making such an unintentional fashion statement. Needless to say he does not recommend the experience.

You should keep in mind, too, that certain cultures do not admire skimpy clothing, especially when worn by women in religious or holy places. In fact in some cultures, they will spit at you in protest.

Climatic Zones

When buying equipment and clothing you need to think of the conditions that you can expect and are likely to encounter. John Coppock produced the following overview for his customers at Itchy Feet who found it a most useful way of focusing on their needs. It splits the world into the four climatic zones.

1 Tropical

EQUATORIAL

Tropical equatorial is found approximately 5 degrees north or south of the equator, where there is no real dry season and rain occurs all year round. As the sun is nearly overhead, it is evenly hot and sticky all year. The most well-known regions are the Amazon rainforest and the Congo basin of Central Africa.

Further north and south, between 5 and 15 degrees either side of the equator, there is a distinct wet and dry season with wet summers and dry winters. Very high temperatures are experienced all year round, though these are moderated by altitude in areas such as Southeast Asia and Central America.

MONSOON

Monsoon climates are caused mainly by temperature differences between land and sea. In these areas, the prevailing winds reverse their direction twice a year, resulting in a hot, wet season followed by a mainly dry, warm one. The best known monsoon affects the Indian subcontinent.

2 Desert

HOT

The true hot desert climates with very high daytime temperatures have little rain all year round and no real cool season, although temperatures may drop sharply at night. The best examples are the Sahara Desert, the deserts of the Middle East and central Australia.

SEMI-DESERT

These are tropical grasslands and the semi-arid edges of hot deserts. There is usually some rain occurring in one season of the year (although the rains can fail several years in succession causing severe drought). Examples are the Sahel region of Africa and the central drier regions of India.

COLD DESERT

Cold deserts occur at higher latitudes in the interior of large continents. The best examples are parts of central Asia and Western China, which are very hot in summer but bitterly cold in winter.

3 Temperate

WARM TEMPERATE

Rain occurs in all seasons, but summer is the wettest and hottest time. Winters are mild with occasional cold spells. These climates are found in the south-west United States, South Africa, China and Australia. Around the Mediterranean and some parts of central Chile, California and Western Australia the winters are generally mild with depressions bringing some winter rain, and summers are warm and hot with little or no rain.

COOL TEMPERATE

The cool temperate oceanic type of climate produces rainfall all year round with less extremes of heat and cold. This climate is found in much of north-west Europe, New Zealand and coastal North America.

Changeable weather is a characteristic of these areas, and they are strongly influenced by large, moving weather systems. Frequent nighttime frosts and generally cold winters are common and can be severe.

4 Cold

MOUNTAIN CLIMATES

Mountain climates occur in all major ranges where land rises above or near the permanent snow line – generally over 3,000 m (10,000 ft) in height. The foothills may be tropical, while the peaks are covered with snow. The Himalaya, Rocky Mountains, Kilimanjaro, Mount Kenya and the Ugandan Ruenzori range are good examples of this climate.

SUB-ARCTIC TUNDRA

In these areas of extreme conditions, summers are often short and hot and winters are long and cold. Vast areas of Canada and Russia experience this type of climate.

POLAR

Near the North and South Poles in Greenland, Antarctica and land inside the Arctic Circle, the Polar climate is dominated by low temperatures, frequent strong winds and year-round snow cover. In all months temperatures are near or below freezing.

Tropical rainforest packing list

For people visiting the rainforest belt (e.g. Southeast Asia or the Amazon), which usually involves some activity in hot, humid conditions.

HEALTH AND SECURITY

- Sunglasses
- Sunscreen – SPF 20
- Biodegradable soap – 100 ml
- Blister spray/treatment
- Hand sanitizer
- Lightweight towel
- Washbag
- Insect repellent – 50 per cent + 100 per cent DEET
- Sterile set
- First-aid kit

- Padlocks
- Moneybelt
- Water bottle
- Water filter
- Water purifier

TRAVEL ESSENTIALS
- Sewing kit
- Knife/Leatherman
- Torch
- Batteries
- Gaffa tape
- Universal plug
- Clothes line

SLEEPING AND LUGGAGE
- Impregnated mosquito net
- Sleeping bag
- Sleeping bag liner
- Travel pack
- Day pack
- Pack-it-cubes

CLOTHES
- Underwear x 3
- Socks x 3
- Swimwear x 1
- Skirt x 1 +/or
- Long trousers x 1
- Zip-off trousers x 1
- Shorts x 1
- Long-sleeved shirt x 3
- Short-sleeved shirt x 2
- Microfleece x 1
- Waterproof jacket/poncho
- Sandals
- Shoes
- Sun hat

High-altitude trek packing list

Individuals travelling independently or in a group going to trek in the Himalaya or similar mountain ranges, climb Kilimanjaro, walk the Inca trail, or take part in any activity over 3,500 m.

HEALTH AND SECURITY

- Sunglasses
- Sunscreen – SPF 20
- Biodegradable soap – 200 ml
- Blister spray/treatment
- Hand sanitizer
- Lightweight towel
- Washbag
- Insect repellent
- Bug proof spray
- Sterile set
- First-aid kit
- Padlocks
- Moneybelt
- Water bottle
- Water filter
- Water purifier

TRAVEL ESSENTIALS

- Sewing kit
- Knife/Leatherman
- Torch
- Batteries
- Gaffa tape
- Universal plug
- Clothes line
- Knife, fork and spoon
- Compass
- Trekking poles

SLEEPING AND LUGGAGE

- Sleeping bag to –7°C
- Sleeping bag liner

- Thermarest
- Thermarest repair kit
- Trekking pack or duffel bag
- Day pack
- Pack-it-cubes

CLOTHES
- Underwear x 4
- Socks x 4
- Long trousers x 1
- Zip-off trousers x 1
- Baselayer trousers x 1
- Long-sleeved shirt x 2
- Baselayer top x 2
- Fleece trousers x 1 or
- Microfleece x 1
- Fleece jacket or down jacket (down is fantastic – light, cosy, warm)
- Waterproof jacket
- Waterproof trousers
- Shoes/sandals
- Boots
- Gloves
- Sun hat
- Fleece hat

Game viewing packing list

A game-viewing holiday on the African savannah staying in lodges or tented camps, but travel can be exposed to the elements, and the weather can fluctuate violently.

HEALTH AND SECURITY
- Sunglasses
- Sunscreen – SPF 20
- Biodegradable soap – 100 ml
- Hand sanitizer
- Lightweight towel

- Washbag
- Insect repellent – 50 per cent + DEET
- Bug-proof spray
- Sterile set
- Padlocks
- Moneybelt
- Water bottle
- Water filter
- Water purifier

TRAVEL ESSENTIALS

- Sewing kit
- Knife/Leatherman
- Torch
- Batteries
- Universal plug
- Clothes line
- Sleeping and luggage
- Impregnated mosquito net
- Travel pack/soft luggage
- Day pack
- Pack-it-cubes

CLOTHES

- Underwear x 3
- Socks x 3
- Swimwear x 1
- Skirt x 1 +/or
- Long trousers x 1
- Zip-off trousers x 1
- Shorts
- Long-sleeved shirt x 3
- Short-sleeved shirt x 2
- Microfleece x 1
- Waterproof jacket
- Sandals
- Shoes
- Sun hat

Gap-year packing list

An adventurous gap year with a three-month work-based project in, say, Africa when smarter clothes may sometimes be required, and then travel on to Australia and Southeast Asia.

HEALTH AND SECURITY

- Sunglasses
- Sunscreen – SPF 12
- Biodegradable soap – 200 ml
- Hand sanitizer
- Lightweight towel
- Washbag
- Insect repellent
- Bug-proof spray
- Sterile set
- First-aid kit
- Padlocks
- Moneybelt
- Pacsafe
- Water bottle
- Water filter
- Water purifier

TRAVEL ESSENTIALS

- Sewing kit
- Knife/Leatherman
- Torch
- Batteries
- Gaffa tape
- Universal plug
- Clothes line
- Knife, fork and spoon

SLEEPING AND LUGGAGE

- Sleeping bag to 0°C
- Sleeping bag liner
- Impregnated mosquito net
- Thermarest

- Thermarest repair kit
- Travel pack with day bag
- Pack-it-cubes

CLOTHES

- Underwear x 4
- Socks x 4
- Swimwear x 1
- Skirt/sarong x 1 or
- Long trousers x 1
- Zip-off trousers x 1
- Shorts
- T-shirt x 2
- Long-sleeved shirt x 2
- Short-sleeved shirt x 1
- Microfleece x 1
- Waterproof jacket
- Waterproof trousers
- Sandals
- Shoes/boots
- Gloves
- Sun hat

Free, independent world traveller

Travelling for an extended period, staying in budget hotels and hostels, sometimes doing casual work to help fund adventures Example: London – Bangkok (travel in Southeast Asia) – Australia (work and travel) – NZ – Fiji – Vancouver (travel in N America) – London, from October to July.

HEALTH AND SECURITY

- Sunglasses
- Sunscreen – SPF 12/20
- Biodegradable soap – 200 ml
- Hand sanitizer
- Lightweight towel
- Washbag

- Insect repellent
- Bug-proof spray
- Sterile set
- First-aid kit
- Padlocks
- Moneybelt
- Pacsafe
- Water bottle
- Water filter
- Water purifier

TRAVEL ESSENTIALS
- Sewing kit
- Knife/Leatherman
- Torch
- Batteries
- Gaffa tape
- Universal plug
- Clothes line
- Knife, fork and spoon

SLEEPING AND LUGGAGE
- Sleeping bag to 0°C
- Sleeping bag liner
- Impregnated mosquito net
- Travel pack with day bag
- Pack-it-cubes

CLOTHES
- Underwear x 3
- Socks x 3
- Swimwear x 1
- Skirt x 1 +/or
- Long trousers x 1
- Zip-off trousers x 1
- T-shirt x 2
- Long-sleeved shirt x 2
- Short-sleeved shirt x 1

- Microfleece x 1
- Waterproof jacket
- Sandals
- Shoes/boots
- Sun hat

Overland adventure packing list

Truck-based travel, say, a group going across South America (probably for more than five weeks). Africa is warmer (though still surprisingly cold at Ngorongoro Crater or in the southern winter at night). Asia varies from bitterly cold to baking hot.

HEALTH AND SECURITY

- Sunglasses
- Sunscreen – SPF 20
- Biodegradable soap – 200 ml
- Hand sanitizer
- Lightweight towel
- Washbag
- Insect repellent
- Sterile set
- First-aid kit
- Padlocks
- Moneybelt
- Water purifier
- Water filter
- Water bottle

TRAVEL ESSENTIALS

- Sewing kit
- Knife/Leatherman
- Torch
- Batteries
- Gaffa tape
- Universal plug
- Clothes line

Sleeping and luggage
- Sleeping bag to 0°C
- Sleeping bag liner
- Impregnated mosquito net
- Trekking pack or duffel bag
- Day pack
- Pack-it-cubes

Clothes
- Underwear x 3
- Socks x 3
- Swimwear x 1
- Skirt x 1 +/or
- Long trousers x 1
- Zip-off trousers x 1
- Fleece trousers
- Shorts x 1
- T-shirt x 1
- Long-sleeved shirt x 3
- Baselayer top
- Microfleece x 1
- Fleece jacket
- Waterproof jacket
- Sandals/boots
- Shoes
- Gloves
- Sun hat
- Fleece hat

14
Health

The old saying 'prevention is better than cure' is the best advice anyone could give to travellers as far as sickness abroad is concerned. With sensible precautions you should not be troubled by illness while away on an adventure into wilderness or unfamiliar places a long way from medical care facilities. Common sense and some specific knowledge of the risks you are likely to encounter are the most fundamental means of protection against disease.

Getting paranoid or irrational about the risk of catching some nasty infection will not help you to make the most of your adventure, so it's important to be properly informed and realistic about the dangers. Once again, developing good habits and routines along with some advanced planning will help to ensure that your journey goes without mishap or discomfort. In the extreme scenario, good sense can save lives.

There are broadly three levels of threat related to health that should concern you. First is the prevalence of diseases, some of which could be life-threatening, others which could cause debilitating effects that could ruin your trip and last long after you return home. Second is the possibility of an accident which would require first aid and prevention of infection in a wound. Third is your general standard of health and the hygiene practices that are necessary for your well-being anywhere in the world.

Diseases

If you take proper precautions, the chances of catching a tropical disease are slight. One problem is that many of them don't show distinctive symptoms for some time. The first signs will be that you feel generally unwell with nausea or headaches or the kind of symptoms usually associated with flu. It's important then to think back to any insect bites or occasions when you may have eaten or drunk anything suspect and get medical advice as soon as you can.

Malaria

Malaria is a serious, sometimes fatal, disease and is by far the most common insect-borne infection in hot regions. There are drugs which give some protection but it is still important to take physical precautions against being bitten, such as keeping your skin covered and your clothes treated with chemical repellent, and sleeping under a net. Once again, prevention is better than cure. If you are going to a country where malaria is present, it is necessary to plan ahead because you will need to take antimalarial drugs over several weeks before departure, following a strict schedule of doses, and continue taking the tablets for four weeks after you have left the area.

There are broadly four types of malaria that infect humans and your doctor or clinic will need to know where you are going as the drugs they prescribe may be determined by the type you are most likely to encounter. Malaria is caused by a microscopic parasite called Plasmodium and it exists in the four varieties, P. *falciparum*, which is the deadliest and most common in Africa, P. *vivax*, P. *ovale* and P. *malariae*.

Malaria occurs in over 100 countries and it is estimated that 40 per cent of the world population is at risk. The World Health Organization estimates that there are between 300 and 500 million cases a year and of those, more than one million people die.

Malaria regions

The malaria-risk parts of the world cover the whole of Africa, the Indian subcontinent, Southeast Asia, Oceania, the Middle East, large areas of Central and South America and parts of the Caribbean, notably Haiti and the Dominican Republic. Outside of Africa, 75 per cent of malaria cases are concentrated in nine countries – Afghanistan, Brazil, Cambodia, China, India, Indonesia, Sri Lanka, Thailand and Vietnam. The malaria mosquito thrives on water, especially in stagnant pools, and the wet paddy fields where rice is grown in Asia are a rich breeding ground.

If you are going anywhere in these regions, a course of anti-malarial tablets is vital before you go and needs to be built into your travel plans. It is a very unpleasant experience if you get infected, but it is largely preventable if you maintain vigilance and good practice to block mosquitoes from settling on your skin and giving you a bite.

When a malaria-carrying mosquito bites, it passes the infecting Plasmodium parasites from its mouthparts into the person's blood. The parasites then go to the liver where they grow and multiply inside red blood cells. This can take as little as eight days or as much as a few months, and the infected person will not notice any symptoms or feel sick. Eventually the infected red blood cells burst and release a toxic chemical into the bloodstream which makes the person feel ill. The new population of parasites is then free to infect other red blood cells and the disease gets progressively worse unless treated quickly. The aim of the preventative treatment over the weeks before any exposure to a mosquito bite is to build up a reserve of chemical agents in the liver and bloodstream to kill off the parasites before they do their damage.

When you are out and about in a malaria-prone area, it is wise to cover up as much as possible, even down to tucking trouser bottoms into your socks or boots. Open sandals are not appropriate on hot days if mosquitoes are about.

Using chemical sprays and burning mosquito coils helps to keep them away indoors, but use chemical repellent sparingly on your skin and never on parts of your arms and legs that are covered with clothing. There are a variety of repellents available today, many of which contain DEET (diethyltoluamide). They should be used on exposed skin such as hands, face and neck. Permethrin is both a repellent and an insecticide and putting it on your clothes will help to ward off ticks and other nasties besides mosquitoes and does not seem to have any toxic side-effects so long as it is not over done directly on the skin. It is wise to wash repellents off hands and face with plenty of soap and water at the end of the day once you are indoors. When you are asleep, you should be protected effectively by a mosquito net. Remember to ensure that the net is well tucked in below your air bed or mattress to keep you enclosed completely.

The symptoms of malaria can be like those of influenza, with a chill, headache, muscle aches and tiredness. Nausea, vomiting and diarrhoea usually follow and a patient may look pale or may have yellow in their eyes and skin because of the loss of red blood cells. Malaria of the type *P. falciparum* can cause kidney failure, coma and death if it is not treated quickly.

Malaria symptoms usually show up first about ten days after the person has been bitten, but it can be as long as several weeks, so you could be home before you start to feel ill. Some parasites can stay in the liver as if resting for months without showing any signs of infection, which is a reason for being strict on yourself about following the dose instructions of anti-malarial medicine, even after you are home from your journey.

If you get a fever or flu-like illness up to a year after visiting a malaria-risk area, you should tell your doctor and get a blood test. The parasites can be seen in a drop of blood under a microscope. Your doctor will need to know where you have been to help identify the type of malaria you may have and give you the appropriate medicines.

Note: If your adventure involves scuba diving in a malaria-risk area, you should tell your doctor. Some anti-malarial tablets contain mefloquine (a trade name is Lariam) which is now known to react badly with compressed nitrogen and cause disorientation. In such circumstances you should take an alternative anti-malarial drug.

Dengue fever

Dengue fever is another disease spread by mosquito bites but it is caused by a virus from a different type of malaria mosquito. There is no vaccination available, though some research is going on in Thailand to develop one. It is not a disease that can be transmitted directly from one person to another, so protecting yourself from contact with mosquitoes is essential to staying healthy.

The dengue-carrying mosquito feeds in the daytime on human blood, so all the precautions described above for keeping your skin covered also apply here. The risk of catching the virus is reduced by taking precautions to limit the places where the mosquito can breed, and this means keeping water covered and using insect repellents to deter them from settling on the skin and biting. The risk to adventurers from dengue fever is quite low if the same care is taken as for avoiding malaria. Dengue fever seems to affect people in urban areas more than forest or jungle, especially where housing is sub-standard and there is inadequate water and sewage treatment.

The symptoms of dengue are high fever, severe headache, backache, joint pains, nausea and vomiting, eye pain and rash. Treatment is mainly by taking painkillers but not aspirin. (In severe cases there is bleeding from small blood vessels and aspirin reduces coagulation of the blood.) An infected person should drink lots of fluids. There has been an increase in the prevalence of dengue fever in the sub-tropical countries of Central and South America over the past 20 years and this is alarming the health authorities. There are four different viruses that cause the disease and they don't provide immunity to each other. Epidemics tend to be larger and more frequent than those of malaria and in Southeast Asian countries, dengue fever has become the most common cause of serious illness among children.

There have been epidemics of dengue fever in east Africa, including Kenya, Mozambique, Djibouti, Somalia, and also in Saudi Arabia and the Seychelles. In the 1980s there was an epidemic in Cuba, linked to a strain from Southeast Asia, and the disease has spread to Venezuela, Colombia, Brazil, French Guyana, Suriname and Puerto Rico. In the 1990s there were also epidemics in Nicaragua, Panama and Costa Rica. Outbreaks have also been recorded in the USA (southern Texas) and northern Mexico.

The global spread of dengue fever is giving health workers cause for concern, and they are comparing it to malaria in terms of the numbers of people at risk. The occurrence of different strains around the world suggests that it is being spread by increased global travel between different regions where the specific mosquite is common.

Yellow fever

Yellow fever is caused by a virus transmitted by a mosquito bite and is most common in sub-Saharan Africa and, to a lesser extent, tropical South America but nowhere else. There is no known cure for yellow fever but there is an effective vaccine available to prevent it, and it is common for other countries to demand proof of vaccination from travellers who have come from infected areas. Many other countries have the type of mosquitoes that could easily pick up and spread yellow fever from infected human carriers. South Africa is one such country which is thankfully still free of yellow fever.

The disease gets its name from the yellow colouration of a victim's skin, caused by damage to the red blood cells by the virus. The first symptoms are bad headaches, fever, nausea, muscle aches and general weakness, and they show up about three to six days after a bite.

It is difficult to get accurate figures for the extent of the disease in Africa because only a small proportion of actual cases are reported from remote areas and the symptoms vary from a mild influenza-type sickness to a severe and sometimes fatal fever. The worst time of year seems to be from July to October, the late rainy and early dry season.

In South America, yellow fever is most common among young men exposed to mosquitoes in the course of working in the forests of Bolivia, Brazil, Colombia, Ecuador, Peru and Venezuela. The worst time of year for infection is from January to March, during the rainy season, especially in Brazil and Peru.

Yellow fever is generally not a problem for travellers who have been vaccinated and take sensible precautions to avoid being bitten by mosquitoes, such as wearing long-sleeved shirts and long trousers in preference to shorts, and using chemical repellents sparingly. Five fatal cases involving Americans and Europeans in the five years up to 2002 were people on holiday at the coast in Brazil who took excursions into the interior without proper protection.

Yellow fever vaccination is available from doctors and travel clinics. You should receive a validated International Certificate of Vaccination which it is wise to keep with your passport as it is valid for ten years. The requirement to show the certificate is enforced strictly by some countries if your passport shows you have been in Africa or South America.

Lyme disease

Lyme disease is a potentially serious illness caused by bacteria spread through tick bites. A circular pink or red rash is the giveaway sign of a tick bite. Ticks are very small so you may not notice their bite, and the distinctive rash does not show up in every case. The symptoms can develop into a fever, headache, muscle and joint aches, nausea, fatigue and loss of appetite. The usual treatment is with the antibiotic doxycycline. Left untreated, Lyme disease can cause arthritis attacks, back pain and mental problems such as forgetfulness and a difficulty in putting words together.

Ticks live in grassy or woodland areas and are widespread in parts of North America as well as large parts of Europe, especially the Black Forest in Germany, southern Sweden, southern and eastern Austria and parts of Switzerland. Lyme disease ticks are also common in central Asia, China, Japan and Australia, but not in Latin America. In Africa, cases have been known in Nigeria, Angola, Kenya, Tanzania and Zambia.

Not all ticks are infective but the normal precautions should be taken. Insect repellent containing DEET and protective clothing are usually enough to protect you from bites, but in areas where ticks are prevalent, it is wise to shake your outer clothing at night to dislodge any that may have become attached during a forest trek.

Leishmaniasis

This is caused by a microscopic parasite picked up from being bitten by a sandfly. It is common in China, Russia, India, Egypt and the rest of the Middle East, East Africa and parts of South America. Symptoms do not show up for at least two months after the bite and the first signs are skin ulcers, accompanied by fever, weight loss, a low blood count and general weakness. Because of the long incubation period, these may not become apparent until after you have returned home, so it is important that you see a doctor and tell him or her where you have been.

Trypanosomiasis

Commonly known as sleeping sickness, trypanosomiasis is a disease picked up from the tsetse fly in Africa. The site of the bite will turn red and become very sore and you will develop a fever, lethargy and headaches. DEET-type insect repellents are usually effective prevention, but it is wise to stay out of areas known to local people to be risky.

Onchocerciasis

Usually known as river blindness, this is a disease caused by a worm parasite after a bite from a blackfly. It is common in equatorial Africa and parts of South America and the Middle East. It is advisable to avoid going into rivers and streams in infected areas.

Japanese encephalitis

This is a viral infection of the brain and spinal cord transmitted by mosquitoes. It is prevalent in South and Southeast Asia from India to Japan and precautions against mosquitoes are essential. A vaccine is available.

Tick-borne encephalitis

As the name suggests, this form of encephalitis is caught from tick bites. It is prevalent in rural areas and forests in central and eastern Europe, including Austria, southern Germany, Switzerland and parts of Russia. Treatment is effective if it is started early enough, but the symptoms are difficult to spot as they can be like a mild dose of the flu. A vaccine is available and treating your clothes with tick-repellent chemicals provides added protection especially if you are going to spend time in a forest.

Cholera

Fortunately cholera is not very common. There is an oral vaccine that gives some protection but the best way is to observe good practice in food and water hygiene. Cholera is a severe intestinal infection that causes acute watery, bloody diarrhoea and dehydration and can be fatal. It is caught by consuming contaminated food and water, and is a problem in areas of poor sanitation in South America, the Middle East, Africa and Asia, and in places where there has been a natural disaster such as an earthquake or severe flooding. Fortunately, it is rare for travellers to be affected by cholera if sensible precautions are taken, and it is aid workers in disaster zones who are most at risk.

Typhoid

This is a water-borne disease and is easily avoided by maintaining high standards of hygiene and water purification. Vaccines are available which are taken orally or by injection. Typhoid can be picked up from contaminated food and water in some countries if you don't stick to the habits of strict hygiene and safe food handling. Polluted water is the most common source of typhoid, along with shellfish taken from waters contaminated by sewage, and raw vegetables grown in fields fertilized by faeces. There is a vaccine against typhoid so a pre-travel jab is recommended if you are likely to be going to an area where typhoid is a known threat.

Rabies

You can be immunized against rabies if you know you are going to an area where it is prevalent, but if you get bitten or licked by an infected animal, make sure you get a booster shot when you return home.

Tetanus

Every traveller should have up-to-date tetanus protection. Any wound, even a graze, that breaks the skin leaves you vulnerable to infection and tetanus is often the first to take hold because the tetanus bug is found in soil the world over.

AIDS

There is no vaccine to protect you from AIDS. AIDS is a serious, life-threatening condition and infection with the HIV virus which causes it can occur anywhere in the world. HIV infection is preventable; the precautions are in your own control, and do not mean that you must never visit a country where AIDS is rife.

Not every country has a full record of the extent of its spread but it is well-known that AIDS is devastating some communities, particularly in parts of Africa.

AIDS is so widespread that it is not the destination that matters as far as the risk to travellers is concerned; what matters more is personal conduct regarding sexual contact and practices such as sharing needles or instruments that puncture the skin. These factors matter just as much abroad as at home and are within your own control. The risk of HIV infection is low wherever you go if you avoid sexual contact with infected partners and protect yourself from direct contact with another person's blood or secretions. This is common sense and not specific to travel.

You should be aware that there is some concern that the blood supplies in hospitals in developing countries may not be screened adequately for HIV, but you must get it into perspective – the likelihood that you would need a blood transfusion while away on an adventure is so low that you cannot plan for it. The benefit of taking reserve samples of your own blood for such an eventuality are far outweighed by the risks from inadequate storage in a camp or lodge in a hot country.

You are at risk of HIV infection if you have sexual contact with an infected person, with someone who does not know their HIV status or with someone who has had multiple partners such as sex workers in bars and clubs, and it does not matter whether it is with someone of the same or the opposite sex. It is the transmission of the virus in bodily fluids which spreads HIV.

Unsafe sex

It is beyond the scope of this book to give adventurous travellers advice about morals but you may be faced with the opportunity for easy sex in a faraway city, such as on a stop-over in Bangkok on the way to a trekking project up country, for example. It's your choice whether you have sex and with whom, but be aware that AIDS is having a greater impact on the brothels of Bangkok than the Thai authorities care to admit. A cynical view might be that sex tourism is a significant part of the city's foreign earning potential so the authorities are not keen to impose restrictions. Young people in Thailand have an easy-going attitude to sex, more so than in the West perhaps, and they can make a lot more money from sex tourism in the capital than they can from scraping an existence in a village or on a farm and their families benefit while they are earning.

Sadly, there is little support for them when they fall ill, not necessarily from HIV/AIDS, but from infections that they are unable to fight because AIDS has undermined their immune system. There are plenty more young people ready to take their places in the brothels of Bangkok. So sex in the city is easy. The advice from this book is that when presented with risk, do not make things worse by your own voluntary actions or omissions.

The other HIV risk factor is infection through the use of contaminated needles for injections or other skin-piercing practices. The issue here is once again the transmission of a virus from one person's blood to another's. This is not confined to sharing needles for injecting illicit drugs. It also concerns ear, nose or other decorative body piercing, tattooing and even acupuncture if it is not carried out to strict standards of hygiene with the needles properly sterilized. Again, it is beyond the scope of this book to advise you on fashion but if you must have a tattoo or a nose stud, can you be sure that the artist has sterilized his equipment since the last customer? That is the risk assessment you must make to protect your own health.

You may be less at risk from acupuncture if it is carried out in a proper medical facility by a reputable practitioner, who will be alert to the danger of cross-infection and will use sterilized needles. The advice here is to check that this is so before you commit to the procedure. If you must have an injection while away, try to insist that the doctor or nurse uses a new needle from a sealed pack. This is not always possible in some developing countries, so avoid the need for injections by arranging them with a doctor or clinic before you set out on your journey.

If you have a condition that requires injections, such as diabetes, or you must take a sample of your blood for a test, then ensure the needle is sterile. Preferably, take enough new replacement needles to last your whole journey. If you must use a sharp instrument to pierce the skin for a blood test, sterilize it by holding it in a clean (not yellow) flame on a stove, or allow it to stand in boiling water for at least 30 seconds immediately before using it to prick the skin.

It is probably apparent to you that the precautions suggested here against HIV infection also prevent cross-infection with other agents of disease, such as hepatitis B, hepatitis C and sexually transmitted diseases (STDs). The point is that they are all transmitted from one person to another by direct mixing of bodily fluids.

Hepatitis

Hepatitis is a viral infection of the liver. It can be very serious because the liver is a vital organ for clearing out toxins and waste from the bloodstream. There are various forms of the disease, two of which are common in under-developed countries.

The symptoms of hepatitis are rather like those of flu with headache, fever, nausea and vomiting, but it usually takes a month for them to develop so you may not know you are infected until after your trip. The Indian subcontinent is the area of highest risk, but hepatitis A is also present in some parts of Southeast Asia, Africa and South America.

Hepatitis A is generally caught from contaminated food. The virus is released in a person's faeces and if the person does not wash properly, it gets on to food by unhygienic handling. The infection can take some weeks to show up and then it is a debilitating sickness that can last for months, but is rarely fatal in adults. Travellers are more susceptible than local people because they have not built up immunity from having the disease earlier in life. A very effective vaccine is available which gives ten years' protection. The best advice, however, is to avoid uncooked food unless it's fruit that you've peeled yourself.

Hepatitis B is more serious and can be fatal. It's caught by contact with contaminated body fluids, especially blood, usually by using needles that have not been sterilized. It is also a sexually transmitted disease so all the precautions described for HIV/AIDS also apply here. Hepatitis B can cause liver damage, and people who recover from a bout of sickness remain carriers of the virus and can suffer ongoing liver problems. Fortunately an effective vaccine is now available.

Altitude sickness

Even if you are in perfect health and at peak fitness, you can still develop altitude sickness, a condition caused by low levels of oxygen supplied to the brain at high altitude. The usual symptoms are shortness of breath, nausea, loss of appetite, dizziness, fatigue, insomnia and a dull, throbbing headache. It is usually caused by ascending too quickly to altitudes above 8,000 feet or through strenuous exertion at high altitudes without giving yourself time to acclimatize. Altitude sickness can occur on high mountains but also in countries like Bolivia. Ecuador and Peru, so it is wise to spend a day or two relaxing when you arrive there. Mild cases are not dangerous and require only rest. If the symptoms persist, it is important to get to a lower altitude as soon as possible.

Some trekking groups carry a Gammow bag (a portable compression chamber) or bottled oxygen to be used in severe cases, as the sickness can worsen and cause you to become confused and unbalanced. Previous experience of high places, pre-ascent training and being in good physical shape do not prevent the onset of altitude sickness – it can strike anyone. The best advice is to eat a diet that is high in carbohydrates to build up glycogen in the muscles, avoid vigorous activity in addition to the climb, don't ascend faster than you need to and spend some time acclimatizing. There are medications that reduce the symptoms but for most people, taking aspirin the day before the climb and for three days at high altitude can help, and will certainly reduce the severity of the headaches.

Dealing with Accidents

Accidents happen. You can't plan for them and you can't always avoid them, but you can prepare for dealing with them when they hit you or your team. A routine precaution for anyone planning an adventure or travelling generally is to be up to date with anti-tetanus immunization and it is well worth taking a course in first aid in the months before travelling. Your local branch of the Red Cross or St John's Ambulance will be able to tell you when one is being held in your area. These organizations have volunteer instructors who would arrange a course specifically for a group as part of your preparations. There are also several commercial organizations that specialize purely in adventure medicine and these are listed in the Gazetteer section.

A course in first aid will not turn you into a medic or a nurse, but it will give you some practical tips and routines to follow in an emergency, and they could mean the difference between life and death for a fellow traveller. First aid is not about giving treatment to an injured person, it is about keeping them alive and safe until you can get medical help or transport to a hospital. At the very least you will have some knowledge of how not to make a bad situation worse.

First aid is also included in survival courses, where you get some additional ideas about improvizing when away from immediate help by the rescue services. A basic first-aid kit is essential wherever you go. While there are several good medical packs available, the Lifesystems Trekker first-aid kit is very popular and for remoter adventures can be combined with their sterile pack. Neither take up much space in a rucksack or luggage and contain the following:

Trekker first-aid kit

- Woven bandage
- Crepe bandage (small)
- Antiseptic cleansing tissues x 4
- Non-adherent dressing (small)
- Scissors
- Safety pins x 6
- Gauze dressings x 5
- Disposable latex gloves
- Micropore tape
- Adhesive fabric strip
- Paracetamol tablets x 16
- Primary care information sheet

Sterile kit

- 5 x disposable sterile syringes (2 x 2 ml 2 x 5 ml 1 x 10 ml)
- 6 x single-use hypodermic needles (1 x 19 g, 2 x 21 g, 2 x 23 g, 1 x 25 g)
- Braided silk suture and needle
- 3 x wound closure strips
- Intravenous cannula (drip needle) (18 g)
- 6 x antiseptic cleaning tissues
- 4 x adhesive dressings
- Scalpel blade and handle
- Latex gloves and information card

For use by trained medical personnel only and designed by doctors for use in medical emergencies. Using this kit in an emergency, the risks of contracting blood-borne diseases from unsterile medical equipment are reduced.

Health and Hygiene

Proper nutrition is one essential for good health. Food provides the energy for activity and minerals and vitamins are essential for keeping your systems functioning properly and fighting infections. In addition, you should not underestimate the importance of sleep for recharging and refreshing the body. Over-doing physical and mental exertion in a strange land with few of the comforts of home can reduce your body's ability to fight off disease. But most important of all is general hygiene.

Washing

Washing your hands with soap and water is the basis of good hygiene wherever you are. Hygiene is an important issue in basic living conditions, and a difficult one, as water is often in short supply. A daily bath or shower is not practical on an expedition and it will be necessary to improvize to keep clean. One useful tip is to pack some anti-bacterial moist tissues for your journey, sometimes called 'wet-ones' or 'baby wipes'.

One way of having warm water for washing is to make a solar shower with plastic bags, which you fill with water and lay out on a flat surface in the sunshine. Some army supply stores have bags specially made for this, with one side painted black to absorb heat more effectively.

Always, and without fail, wash your hands with soap and water after going to the toilet and before handling or eating food. This means washing your hands thoroughly, not just giving them a quick rinse. One of the most common ways to become ill in the wilderness is from infections picked up through poor personal hygiene. But do respect the environment by not using soap in a running stream or a lake; it is better to reserve a bowl of lake water for hand washing. Always use biodegradable soap.

Cleaning up after a meal should be handled in a similar way, treating waste food and washing waters as compost to be buried away from natural water supplies. Dishes should not be rinsed in a lake or stream because not only will this pollute the water, but the water itself may contain pollutants, micro-organisms and parasites that could settle on the drying dishes and be revived when they are next used for eating. Dishes, cups and cutlery should be washed with heated water and rinsed with clean water that has been treated with a filter or purification tablets. Anything that is not food – such as packaging and disposable containers – should be bagged and carried away to be disposed of carefully or recycled.

Dental hygiene is also extremely important. It may not seem very important when you are in the jungle or desert coping with many other strange things but cleaning your teeth with a little purified water should still be a daily routine.

Poor personal hygiene is the cause of the most common travel illness, diarrhoea. Apart from discomfort and embarrassment, the main problem with diarrhoea is that it can result in the loss of a lot of fluid and essential mineral salts from the gut. In extreme cases, this can lead to dehydration, which could leave you vulnerable to other problems. There is a simple remedy. Dioralyte, which is a commercial product readily available from pharmacies which helps to replace body fluids and salts lost in bouts of diarrhoea and is good for preventing dehydration. It comes as a pack of sachets containing blackcurrant- or citrus-flavoured powder that dissolves easily in water to make a pleasant drink. As with any medication, read the patient information in the pack before use.

Foot care

Proper foot care is vital and blisters need to be treated and protected from infection right away. In the heat of a tropical country, and on a walking holiday anywhere, athlete's foot can be a nuisance and a health hazard. It is caused by a fungus in the skin that thrives in the warm, moist conditions of boots and shoes, so take any chance you get to wash and dry your feet thoroughly. Avoid walking around in bare feet in tropical countries because the soil contains micro-organisms and parasites that can get under the skin.

Latrines

The most difficult issue about personal hygiene is how to go to the toilet when there is no bathroom in the great outdoors. This may be taken care of in a base camp that is set up for constant use, but on a trek where you set up camp along the route, it can become an issue of health, environment and dignity. If no latrine or portable loo tent is provided, the best advice is to imitate a cat and dig a shallow hole and cover your own waste with earth. Some may wish to use a sarong as a wrap to create some privacy.

An earth latrine is an area about 30 metres away from any natural running water and away from where the rest of your group may be gathered, possibly shielded by bushes or trees. If you go to the toilet too close to a stream or lake, the water will become polluted with, in effect, untreated sewage which is not good for the environment, the living things in the water or other human beings who may be in the area or downstream and who could become infected with bacteria or parasites which you were not aware of.

A plastic bag or bottle of water and some soap should be kept close so that you can wash your hands straight away. The hole needs to be about 10–20cm deep. The soil placed on top of your solid waste contains microbes which will digest it and help to degrade it like compost. Avoid digging a latrine hole on a slope or in very wet soil because water running off can carry away the harmful pollutants, when what you are aiming to do is to confine it until the soil organisms have turned them naturally into fertilizer. There are two schools of thought on how to dispose of toilet paper; some people say bury it with the human waste, others say bag it and burn it at the next opportunity on a camp fire or at the next lodgings. Hard-core expedition trekkers say don't use paper at all and clean yourself with readily available leaves and grass from where you are sitting.

15
Food and Water

Getting enough to eat is vital for any activity and food is your core source of energy. Deciding on the right selection is important to the success of any adventure. Exploring the range of things to eat in another country can itself be an adventure and an education.

Any adventure or expedition is going to involve greater physical activity than staying at home so your choice of what to eat must take this into account. You need high energy food and it has to be appealing and varied. Missing out on a meal because it is not appetizing can leave you feeling drained and out of sorts. You can't be fussy when you are abroad because your favourite items may not be available. Your meals must be balanced in terms of nutrition if you are to stay healthy and lively, with the right proportions of protein, carbohydrate, fat and vitamins.

It's important also to drink plenty of fluids as part of an active lifestyle, in both hot countries and cold climates especially on high mountains and in the polar regions. As much as 30 per cent of body heat and moisture is lost through the head, neck and mouth in these environments. Dehydration can have a bad effect on your performance, not least because it interferes with the efficiency of your body to make the best use of solid food. You will be surprised how much fluid is lost through overall perspiration when you are active in a hot, dry climate because you may not be aware of sweating if it evaporates quickly.

You will also lose essential salts rapidly. Don't wait until you are thirsty – drinking a little at regular intervals is more effective, especially if you take in some replacement salts from fruit juice, a commercial sport drink or a sachet of prepared powdered salts made for the purpose. At the very least, a little sugar and cooking salt added to some clean drinking water would help.

Eating Out Locally

Trying out unfamiliar dishes and experiencing new tastes and aromas is a way of exploring what the world has to offer. Part of the enjoyment of visiting an unfamiliar country and another culture is experiencing the local food and drink in a restaurant, cafe or lodge. Even better, you may get the chance to sample local hospitality if you are invited to someone's home. Eating is one of life's pleasures and when you are away on an adventure, mealtimes are social occasions for your group and also opportunities to meet local people and make new friends.

One of David Browne's adventure trips was a tour of Pakistan with the aim of visiting places associated with the history of British colonial rule. On the way he met up with some students from Karachi who were in Peshawar on their way back from a visit to the mountains in northern Pakistan. The next day he was invited to the home of one of the students to share a typical family meal of rice, dahl, spicy chicken and flat bread, with the sweetest honey and almond pastries. The occasion made an unplanned cultural and memorably delicious highlight to his tour.

In Morocco, Tunisia and other parts of north Africa, you might get the chance to try a genuine tajine – a stew made with marinated meat (usually lamb or goat) and vegetables prepared in a clay pot with a curious cone-shaped lid, served with cous-cous, a grain dish made from wheat.

Typical dishes to try in South America are empanadas, which are pastries filled with a variety of diced meat, potatoes and peppers, or feijoada, which is a thick stew made from black beans and the meat from pig's ears and tails. It is said to have been devised by slaves in colonial Brazil to make use of the meat discarded by the farmers they worked for. Llapingachos are common in Ecuador and consist of pancakes or patties made with mashed potato, onion and cheese. In Mexico and parts of Central America, you must of course try tortillas and tacos but expect a treat for the taste buds that far exceeds anything you get in a Mexican-style restaurant in Europe.

Travelling the Silk Road countries of central Asia, you will almost certainly encounter plov, a dish which has various ethnic variations, but is basically a meat and rice stew made with turnip and carrot and sometimes apricots in a heavy cooking pot with the oil from cotton seed or ground nut. It is very popular in Turkmenistan and Uzbekistan, as is shorpa, a soup made from vegetable stock and really fatty pieces of lamb which are considered a delicacy.

In India and the Far East there will be endless opportunities to try food prepared on stalls that line the streets or on river boats. The main thing here is that the food you eat must be freshly prepared and served piping hot straight from the wok or pan. It is not wise to go for food that has been standing for any length of time. The local people may not suffer, but warm food in a hot climate attracts flies and is a rich breeding ground for the micro-organisms that could cause you an upset stomach or worse.

Eating Strange Food Safely

With proper planning and a good measure of common sense, a trip to even the most remote and exotic environment can be completed without any ill-effects from food and drink. There are some basic rules to follow which should become ingrained as good habits for adventurous travellers and help you avoid becoming paranoid about life-threatening diseases or embarrassing discomfort. Horror stories about what can happen should not stop you enjoying your food while away from home, just take practical precautions and your trip should be trouble free.

Travellers' diarrhoea is the most common upset from food and drink. It is caused by a wide range of micro-organisms but particularly, one called Campylobacter which is common in tropical climates. Even a brief bout of diarrhoea can spoil a trip and the discomfort is usually accompanied by nausea, vomiting and fever which can last up to two or three days. The risk of contracting travellers' diarrhoea is highest in countries with low standards of hygiene and sanitation and poor infrastructure for controlling the safety of food and drinking water. While the risks are greater in poor countries, locations with poor hygiene can be found in any country.

Apart from diarrhoea remember that other more serious illnesses, including cholera, typhoid and hepatitis A, described in Chapter 14, can be caused by contaminated food and water so it is vital to maintain good habits of clean food handling at all times.

Things to Watch out for

It is not necessarily the type of food that poses a risk, so much as how well it has been prepared and stored. While you may be partial to a medium-rare steak or soft-boiled eggs at home, it's safer to insist on having them well done when you are out and about in unfamiliar places.

Summary of food risks abroad

Usually safe	Risky	Best avoided
Freshly-prepared hot food	Food from street vendors	Food left standing warm
Freshly-peeled fruit	Unpeeled fruit	Shellfish
Tinned food	Salad unless well washed	Broad-leaf salad
Dried food	Ice cream	Rare meat or raw fish
Bottled water or drinks	Ice cubes unless made from purified water	Unpasteurised dairy items including milk and cheese
Freshly-baked bread		

Freshly-cooked hot food is not usually a danger, but avoid food that has been sitting for any length of time, on a buffet table for example, or on which flies have settled. A general rule for eating fresh fruit and vegetables is: 'peel it, boil it or forget it'. Fresh salads are best avoided unless you can scrub the leaves clean. Fresh fruit and vegetables with thick skins are considered safe because they can be peeled with a clean knife.

Don't eat cheese or milk products as they are likely to be unpasteurised in countries that attract adventurous travellers. The problem with unpasteurised milk products is the risk of brucellosis but this is easily destroyed if the milk is boiled. Indian chai, which is a brew of tea and milk boiled together, is not a problem, but by contrast, home-made goat's cheese is notorious for containing brucellosis. Local people build up some resistance to its effects so you may think it's all right but a polite refusal is a wise response if it is offered to you.

On any list of foodstuffs to avoid, fish, particularly shellfish, comes quite high. This is because they feed by filtering large quantities of water and any toxic substances from water contamination tend to be retained and concentrated in their flesh. There is a particular toxin called ciguatera that is common in fish in tropical areas and it can cause illness in humans even after the fish is cooked.

Dangers lurk also in the cutlery and utensils, including cups and mugs if they have not been washed properly. So it is essential that this aspect of food hygiene is not overlooked. If you are very concerned at the state of things in a restaurant, one tip is to discreetly wipe the items with an anti-bacterial moist tissue.

Precautions for avoiding unsafe food and drink

- Avoid cooked food that has been kept at room temperature or in the open air for a long time.
- Eat only food that has been cooked thoroughly and is still hot.
- Avoid uncooked food, apart from fruit and vegetables that can be peeled or shelled, and avoid fruits with damaged skins.
- Avoid dishes containing raw or undercooked eggs.
- Avoid food bought from street vendors.
- Avoid ice cream from unreliable sources, including street vendors.
- In countries where poisonous chemicals may be present in fish and shellfish from sea pollution, obtain advice locally.
- Boil unpasteurised (raw) milk.
- Boil drinking water if its safety is doubtful; if boiling is not possible, use a certified, well-maintained filter or a chemical agent to treat the water.
- Avoid ice cubes unless you are sure they are made from safe water.
- Avoid brushing teeth with unsafe water.
- Bottled or packaged cold drinks are usually safe provided that they are sealed; hot beverages are usually safe.
- Don't drink water from wells or streams unless you put it through a purifier first.

Water

You need to be extremely careful about cold drinks and ice cubes. Bottled water will be safe, so long as the cap seal is not broken. Beware of bottles that have been reused and filled with the local tap water! Sealed bottles of carbonated (fizzy) drinks cannot easily be faked, so you can usually rely on those. The standards of hygiene in factories and bottling plants are likely to be higher than in a local cafe because a commercial enterprise stands to lose a lot more business if its reputation is damaged by reports of sickness traced back to its products.

Tap water is safe if it has been through a well-maintained purification plant before being piped around to consumers. This is rarely the case in developing countries. Where there is a public water-purification system, the level of chlorine or other chemicals in the tap water can still make it unpleasant for visitors to drink.

It is a good precaution to avoid using tap water for cleaning your teeth if you are in any doubt about its purity. When you are out in the field, trekking or camping, there is nothing wrong with brushing your teeth with toothpaste and a mouthful of fizzy drink. It may not taste so good but at least it eliminates the risk of water-borne infection.

You cannot do without water wherever you go, so treasure your supply of bottled water if you are venturing out to remote areas. If you are a long way from a shop that sells commercially bottled water, ensure you have some means of purifying the water taken from local sources. Even in crystal clear streams, rivers and lakes, the water should be considered unsafe to drink.

Purifying Water

If you can, boil the water and then keep it covered while it cools. This may not be possible if, for example, making a fire in a forest or dry scrubland is going to be a hazard. Do bear in mind that if you are at high altitude the atmospheric pressure is lower than at sea level and water boils at less than 100°C. If you are melting snow for your drinking water or for cooking, allow it to boil a little longer than usual to ensure all the nasty microbes are killed off.

As an alternative to boiling, filtering and chemical treatment will ensure your water is safe. There is a wide range of filtration systems and chemical treatments on the market and deciding what to take will depend on the nature of your adventure.

If you know you are going to have to use water from open sources such as rivers, streams or wells, make sure you have effective means of filtering it. Filtering first is necessary to get rid of parasites and organic particles that could be resistant to chemical treatment. The Aquapure Traveller, available from MASTA Travel Shop (www.masta.org), turns any tap, river or pool water into fresh, pure drinking water, free from harmful organisms such as Giardia and Cryptosporidia. It consists of a 750 ml water bottle and a filter unit with iodine sleeve and produces around 450 refills or 350 litres of safe drinking water before a replacement filter cap is needed. The MSR Miniworks EX Ceramic Water Filter is compact and easy to use and is the filter chosen by the Amphibious Raids and Reconnaissance Division of the US Marine Corps. It purifies a litre of water in about a minute and includes a solid block of carbon that eliminates odour from iodine and most chemicals including pesticides.

Once you have filtered your water, if still unsure, a simple and effective chemical treatment is iodine. Two or three drops of tincture of iodine in a litre of clear water will do the trick, but tends to give drinking water an unwelcome taste. Leave it to stand for about 15 minutes, and you can add flavouring or fruit juice once the iodine has had time to take effect. A vitamin C tablet dissolved in the water gets rid of any unpleasant taste left from the iodine and keeps you healthy at the same time. Iodine should be used sparingly and not for longer than about six weeks, and should be avoided by anyone who is pregnant or has thyroid problems.

Tincture of iodine is available from any chemist. Lifesystems Iodine Drops or Tablets, available online from Gear-Zone (www.gear-zone.co.uk), have been specially produced for travellers and are a low-cost, effective way of ensuring clean water free of disease-causing bacteria. Another brand is called Potable Aqua Plus and these tablets are made to strict US military specifications, based on iodine as the disinfecting agent. They can be purchased online through various websites and from outdoor pursuits shops.

Chlorine tablets are also available to make drinking water safer by killing pathogenic organisms and have the advantage that they don't cause the iodine taste. Chlorine can also be used to disinfect water for cleaning teeth and washing fruit and vegetables. The tablets come in a small plastic bottle containing 75 tablets which will purify up to 75 litres of water.

As a real emergency measure, you can add a few drops of bleach to the filtered water and leave it to stand for a few minutes, but this is likely to give it a slight taste of chlorine.

Cooking for Yourself

Expedition planning needs to include some attention to the detail of what you are going to eat on your trip. You can't take a supermarket trolley-load with you so you need to keep in mind economy of space and weight while considering the things you need for a varied, nourishing diet.

You can eat well in even the most extreme conditions. Your meals should be appetizing and as close as possible to your usual diet. In the early days of space flight, NASA astronauts were fed on a scientific diet of prepared foods in tubes and sachets that supplied all their nutritional and energy requirements, but were seriously unappealing. As a result of feedback from the astronauts, the decision was made to provide food in more familiar styles that looked like proper meals. The lesson was that food is not just functional but is also important for morale on a long journey away from home, and this applies to Earth-bound adventurers too.

You don't need to be a star chef, but you need to be confident that you will enjoy the meals you are going cook for yourself. Don't assume that there will always be someone on hand to do the cooking for you, even on an organized tour. Basic dishes do not need elaborate preparation or technique to turn out appetizing, tasty and nutritious.

Menu planning is important to ensure that you have a balanced diet to keep you healthy and fit for the rigours of an adventure or expedition away from hotels and restaurants. The essential requirements are the same wherever you go: a balance of carbohydrates, protein and fats along with sufficient vitamins and minerals.

Part of an adventure to a strange or remote country is the excitement of trying local dishes so it's not a good idea to be too fussy about what you will eat or you could go very hungry indeed. You should plan to buy some fresh items wherever you go. In the planning stage, do some research about the staple foods of the countries you intend to visit and even try out some unfamiliar dishes at home. If your trip is going to involve you doing your own cooking on a camp stove, then it's wise to get some practice at basic cooking before you set out.

Nutritional Requirements

Menu planning should begin with a consideration of what the body needs to bear the strenuous activity of an expedition. A rule of thumb is 3,000 kcals (kilocalories or calories) per day with a further 1,000 kcals if there is tough climbing or mountaineering involved.

Breakfast should provide about 20 per cent through cereals, milk, bread, jam, perhaps peanut butter. Lunch and a variety of snacks en route should account for 50 per cent of the day's energy intake and include a hot drink. It's not wise to have too much all in one sitting because the body takes time to digest food and that process takes up energy, so a lunch break is essential for a rest to allow the food to settle. The evening meal should be the remaining 30 per cent of the day's requirement and is also an opportunity for a morale-boosting period of reflection on the day's achievements. This is the time for a full cooked meal as there is no pressure to move on. Try to make it a simple three-course affair even in a tent on a mountainside. This may seem extravagant and complicated, but it's worth it because the action of preparing an appetizing meal at the end of a strenuous day in an unfamiliar part of the world is actually quite relaxing and a great morale booster.

Carbohydrates are the main source of energy, and there are two broad types: simple and complex. Simple carbohydrates are items such as sugar, glucose and honey which are easily digested and provide a rapid boost of energy; complex carbohydrates include bread, potatoes and pasta which take longer to digest and release their energy more gradually.

Protein from meat, dairy products, pulses and soya beans is essential for keeping the muscles in good form. Fats, such as butter, and oils from fish and nuts are a concentrated source of energy and are also essential for the proper digestion of protein.

On a trip of up to two weeks, it is highly unlikely that you will have a vitamin and mineral deficiency but if you are travelling for longer periods, it is wise to carry a supply of supplements in tablet form. Vitamin C tablets that dissolve in water make a healthy and refreshing drink now and again. As an added benefit, you might take some further nutritional supplements in tablet form such as B12, and iron, if you are going to be away for several weeks.

If you are planning the menus for a group, you need to be aware of special needs. Some people are allergic to nuts, and it is easy to overlook the fact that cereals such as muesli – which makes a fine, lightweight expedition breakfast – may contain particles of nuts. Some people prefer not to eat meat and there is no reason why vegetarians should not be able to enjoy an expedition; there are other sources of protein besides meat products, such as soya and textured vegetable protein (TVP).

For journeys that involve arduous trekking or climbing between planned mealtimes, everyone should have in their packs some reserve items such as snack bars and chocolate for an extra shot of energy on the way, and in case of an emergency when the trek is held up or takes longer than expected. Kendal Mint Cake was invented especially for such occasions and is still a favourite reserve item among climbers and trekkers, even though they may not admit it!

Suggested Foods for an Expedition

Breakfast should be warm and filling because it sets you up for the day, and it could be some hours before lunch. Porridge is a good base, is easy to prepare and can be eaten with fruit and sugar to give it some variety. Commercial products like Readybrek and Quaker Oats are available in meal-sized packets which are compact, lightweight and contain a balance of nutrients and fibre. A drink like hot chocolate or cocoa is also a good breakfast item, and you can make enough to put some into a thermos flask for later. If you have only one cooking pot or a single stove, it makes sense to make the porridge first and get the drink ready while you are eating.

Lunch on the move may be a just a nourishing snack of fruit and nuts with a hot drink if you have time to prepare it and you have a sheltered spot to sit and wait for it. But on a high mountain you really don't want to hang around. Remember, the higher you go, the longer it will take for water to boil because the air pressure will be reduced compared to sea level. This is where a flask that you prepared earlier will be welcome.

In between meals, an oatmeal snack bar or some biscuits and dried fruit such as apricots and dates will give you an energy boost. Mixed nuts are also good for a snack because they are filling and contain protein. Chocolate is a good source of nourishment too, but some experienced expedition leaders recommend reserving chocolate as an emergency ration.

The evening meal will be the main meal of the day for several reasons. It has to be filling to last you through the long hours of the night and it is a time for morale boosting, whether you are alone or in a group, in extreme conditions. Soup is an obvious starter and can be different every night, according to your taste. Rice could be the basis for a variety of appetizing meals and has the advantage that you can add almost anything to make a risotto or paella-style meal in a single pot. Pasta is also a good expedition staple and can be prepared with meat or vegetables. A bean stew is another possibility for a main course. Mashed potato powder is popular with some people for camp cooking, but is not so adaptable – you need to prepare it separately from other ingredients, which is fine if you have more than one stove. You do not need to skimp on dessert just because you are out on the trail. Some fruit or a local sweet pastry makes a pleasant pudding, and you can round off with a hot drink.

Do some research about the foods available locally in the places you intend to visit. Be prepared to be adventurous in your eating habits as much as in your travel plans and you will be pleasantly surprised to discover some tasty treats. Fresh papaya is delicious and easy to prepare, for example, so don't waste space packing it at home.

A regular basic meal in Nepal, for example, is daal bhaat-tarkari. This is a plate of boiled rice with fried curried vegetables and lentil gravy. This is easy to prepare on a camp stove. Rice and pasta are the kind of foods that do not take up much space in a pack but when boiled in water expand and produce a substantial part of a meal.

Dehydrated foods are light and easy to pack. Powdered soup is better for taking on a trek than tinned varieties; milk and mashed potato also come in powder form. It's possible to buy complete meals in dehydrated packs but these can be expensive compared with basic ingredients. Dried food packs such as freeze-dried vegetables, chicken cubes or soya mince are light to carry and easy to turn into a satisfying meal even on a mountainside, cooked in a pot of boiling water made from snow.

16
Personal Safety

Terrorism is now the single biggest reason why people take a greater interest in all aspects of their safety while travelling. No international travel is risk-free, and it never has been. Potentially, terrorism *could* affect your adventure, but this does not mean it *will* happen to you or that you should not go. You must keep this and other possible threats to your safety in perspective, and that is partly what this chapter is about. Before looking in detail at terrorism, for example, it is important to remind yourself of the more prosaic aspects of personal safety.

Urban Survival

As a foreigner in another country you are vulnerable and likely to be the subject of special attention by local people, not least because they will have the impression that you are rich. You may not think you are, but it's worth bearing in mind that in very poor countries even the clothes you stand up in would be beyond the means of some people. So the question of safety and survival starts as soon as you arrive in a new country and pass through towns and cities. Part of the thrill of adventure is to experience local life and meet people, but this has to be done in a way that does not invite trouble.

To avoid becoming a victim of crime you should be alert, sensible and vigilant without being paranoid that there's attacker waiting for you round every corner. Urban survival is about being sensible and taking practical precautions, and that applies in Britain, Europe and the USA just as much as in Afghanistan, Botswana or Colombia. If you are streetwise at home, then learn to become worldwise when you travel abroad.

Being worldwise is the theme of the travel advice from the Suzy Lamplugh Trust, a leading authority in the UK on personal safety, which has a very informative website on the precautions to take to ensure you have a trouble-free visit to unfamiliar places. Its role is to encourage people to think about the risks ahead and minimize any damage that might be caused to individuals from aggression in all its forms – verbal, physical and psychological.

The Trust cooperates with public and educational bodies to provide information and advice and its website (www.suzylamplugh.org) is well worth consulting before you go abroad. There is a country-by-country directory which outlines specific risks and precautions and the information is also in a handy, pocket-sized book, *Your Passport to Safer Travel*, published in partnership with Thomas Cook Publishing. The Trust was founded in memory of the London estate agent Suzy Lamplugh who disappeared while meeting an unknown client, and over almost 20 years it has grown into an organization with a network of 700 tutors and consultants who provide talks and courses. The emphasis is on the reduction of crime and violence against the individual and it operates now on an international basis, with statutory and voluntary organizations, to gather information, to campaign for changes in attitude and to promote good practice and advice. Urban survival is about keeping out of trouble and not taking unnecessary or avoidable risks.

Tom Brosnahan is a travel writer who knows Turkey very well and has created an extensive website about travelling the country, called Turkey Travel Planner (www.infoex change.com/Turkey). He is in no doubt that Turkey is a safe and friendly place and says he has never been attacked or had a penny stolen in 35 years of regular visits. He takes precautions that take him out of the 'easy' category for the minority of locals bent on robbing visitors. In crowded places, for example, keep bags close to you and in front of, not behind, you.

Precautions before you leave

- Obtain comprehensive travel insurance.
- Make copies of tickets, passport, insurance policy, itinerary and contacts, and leave a copy of each at home.
- Take sufficient money. British consular staff can't send you home if you run out.
- Find out about local scams used on tourists.
- Read up on local laws and customs to avoid causing offence or unwittingly breaking the law.
- Consider taking a roam-enabled mobile phone with you or a prepaid phone card, and use email to keep in touch with home.
- Take a simple wooden door wedge to ensure that your bedroom door is properly locked when you are in it.
- Pack a 'Jif' lemon squeezer as an eye squirter for self-defence against physical attack.
- Carry a shrill whistle to draw attention if potentially threatened.
- Buy a Telco emergency 'phone home' card.

Common Problems

There are scams that you need to avoid, and these are not specific to any particular country. For example, a group of local people, usually young men, will strike up a conversation with tourists and offer to take them off to a better bar or club. They can then get them into a taxi and take them anywhere they want. It has been known for them to spike drinks with a drug and for tourists to wake some hours later with no money, no passport and no bag.

Such incidents are rare and easily avoided with a modicum of common sense, and should not deter you from talking to the people of your host country. If you are invited out with some local people, make sure someone in your group or at your accommodation knows where you are going.

Being streetwise abroad

- Avoid crowds where you have to slow down. Every time you slow down while walking in a street you become an easier target.
- Be suspicious if somebody slows you down by, for example, falling in front of you or getting his clothes stuck in something, as it may be a pretext for an attack by an accomplice behind you.
- Be aware of who is behind you. If the same person is behind you for a few minutes, be suspicious.
- Don't keep all your money in one place. Keep your passport and air ticket separate.
- Avoid travelling with big luggage. The bigger the luggage, the more visible you are and the harder it is for you to defend yourself or chase a thief. Backpacks can be easily opened even while you are walking.
- Use taxis that are recommended by the hotel you are staying at, and let the hotel know where you are going in it. Always be wary of taxis you hail on the street.
- Be on your guard and be careful when talking to strangers. Anybody who approaches you should make you a little suspicious. Once they force you to behave in a friendly manner, they have the upper hand psychologically. They know that you were raised to be nice to people who are nice to you.
- In most countries of the world women never respond to strangers. For a foreign woman it is never a good idea to respond to men who approach. The appropriate behaviour is cold silence and indifference. Even a 'no' is viewed as beginning a conversation. A smile is the worse course of action if

the uninvited stranger won't go away.

- Avoid being an easy target. Walk fast all the time. Every time you stop, to browse in a shop or to take a picture, for example, stay alert to what's going on around you.

- Don't wear expensive clothes or jewellery. An expensive-looking watch can be very attractive to a thief, so keep it out of sight.

- Try to dress in a similar style to the locals to give the impression you live in the country and are not just travelling through it. Dress conservatively and modestly and not in a way that would be provocative in the local culture. Legs, for example, should be covered most of the time and shorts would mark you out as a tourist.

- If you are attacked, move slowly and take a moment to recover from the shock. Only fight back if the attacker is clearly disorientated by drink or drugs, otherwise you may be risking serious injury. Your attacker probably has more experience at this sort of thing. Most attacks will be for money, so let it go, having taken the precaution of keeping some in another wallet or pocket.

- Try not to look like a tourist who is lost, helpless and desperate. Hold yourself like a person who lives around there, minding your own business.

It is a very good idea for women travellers to do things together. Sexual assault is not common but the attention given to a single woman traveller can be very irritating and off-putting. Safety and survival is again down to being streetwise, blending in by dressing conservatively and not drawing the attention of strangers, especially at night. It helps also to look like you know what you are doing and where you are going, even if you don't. Getting out a map in the street is a sure sign that you are lost and vulnerable.

Highly populated areas such as bus stations, railways and airports are potentially concentrated trouble spots. They are favoured 'soft' places for theft and places where conmen operate. Be vigilant and spend as little time as possible in public areas such as concourses, public waiting areas or shopping mails. In airports get 'airside' as soon as possible, as it is 'controlled space', and therefore safer. Do not leave luggage unattended and never let your possessions out of your sight. In congested areas, beware of being distracted by someone as your pocket is picked by someone else. Do not carry travel documents, wallets and credit cards in obvious pockets such as the back of trousers or jeans.

Drug running – how it could happen to you

- You may have been targeted as a narco-mule for weeks, by one or more people who have befriended you, or simply observed you without you noticing.
- The person/persons who have been targeting you are unlikely to be the people who will compromise you. They will have reported on your habits and movements to others. You may even be having regular sex with them.
- The 'bag switch' is a classic, often done at the hotel or in the boot of a taxi.
- Accept no gifts: especially those that could have a dual purpose.
- You could be used as a decoy and 'set up' with the authorities.
- 'Everyone has a price.' Any money you have accepted in such circumstances is likely to be counterfeit.
- Use reliable locking systems on your luggage.
- Do not have an 'open to see' label on any of your luggage.
- Do not carry anything for anyone – even your travelling friends – especially not any new acquaintances.
- Never let your luggage out of your hands or sight (no matter what the circumstances).
- Use your common sense. Be responsible for yourself and no one else.

Drugs

For your own protection, don't get involved in illegal drugs in a foreign country. You have no control over their quality or potency and you could be drawn into a scene that could be very dangerous. Apart from your personal safety, there is an issue about foreigners fuelling the underground drugs market. It has been known for police drug squads to offer cash or other rewards to local drug dealers for reporting a tourist. Stay alert, streetwise and worldwise and keep out of avoidable trouble.

Terrorism

Terrorist threats come in many forms and from many sources of discontent. The feature common to them all is their effect on so-called 'soft targets'. Violence and warfare are no longer constrained by the rules of war and military targets. Ordinary people are in the firing line. One of the main lessons from the 9/11 attacks in the USA is that aircraft are vulnerable to being taken over by a determined terrorist as a weapon for destruction and publicity.

Terror groups thrive on the oxygen of global publicity, because it draws attention to their cause. They care little for the effect on the immediate victims who are powerless to influence any events or decisions that could advance the cause being pursued by the terrorists. This is different from kidnapping and hostage taking, where the victim is chosen for their connection to decision-makers. Either way those caught up in their acts are 'message generators'.

Anyone could become a victim of terrorism and there are no foolproof ways to make yourself immune to the threat. All you can do is assess the risk and make your travel decisions on the basis of the best information and advice available at the time. Becoming paranoid is no basis for an adventure. No airline or government can guarantee 100 per cent safety, but a 1 per cent risk of a terror attack is not a basis for cancelling a trip. Look at Spain, a modern, prosperous industrialized country that is popular with a wide cross-section of travellers and beach-loving tourists. Spain has an active terror group in the Basque separatist movement, ETA, which threatens to draw attention to its aims by attacking economic targets such as the travel and tourism industry.

Assess the risk by collecting together all available information and deciding how closely the threat should concern you. Clearly there are some places where an attack is more likely to happen than others. The biggest clue is whether there is a pattern of recent disturbances, and the state of play in the locality at the time. If there's tension, there's a greater risk, so the place is best avoided.

As I write, there is continuing unrest in Chechnya, parts of Israel, Kashmir and various parts of Africa, so a careful assessment of risk would lead you to avoid those particular places. But who would have said avoid Moscow, yet Chechnyan sympathizers blew up a theatre in the city in 2002? Who would have said avoid Bombay, yet a bus was blown up there in the summer of 2003? No one has a crystal ball on terrorism.

It is an essential part of planning an adventure trip that you research the destination and your route for *known* risks, especially if you intend venturing into areas little used by foreign visitors. Advice on making a detailed risk assessment is provided in the next chapter.

To avoid being a terrorist 'message generator'

- Undertake good, sound research from the media and the Internet, as this will allow you to make your own assessment of perceived and real risk.
- Ensure continued vigilance and regular reassessment while travelling.
- Do not be opinionated or overbearing with local people.
- Do not try to impose political or unsympathetic views on local people or other travellers.
- Show respect for people, their beliefs, sacred places and their environment.
- Be vigilant and look out for suspicious people in areas preferred by Westerners or where Americans gather. These may well become the new soft targets.

For travel information, the government advice services, such as websites of the FCO in the UK or the US State Department, are the first places to look. There is also information available from the national governments of the countries you intend to visit. The people on the ground can be a valuable source of information, and your tour organizer should be able to get in touch for the latest news. Local knowledge is vital for your planning; local people may know things that never reach the Western media. Quite often, terrorism is localized and large parts of a country are peaceful. This was very much the case in Sri Lanka where Tamil Tigers were fighting the government forces for control of the northern part of the island. In some countries, however, the general state of lawlessness poses a problem wherever you travel.

The intelligence services may have been aware that a terror attack was likely in Bali, Indonesia, in 2002, and certainly it was well known that the country was tense, but no one could have predicted that the Sari Club would be hit when it was, to devastating and tragic effect. Terrorism happens. It's part of modern life, regrettably. The question is, how can you avoid being a victim?

At least one of the lessons from the Bali bomb applies to many adventure destinations, especially in areas where you go to unwind and party a little after your adventure. Ros Coward of the *Ecologist* magazine noted about the Bali incident, 'There had been fights with locals over religious disrespect, and offensiveness to local culture.' The lesson here is simple. Some people may need to act with a little more modesty, more grace, more attention to cultural, religious and political frustrations. Better behaviour of this kind will not only be greatly appreciated, but will build friendships and relationships that can last for years and give a greater understanding of both cultures.

Heading for Conflict Zones

Most trouble spots for civil unrest can be avoided. Demonstrations, whether political, industrial or religious, are often noted in advance by the media. If caught unawares, either quit the area without looking panicked or make for a cafe or place where you are out of the main surge of the event. In some instances however, you may have little choice but to travel through a dangerous zone.

Environmental Threats

Natural disasters – floods, earthquakes, hurricanes and land-slides – are often overlooked and can be even more catastrophic than the disasters man makes solely for himself. Check for up-to-date information on the areas you are visiting along with historic environment events. You may notice a pattern emerging that it would be as well to avoid.

Stay in Touch

A last piece of advice – ensure you maintain some line of communication with home, in case things should go wrong. Many people assume that if they are in trouble, British consular staff have the remit to repatriate them or 'get them out of gaol' in any circumstances, and this is not the case. Consular staff may make a maximum loan of £100 to a DBN (Distressed British National) and there is no such thing as a 'get-out-of-jail-free card'.

Before you go, reassure your family and friends that you have carefully thought through your itinerary. Talk to them and spend quality time with them before your departure. Let them have ample chance to express their concerns and address them with care and consideration for their peace of mind. Give honest reassurance at all times. Promise to communicate regularly by each and every available means that they can use as well.

Travel in combat zones

- Be aware that safe passage in one area could cause real trouble or even death in another. (Do not have an Israeli stamp in your passport in Middle Eastern countries.)
- Always travel with the correct permits and permission of the relevant commanders.
- Make sure you have a thorough understanding of where the combat lines are.
- Make sure you understand the rules of engagement in place with the warring factions.
- Understand local customs, beliefs and their real and perceived threats.
- Never wander aimlessly around. Always look as if you have a purpose. If you are wanting to see an official, always try to know their name.
- Always stay alert, with your possessions packed, so you would be ready to move very quickly.
- Always sleep in places which are well-protected from shell and mortar attacks and shrapnel.
- Carry all personal documents and any relevant information about blood group and allergies with you at all times in a waterproof sleeve.
- Always have to hand a comprehensive first-aid kit with syringes, needles antibiotics, painkillers, etc.
- Reduce hostage risk by always meeting in public, well-lit places.
- Do not stand out. Dress soberly and conservatively.
- Be a good listener and be soft and mild mannered at all times.
- Never discuss politics.
- Never carry too much money and disperse it about your person.

17
Risk Assessment

Adventurous travel is only marginally more risky than conventional travel. That said, you cannot have an adventure without some element of risk. Some of these risks you can control or minimize, while with others, you can prepare for their likelihood to either negate or reduce their impact on the adventure.

The activities that standard travel insurance policies will not cover are the best guide to what is considered to be adventurously risky, or even dangerous. It does not necessarily follow that these activities are directly connected to travel. The heightened and perceived risks, other than in the obvious scenarios (the biggest risk for 99 per cent of us travellers is still being robbed or getting sick), are mainly in specific situations and locations and can be prepared for in advance and managed in pursuit of the adventure without detracting from its purpose or enjoyment.

Risk assessment should always be part of your pre-departure planning and should continue to be evaluated and updated as necessary throughout the adventure.

Most adventure travellers have a healthy respect for their physical limitations and/or their 'comfort zone'. You should never disregard these limitations – they are a key to constant and regular checks at every stage. As an adventurous traveller you are also likely to start out with another very important advantage – a mind set of self-responsibility. An acceptance of being responsible for oneself is a vital part of carrying out a personal risk assessment and certainly as a leader or manager of an adventure you should accept that you are ultimately responsible.

Risk Assessment Before You Go

Undertaking a risk assessment before you set out is strongly recommended for all types of adventure, whether you planned it yourself or used the services of a specialist. A risk assessment is a logical and careful examination of what could cause harm to you or your companions on an adventure. It allows you to look at the precautions you should take to prevent anything untoward happening to yourself or anyone travelling with you or helping you, as well as any loss or damage to your equipment and stores. Remember that accidents and ill health can ruin lives and in a worst-case scenario, you could be taken to court for not taking enough care.

In an assessment you need to consider whether a risk is relevant and significant and whether you have taken, or can put into place, measures to minimize the risk. Ciaran Elliott of The Robert Gordon University, Aberdeen uses this example. You are planning to travel across a desert in a vehicle and need to assess the potential significant hazards associated with this activity. The list could include:

- lack of water for the occupants of the vehicle
- getting lost
- insufficient fuel
- getting the vehicle stuck

- medical emergencies
- vehicle breakdown
- hijacking and kidnapping
- vehicle accidents – hitting other vehicles, camels, etc. either through carelessness, tiredness, etc.

The list could go on and on.

There are also hazards that are significant but not relevant, for instance:

- Polar bear attack
- Meteorite impact.

The list could continue into madness!

There are also hazards that are relevant but not significant, for instance:

- Worn upholstery on the driver's seat
- Lack of haute cuisine during the desert crossing.

There are obviously also hazards that are neither significant nor relevant but there is no reason to list these now as the point has been illustrated.

Control Measures

A risk assessment requires you to look at the hazards and consider the control measures needed to reduce them to a manageable or safe level. For instance, running out of fuel is a possibility and this hazard can be controlled by:

1 Estimating how much fuel you will need for a particular journey.
2 Ensuring your fuel tanks are full at the beginning of the journey and that you are carrying sufficient spare fuel.

With these control measures in place, you have reduced the risk to a safe or manageable level.

A control risk assessment – white-water canoeing in the Ardèche

Activity/ Element (Step 1)	Hazards identified (Step 2)	Existing controls (Step 3)	Residual risk (Step 4)	Additional controls required (Step 5)	Residual risk (Step 6)
(a)	(b)	(c)	(d)	(e)	(f)
White-water canoeing in Ardèche	Drowning	Swimming tests, capsize drills, rescue techniques, buoyancy aides, river not in full flood, instructor ratio 1:3	No	All require prior experience of fast-flowing rivers. Exercise arranged in Snowdonia prior to expedition. Gradually increase level of adventure and demand not exceeding participants' mental and physical ability	Yes
As above	Capsize resulting in injury	Training and proficiency	No	Ditto	Yes
As above	Cuts and abrasions	First-aid kit. Trained first aider	Yes		
As above	Head injuries	Helmets worn all times	Yes		

As above	Hypother-mia	Wet suits, towels, dry clothing	Yes		
As above	Waterfalls/barriers	Guide book, knowledge/experience of river	Yes		
As above	Water-borne diseases	Guide book, local knowledge, medical kit	Yes		
As above	Canoe/paddle failure	Canoes/paddles maintained and inspected	Yes		

Active and Under Pressure

Active risk assessment will come into play once you are under way. For example, it might be a quick discussion with your companions before running a river, setting off on a climb, entering a cave system or starting a scramble. Sixth sense, experience, the ability to think clearly under pressure – which skydivers would describe as 'non-relative time' are all key parts of this type of assessment.

The ability to make on-the-spot assessments is an important skill to acquire, and requires you, if necessary, to control your imagination. Uncanny as it may seem, if you imagine it will happen, it probably will. Have you ever been determined to avoid skiing into an obvious tree on a ski slope and then hitting it fair and square? Perhaps you've reversed the car into something you were trying to avoid. Try to think in two separate forms. One form you could call, 'factual form' and the other 'imagined form'. The key is not to let the imagined form flood the factual form – the realism of the situation.

Never forget common sense. This is the stable foundation on which both pre-departure and on-going active assessments must stand. It is amazing how many people forget to apply it.

Unfairly Factored In

There have been people who have set out on an adventure with the intention of relying on the rescue services when no longer able to cope. Some of these people never asked in advance for their support, they just knew that because of the ethics and personal code of rescue organizations, they could take advantage of their commitment to preserve lives. Sadly, and whether right or wrong, Pen Haddow's Herculean achievement of a lone, one-way journey to the North Pole has been criticized in these terms.

Pen Haddow had to be rescued in March 2003 after undertaking the first solo, unaided trek from Canada's War Hunt Island to the North Pole. He was picked up after a rescue plane managed to land on a makeshift runway he had marked out on the floating ice using plastic bags. However, two earlier attempts to retrieve him had failed because of breaking ice and thick clouds. Steve Penikett, a spokesman for the airline company involved, pointed out that the ice moves rapidly at that time of year, making the rescue mission difficult for everyone involved:

> I wish it hadn't taken place at this time of year. This is the latest we have ever done a pick-up. It's not the issue of him running out of food. It's the issue of going to the pole at this time of year is just a bit stupid and you are putting a lot of people's lives at risk doing it.

'Laying Off' the Risk

It is surprising how many people plan their adventures themselves and forget to take out insurance or fail to protect themselves with an appropriate policy. Insurance cover for just about any adventure and all travel is available – including war zones. The key is to get the cover at a fair price for what you intend to undertake and always bother to read the small print.

Approximately two-thirds of travellers who make a claim on their travel insurance end up having their claims fully or partly rejected. The most common reason is that the travellers are not fully covered for the claim they are trying to make. Medical costs are the most frequent claim on travel policies, followed by lost money, lost luggage and holidays being cancelled or cut short.

There are some very good specialist companies today who have a complete understanding of adventurous activities and the travel risks involved, as well as the environments they are best undertaken in, the best time of year and the locations to avoid. Some of the adventure package tour operators sell insurance with their programmes, and this has to be a common-sense option for you if booking with an operator as they will be the ones who have made sure that the cover is suitable for your adventure. Remember not to make an inaccurate or false declaration of your health and physical abilities. There are some blanket situations where cover is automatically withdrawn. Many travellers affected by 9/11 who were unable to get on their booked flights as governments around the world grounded incoming and out going aircraft were left out of pocket due to the act of terrorism clause that came into play. However this is changing slowly and some of the major insurance providers have decided to cover some aspects of indirect loss created by terrorism and *force majeure* (acts of war). Do check to see that you can get a policy that includes this cover. In many instances it is being offered with no increase of premium.

Official Risks

It is up to you to determine what is acceptable as a risk for you, as long as you are operating inside the law and are not going to put other people at risk unnecessarily. For example, three UK tourists recently signed up for a tour of Iraq, on an organized trip designed to enable travellers to see what has happened to the country – despite ongoing looting, violence and general instability in much of the country. The organizer explained that 'the idea of the trip is to see what has happened to the country as well as to visit the ancient sites'.

However, the UK's Foreign and Commonwealth Office (FCO) unsurprisingly advised against visiting the country. A spokeswoman commented: 'Anyone organizing a trip or planning to go should not do so.' Note the emphasis the official spokeswoman placed on *not* going to Iraq. Beware that some insurance policies have in their small print a note that they become invalid if travelling against FCO advisory bulletins.

The area of personal insurance, travel trade responsibilities to clients and the due diligence that airlines and tour providers are liable for is rapidly changing and this will affect your adventures. British Airways has been penalized in the French courts for flying French nationals into Iraq's Baghdad airport, when fully aware that the airfield was under military attack and under occupation by Iraqi forces prior to the Gulf War of 1991.

Just remember that you cannot eliminate all the risk. Be flexible in your thinking and if your aim and your objectives have to change because of unacceptable risks, let your common sense, if nothing else, lead you back to safety. Remember to take out insurance and keep constantly in mind that if it doesn't feel right . . . then, IT ISN'T!

The greatest hazard in life is to risk nothing

To laugh is to risk appearing a fool. To place your ideas and dreams before others is to risk their loss. To live is to risk dying. To try is to risk failure.

But risks must be taken because the greatest hazard is to risk nothing.

The person who risks nothing, has nothing, knows nothing and is nothing.

Chained by their certitudes they are slaves, they have forfeited their freedom.

Only a person who risks is truly free.

Author unknown

18
Emergency Survival

You cannot plan for the unpredictable but you can learn some basic things to do in an emergency, and like many aspects of adventure, they are habits that should become instinctive. They are attitudes that could save your life.

The first habit of survival in a new or unfamiliar environment is to be prepared. It may sound like old-fashioned advice, but it applies wherever you go. Another way of putting this is: don't leave out something in the planning stage which could cause or turn into an emergency when you are out in the 'field', whether it is up a mountain, out at sea or deep in a jungle. The second habit for coping with hazards is: don't do anything to make things worse.

There are risks in ordinary daily life but travelling abroad brings additional risks and along with them the fear of going into unknown situations. Some preparation and knowledge will reduce this fear and boost your confidence. As with so many things to do with safety, preparation is better than cure and knowing what hazards are out there is the first step to avoiding them and not letting them spoil your journey.

Survival Courses

There are plenty of man-made and natural hazards that might conceivably face you on an adventure travel, from an aircraft crash to an earthquake or landslide. But common to most emergency scenarios is the issue of survival in a remote location. For visits into extreme conditions, some preparation is needed to cope with living with the minimum of comfort and support. If you are just starting out on your adventure travels, you should seriously consider taking a course geared around survival in wild or remote environments. The course would be an adventure in itself and would provide you with all-important survival habits and build your confidence for later, perhaps more advanced or exciting, expeditions.

One company which runs survival training programmes is Survival Extreme, who have two bases in Britain and training facilities also in Africa and South America. They have a website at www.survival-extreme.co.uk. A basic weekend survival course takes place in Exmoor National Park in the south-west of England. Health is the highest priority and the course is geared around having an adequate supply of water, food and shelter. For the more advanced, there is a 14-day training expedition to Victoria Peak in the Maya Mountains of Belize in Central America. This is ideal for coping with jungle conditions and an environment that becomes progressively more challenging as you climb from the base camp to the top of the mountain.

The principles of survival taught on all introductory and advanced courses are the same, because our basic needs are common to any adventure into unfamiliar territory. But there are specific requirements and strategies for the different terrains such as desert and jungle, and different climates that range from high mountain snow to hot humid rainforest.

Coping in a plane crash

It's the ultimate emergency nightmare of international travel, so what do you actually do when you are involved in a plane crash and survive?

In the first place, you will get some warning or indication that all is not well and the aircraft is going to hit the ground. This could take a number of forms, but it is likely to be either something you feel – like a jolt or an abnormal angle of flight – or a sound or smoke and fire. Oxygen masks will then drop down and the captain will call out a warning to 'brace', which means to fold yourself forward with your head to your knees. You will have a few moments to think before impact, so don't waste those moments by going into a screaming panic. You will have more chance of surviving if you stay calm and work out what to do next.

According to statistics, two-thirds of the people involved in air crashes survive, and about one-third of those who die could have survived if they had known what to do. If it seems certain the plane is going to crash, here are a few tips on what to do.

1 Fasten your seat-belt as tightly as possible. This will help to prevent you being thrown around the cabin on impact with the ground.
2 Check where the emergency exits are and plan your route to each one. Interviews with survivors of air crashes confirm that this is a crucial part of getting out alive. You may not remember the presentation by the cabin crew at the start of the flight, so check the safety leaflet in front of you. In these circumstances you will realize what it's for.
3 Take any sharp items such as pencils and pens out of your clothes and remove high-heeled shoes.
4 Moisten a handkerchief, headrest cover or piece of clothing with water, so that if there's smoke after impact, you can hold it over your mouth. If no other liquids are handy, use your urine. Smoke is a major cause of death among passengers who survive the fall to Earth.
5 If you've got time, gather things you will need outside the plane, such as a sweater or coat to keep you warm and any medicines.

6 Cover your head, preferably with a pillow. Then cross your arms over your legs and fold into the brace position with your head down to your knees and your feet directly in front of you as far forward as possible.

7 If you're still alive after the plane comes to a stop, get out of there as fast as you can. Don't wait to be told what to do, as even the cabin crew may be stunned. Just undo your seat-belt and get to your nearest exit.

8 Make sure you have both hands free to clamber out of the wreck, as the cabin may not be the right way up.

9 Don't waste time crawling on the floor to avoid smoke, it will get you anyway if you delay your exit, and your progress could be held up by other people trampling over you. If there is smoke, keep your head down and your face covered with your wet cloth.

10 When you get to an emergency exit, look through the window and check to see if there is any fire outside before you open the door. If there are flames, get to the exit on the other side and leave by that door and get clear of wreckage to await rescue.

Number one priority is to stay alive, and not to put your own or anyone else's life in danger by doing anything stupid or omitting to do something essential.

Need For Water

You cannot live without water, but water from natural sources such as streams and pools is a rich environment for all manner of organisms that can be harmful to humans. There is more detail about purifying water in Chapter 15. Here we are concerned with regarding clean water as basic to survival in any hostile environment and the importance of getting enough of it. You lose water rapidly through perspiration on hot days, that much is obvious, but you also use up a lot of water during exercise and exertion in the cold. Your body's fluids need to be topped up regularly and an average adult requirement during a stressful activity such as trekking or climbing is about two litres of water a day to maintain peak performance.

Securing an adequate supply of water is one of the objectives of an adventure into wild or unfamiliar terrain. When water is in short supply, the fundamental rule is to conserve it. I have a personal rule never to be without a reserve of water. A plastic bottle doesn't add much weight to a backpack and it can be a life-saver. I would rather go thirsty for a bit longer than drink the last drop – in other words, do not drain your water bottle until you are in a position to refill it. It's inevitable that you will be thirsty on a long walk on a hot day, but thirst is not a problem – dehydration would be. So it follows that knowing where to find water is vital to the safety and success of any adventure or expedition and this should figure large in your planning.

There are various estimates of how long you can go without water in dire circumstances and it's not long – days rather than weeks. I prefer to keep that knowledge as a theoretical concept; it should not have any practical bearing on a planned expedition. But accidents do happen and you could be left, literally, high and dry. Whatever the circumstances, be it a grave emergency such as a fall down an inaccessible ravine or a light aircraft crash on a mountainside, it is vital to have some water available while a physical rescue is being organized.

Sources of Water

Getting water is not usually a problem in a town or village, of course, although the quality of it and its suitability for drinking must be checked and taken care of. Out in the wild, access to a water source governs such basic decisions as where to establish a camp for the night.

At high levels on mountains, or on a trek in polar regions, snow and ice provide a plentiful supply of water, but take particular care to melt and purify it first, because eating it can have the effect of reducing your body temperature in an extreme environment and that would not help your quest for survival.

Out at sea, surrounded by water, do not be tempted to drink saltwater without first using some means of desalinating it. The salt in sea water can have serious effects on the balance of minerals in your blood and other vital fluids. It is better to collect and save rainwater by catching it in anything you can lay your hands on, such as tarpaulin or waterproof clothing, provided it is not encrusted with sea salt. If you are fortunate enough – or perhaps unfortunate enough – to be stranded on a beach after an emergency at sea, here's a tip for extracting a minimal amount of drinking water. Dig a hole in the sand and allow some seawater to gather in the bottom. Light a fire nearby in which to heat some rocks. Place the hot rocks into the hole in the sand and cover it with a cloth to absorb the steam. Squeeze out the cloth and you will have a few drops of precious clean water free of sea salt. It may seem extreme, but in these circumstances extreme measures can save your life.

In the desert, keep an eye out for cacti. These are some of the plant world's best survivors of harsh conditions precisely because they conserve water. To extract water from a cactus, you need to slice through its thick skin to get at the pulp inside. Crush the pulp and strain it through a cloth – it could be a T-shirt – by squeezing it downwards and catch the falling drops in a container. You could get some water by putting the pulp straight into your mouth and sucking on it, but do not eat the pulp itself, spit it out.

An old Aborigine technique for gathering water in extreme areas of Australia takes advantage of the early morning dew on vegetation. The method involves tying pieces of cloth around the ankles and walking around in the grass before sunrise. The cloth picks up the dew and it is said that in this way, they can get as much as a litre of water an hour from the squeezed-out cloths.

Bamboo is a plant that has a reserve of water which you can use with a bit of ingenuity gained from the experience of native dwellers. Choose a long, green bamboo shoot and cut off the top. Bend the plant over and tie it down with the top of the plant pointing down into a container. Overnight, the bamboo will yield a small supply of fresh, drinkable water.

One word of caution about coconuts. The milk from green, unripe coconuts is a good thirst quencher but the fluid from mature coconuts contains a small proportion of an oily substance that has a laxative effect, so drink it only in moderation. If you are trekking through jungle, you could go for a long time without meeting a stream, so keep your eyes open for other sources such as edible fruits and other vegetation. As a source of water, fruit has the added value of extra nutrition such as vitamins and minerals. It may not quench your thirst immediately but your body has ways of extracting the water in the juices for the proper functioning of your vital organs and muscles.

Survival Food

Whatever the climate or terrain, wherever there are living things, there will be water in the earth. It follows also that where there is vegetation, there is food, which is the second most vital requirement for surviving hostile conditions. It helps on an adventure to have food with you in your backpack and the kind of food to take on a trip is discussed in Chapter 15. But what do you do when things go wrong and you are stranded with little or nothing left of your carefully planned supplies?

First, don't panic. So long as there is water, the human body is resilient and you can survive a long time without much food. In an emergency situation, don't be guided by hunger pangs. You know that you feel hungry after a few hours of ordinary living at home with no particular stress on your system.

Know your plants

Before setting out on your travels, consider buying a book on the subject of food from nature such as *The Really Wild Food Guide* which contains over 350 recipes for wild food and a lot of information about what plants you can eat. The book only cover the wild plants that can be found in Britain, so would not apply to every country that adventure travellers would go to. Its value is that it would help enormously in the training stage of an expedition plan. If you can get used to preparing a meal from British wild plants, you will have the confidence to survive off vegetation anywhere in the world.

Another book that should be in the library of a serious adventure traveller is the US Army Field Manual 21–76, which is available for online purchase through the Amazon website. This has a great deal of advice about survival in extreme conditions, and topics cover techniques for identifying and using edible plants and trapping animals in the wild for food in an emergency. It is used throughout the US military and is one of the finest books around on wilderness survival.

Out in the wild, circumstances can overtake your careful preparations and it is important not to let your fear of going hungry cloud your judgement. Rely on your instinct for survival, but help it along by learning a few tricks about foraging for food from natural sources.

You can't expect to become a fully-fledged botanist just for an expedition, but it would help enormously if one of your team is. Some research into the plants native to the country you are intending to explore would certainly not go amiss. The acacia, for example, flourishes wild in tropical regions of Africa, Asia and Australia. Its young leaves, flowers and pods are edible raw and cooked. The almond tree grows wild in temperate conditions and semi-desert scrubland, in southern Europe, the eastern Mediterranean, the Middle East and China. Its highly nutritious kernel can be extracted by cracking open the hard shell and removing a tough coating.

Almonds are an excellent survival food and if you find them they can be collected and saved for later as a reserve food store. The Arctic willow is a shrub with succulent shoots at ground level with an inner core that can be eaten raw or cooked and is much richer in vitamin C than oranges. As its name suggests, this shrub grows wild in Arctic and high mountainous regions of northern Europe and Asia. Obviously, these are just a few examples of survival foodstuffs; you can find out more from books and Internet sites in the course of planning a trip to your chosen destination.

Hypothermia

Having dealt with the vital need for water and food in the outdoors, the next priority for survival is shelter. Cold is a major threat to survival, not only from the risk of freezing to death. Long before that happens, extreme cold has the effect of impairing your judgement and you can lose the energy and the will to do the very things that would save you. You can, in effect, lose the will to live. Hypothermia is a killer because of this.

Hypothermia happens as a result of the body's own mechanism for surviving cold winters, by drawing warm blood from the surface tissues to maintain the temperature of vital inner organs. In evolutionary terms, we are supposed to reduce activity and go to sleep for the winter, not go around burning energy and pumping warm blood to the muscles in our limbs. The problems arise as the warm blood comes into contact with the cold air at the surface tissues and returns to the heart and lungs a few degrees lower in temperature. In a way, the debilitating effect of hypothermia is not so much losing the will to live as the activation of a survival instinct to go into hibernation for the winter.

The human body is very good at maintaining a steady allround temperature of about 35°C. If the temperature of the heart and lungs begins to fall below that level because of chilled blood returning from the cold extremities, drastic action is needed and the body's biochemistry reacts to protect these organs and keep them functioning for as long as possible at their optimum temperature. The legs and arms have to wait until the environment warms up. Hypothermia can be fatal so it is essential to do everything possible to prevent it from occurring.

Shelter from Cold

Even in regions known for having a hot climate, the nights can be extremely cold, largely because there's very little cloud cover to act as an insulation blanket in the atmosphere. You may have had holidays where you slept in the open on a beach in the Mediterranean or on the Canary Islands, but this would not be wise in a semi-desert area. For many adventure trips, a tent is the most practical piece of equipment for shelter. The question of survival arises when conditions overtake you and you are forced by circumstances to improvize, and this is where some advanced preparation comes in.

The weather on mountains is notorious for changing without warning, so if you were caught above the snow line unable to reach the safety of base camp or a known lodging such as a cabin, would you be able to cope? Snow is a wonderful material to work with. It may be cold and wet, but its fluffy structure holds a lot of trapped air. That makes it a good insulating material in an emergency. There are numerous examples of climbers who have been caught out by a change in the weather who have survived by digging a snow hole in which to spend the night.

The main thing is to avoid having your body in direct contact with snow on the floor, and you do this by using whatever you have to make a mat to sleep on. The warmth of your body inside a sleeping bag may warm the air around you in your cocoon, but rather than melt the snow and leave you dripping wet and cold, this actually helps to make an inner crust of ice which remains solid because of the intense cold of the snow above it. This is a practical application of the principle behind the igloo that Eskimos are famous for.

If you do find yourself lost or detached from your group and forced to spend a night out in the open in hostile conditions, build yourself a shelter from whatever comes to hand. Don't just lie down to sleep in the open, as even in tropical countries and deserts the nights can be bitterly cold and your defences are down when you are asleep. Broken branches from trees can be put together to form a framework like a tent and covered with twigs and leaves. This simple shelter will act as a wind break and help to keep the rain off, which is essential, and the trapped air will provide some heat insulation for the night.

Clothing for the Cold

Alongside shelter it is important to consider clothing – in effect our personal portable shelter – in any thoughts about survival. It goes without saying that it is essential to have the most appropriate clothing for the type of expedition and the conditions that you will be living in. When I am out in the mountains, I prefer to have several layers of light materials rather than a single, big, woollen jumper underneath an anorak or waterproof. There are two reasons for this. The layers help to trap air which acts as a natural insulator and, close to the body, it takes on the warmth of the body. The other reason is that if conditions are good and you begin to perspire during an arduous trek, it's easy to remove some of the layers for a more comfortable walk.

As well as the cold, the other enemy of adventurers in cold climates is the wet. Water retains a lot of heat and in the cold, wet clothing will draw heat out of the body which can give rise to a chill. It follows that you should do all you can to keep clothes dry. Store spare clothing inside a substantial plastic bag within a rucksack or backpack, and change into dry clothes at night. On a long, lightweight trip with several overnights, try to retain at least one set of dry clothes, so if the weather is wet the next day, you can change back into the wet clothing from the previous day before setting out again. It's uncomfortable at first, but the inner layers soon get warmed up to body temperature.

In cold conditions, heat is lost rapidly from the head, so a woollen or fur-like hat is not a fashion item but a safety aid. The fibres of wool or fur (and it can be man-made fibre rather than real animal pelt) once again trap air and make an insulating layer for the hard, heat-radiating surface of the skull.

As if the cold and the wet were not enough to cope with, the wind can make their effects even worse. This is a matter of simple physics. The wind encourages water to evaporate from the surface of your clothing and this has a cooling effect. The wind also makes the air feel colder than a thermometer in still air might indicate. This effect is known as the wind-chill factor, a term coined by the Antarctic explorer Paul Siple in 1939. It can be a killer if you are not prepared for it by having a wind-proof item of clothing in cold conditions.

A temperature of −18°C is not unusual for a normal day in the Arctic, but a 30-mile-an-hour wind would have the effect on exposed parts of the body − such as ears or face − of a temperature closer to −40°C, which would be very dangerous if you were not wearing enough warm clothing. Frostbite would set in within 15 minutes. It's particularly important not to let the wind through to the inner layers of clothing where it will increase the rate of evaporation of moisture and cool down the surface of your flesh with disastrous results.

Protecting yourself from the wind is vital in a cold climate, and never more so than if you are caught up in an emergency at sea. It's practically impossible to keep dry, so put on as many layers of clothing as you can and, if at all possible, use something to make a wind break. If there are several people with you, huddle together to reduce the total amount of surface exposed to the wind while you await rescue.

Clothing in the Heat

The reverse is true in a hot climate. You want wind to blow and evaporate the surface moisture as your perspire. Light, flowing cotton clothes act as a kind of wick by soaking up the moisture and the wind keeps you cool by increasing the rate of evaporation. This is why it is better to wear a shirt on a hot trek than risk overheating by wearing a skinny top or going bare-chested. Take a lesson from people who live in hot climates all the time. The Arabs, for example, wear long, cotton robes, not to protect themselves from sunburn, but to keep cool.

As with everything to do with mounting an adventure into an unfamiliar environment, you should be prepared for the unexpected. In towns and cities, be streetwise, and be world-wise when travelling abroad wherever you go. In the wilderness, desert or up a mountain, stay safe by knowing the risks and taking action to reduce them. In a situation of immediate danger, don't make things any worse for yourself or your companions while you seek assistance.

19
Cultural Differences

As a traveller, you are a guest in someone else's homeland and you must conduct yourself accordingly. It can be uncomfortable, but stop and think now and again how uncomfortable it must be for them at times. You may feel culture shock as an anxiety from being in unfamiliar surroundings, but it need not all be negative. It's part of the adventure to be in a different place where you will learn new aspects of life and get a new perspective. Culture shock is a transition phase that you need to go through to achieve the objectives that are the reason why you undertook your journey in the first place.

Culture shock is a term that was invented in 1958 and has come to signify the experience of encountering people in other parts of the world who have a different way of life and a different set of customs, values and traditions from the ones you are used to at home. You can't always put your finger on it, but it often hits you in very practical ways, especially when you visit a non-industrialized country. It's not just a difference of language, dress, food or religion, though these are manifestations of it. It's a totality thing. People have a different way of life from you, and you are the foreigner when you visit them.

This is not how the pioneers of the age of the British Empire saw it. The British civil servants who administered India were legendary for importing their English ways of doing things. Prospectors in North America cleared Native Americans off their lands by force of arms. The Crusades were mounted on the notion that the native peoples of the Holy Land were pagans or 'infidels', lacking the true religion, Christianity. Explorers who 'discovered' Africa and Australia treated the indigenous peoples as savages and lacking in 'civilization'. This undercurrent of disrespect goes back a long way but the effects are still with us in the twenty-first century. A whole book could be written about the roots of racism and the destructive nature of imperialist ignorance, but that's not the purpose of this one. This chapter is concerned with the practical aspects of meeting people of different cultures in modern times and treating them with respect, courtesy and equality.

Culture Shock in Action

The symptoms – if that is the word – of culture shock may hit you at different times. Coping with a strange language and the difficulty of making yourself understood is an obvious manifestation. English is practically a universal language, but it does not reach into every community, especially in the non-industrialized countries away from tourist resorts.

More striking will be the differences arising from the relative economic poverty of peoples in the developing world. This has profound effects on how people live and you may find it hard at first to get used to being without the comforts of home. Social practices, family life, food and standards of cleanliness may seem off-putting.

Then there will be differences in customs and traditions that derive from religion, and these will most often show up as very conservative attitudes to practical issues such as the way you dress. All of these are aspects of discovery that will contribute to the fulfilment of your dream of an adventure if you face them with a positive and enquiring frame of mind.

You would be amazed at the number of people who don't prepare for a foreign experience, and end up ruining it for themselves and for those around them. On holiday in a resort in Greece, Italy or Spain, perhaps, you may have encountered people who do nothing but complain about things not being like they are at home. People like this are usually experiencing a form of culture shock and are not interested in doing anything to get out of it. This is not the spirit of an adventure where travelling around another country is part of the purpose of your visit.

Tips For Dealing With Culture Shock

Remember you are the stranger in another land. You are there partly to learn and participate in the culture, to live and survive for a short while in conditions that local people endure all the time, and you will soon enjoy discovering what other cultures are about.

It may come as a shock to see how people live in villages in India or South America, with few comforts or luxuries. Often an extended family of several generations will live in one house, with grandparents, aunts and uncles and children all sharing the living space, which may be just one big room. If you get the opportunity to visit a home while on your journey, do take it up; you will find you are welcomed as a friend.

In remote areas, few homes have much furniture and you will be sitting on the floor a lot. It's no hardship, and don't be put off if people you are meeting sit close together and make bodily contact or touch your arm or leg when they are conversing with you. It's nothing to be afraid of and just shows that they don't have the Western reticence about physical contact. Shying away from it might be taken as a discourtesy.

When you are drawn into conversation, don't go on about politics, religion or world poverty. For one thing, you won't know enough about regional affairs in that part of the world and your hosts may not know enough English to be able to hold their own in a debate with you, so don't cause offence by playing the foreign policy expert. Take the opportunity to learn some words and expressions in the local language; they will come in useful and show that you are genuinely interested in the people you are meeting. Listen and learn.

Remember again that you are the foreigner abroad and it is you who may look strange. Be prepared to be stared at and watched closely. No offence is meant – it's natural curiosity, especially if you are out of the city and the local people don't get many travellers passing through. Be aware that how you dress is important, and the sight of bare flesh, especially shoulders and legs, can attract unwanted attention. It is rarely appropriate to sunbathe in swimming costumes or shorts anywhere apart from a beach, but you would be surprised how many people take liberties about this and then become uncomfortable when people stop and stare.

Every country is different, and there are regional cultural variations within a country, but some commonsense advice applies to all, such as respect religious sites and rituals.

Good manners

Ignorance of forms cannot properly be styled ill manners; because forms are subject to frequent changes; and consequently, being not founded upon reason, are beneath a wise man's regard. Besides, they vary in every country; and after a short period of time, very frequently in the same; so that a man who travels, must needs be at first a stranger to them in every court through which he passes; and perhaps at his return, as much a stranger in his own; and after all, they are easier to be remembered or forgotten than faces or names.

Jonathan Swift, *A Treatise on Good Manners*

Find Out in Advance

Visiting another country with the purpose of learning about how people live is a great aim for an adventure. It pays to do some research. Find out about the country you will be visiting and learn about its customs and traditional style of life. Learn a few words of the language to be able to say a simple greeting and be polite with 'please' and 'thank you'. Little things like this will help you to make new friends. Try to find out in advance about social practices in case you get an opportunity to visit someone's home, such as whether you should remove your shoes. As your mother may have said, good manners cost nothing.

There are many countries where women get something of a raw deal as far as cultural customs go, and this applies to women travelling alone or in a group without men. Local males can be uncomfortably forward and assume you are there on the lookout for a boyfriend. Jamaica, Belize, The Gambia, the coast of Turkey and Brazil are noted for a kind of gigolo culture. Don't rise to the sweet talk, and a cold, unsmiling dismissal is usually the best way of dealing with unwanted male attention. Avoid getting into polite conversation or you may not be left alone.

In many countries it is not acceptable to use the left hand for handling food. The left hand traditionally is considered unclean even where there are modern toilet hygiene standards.

Many traditional communities are not used to cameras, and photographs and filming may make people feel uncomfortable. It is wise to be over-polite and ask permission first rather than risk causing offence. Taking pictures of military establishments is a crime in many countries.

National customs

There is not space in this book to give details of the entire world's customs but below are some of the things to look out for or ask about, to avoid giving a bad impression or causing offence by conduct that might seem impolite or vulgar. This is not a comprehensive list of what to do or not to do, and some of the examples may seem curious or amusing, but they show that a little thoughtfulness goes a long way.

AFGHANISTAN
Afghans usually sit with legs crossed. Pointing the soles of the feet towards someone else is considered impolite. During meals, food is served in a communal dish on a mat in the middle of the floor, and eaten with the fingers of the right hand only.

ALBANIA
Albanians greet with a handshake and use their hands a lot when talking. Visiting is considered a happy event and unplanned visits are common.

ARAB COUNTRIES (SAUDI ARABIA, KUWAIT, BAHRAIN, QATAR, UNITED ARAB EMIRATES, ETC.)
These are very conservative in social etiquette. You do not greet a female with a kiss or embrace and only with a handshake if she offers it. A few polite words are sufficient. If you are in a group visiting a home, the male and female guests will be entertained in separate rooms at first. Arab culture makes a great deal out of honouring guests; at a meal, the host and his sons will be the last ones to start eating as a sign of respect to their visitors, so don't be embarrassed about starting first. Do not take alcohol into an Arab country.

ALGERIA
Greetings are often cordial and warm with a handshake and an embrace between members of the same sex. Men and women socialize separately. It is considered impolite to point directly at someone. Local women are required to observe a strict Islamic dress code and Western visitors should dress

conservatively, with a headscarf, to avoid being harassed by officials or police.

ARGENTINA

The national language is Spanish, but English is spoken and widely understood in cities. All the same, a few words in Spanish is appreciated. The most popular topic of discussion is sports, particularly soccer. Women travelling alone will find Argentina generally safer and face less hassle than in most other Latin American countries.

AUSTRALIA

Visitors may be surprised by the negative attitudes that some white Australians hold towards the indigenous people, the Aborigines. Always ask permission before taking photographs of Aborigines.

AUSTRIA

In Austria, it is impolite to begin eating before everyone else is ready. Austrians tend to be quite formal even when they are being friendly and they are strict time-keepers.

BAHRAIN

Generally one of the friendliest countries in the Gulf region and more liberal in attitude than others Western women may wear short skirts without any problem. Bahrainis often invite relatives, friends and foreigners to their home. Guests usually bring a gift to the host, such as sweets or flowers. If you are offered tea, it is usual to drink two small cups. Non-Muslims are usually allowed to enter a mosque. The official language is Arabic although English is widely used and understood.

BANGLADESH

When introduced to a man, it is customary to shake hands with him, while women just nod. A standard Hindu greeting is the palms held in prayer in front of your chest. Use the right hand only for eating. The thumbs-up gesture is considered rude. Local women should not be photographed. Rural communities are not used to foreign visitors.

BELGIUM

Meals are an important social and cultural event, so relax and enjoy yourself. Most Belgians are thrifty and do not like waste, so you will be expected to finish your food. Be aware of the language issue (do not call it a problem); some Belgians speak only French and others speak Flemish, a variant of Dutch; it depends which community they belong to, so beware of making assumptions.

BELIZE

Belizeans are informal and friendly when greeting one another and like to use first names. When visiting, you will be offered a refreshment; if there is no refrigerator, it is likely to be fresh coconut.

BERMUDA

The pace of life is relaxed, friendly and welcoming and urban areas are very English.

BOLIVIA

Bolivians tend to stand close during conversations. They use their hands and facial expressions to communicate. Eye contact is considered essential and avoiding another's eyes shows lack of trust, suspicion or shyness. Rural Bolivians are 'campesinos' and not 'Indians' which is taken as rather insulting.

BRAZIL

Brazilians enjoy conversation, jokes and getting to know you, so take your time to enjoy their company. You can't go wrong if you enjoy football; Brazilians take soccer very seriously, and consider their national team to be the best in the world. Women travellers may get a lot of hassle from local young men, so it is best not to get into casual conversation. The official language is Portuguese, not Spanish.

BRUNEI

Women should ensure that the head, knees and arms are covered at all times. Women do not usually shake hands. Avoid sitting with the soles of your feet facing anyone.

BULGARIA

In Bulgaria, 'yes' is indicated by shaking the head from side to side and 'no' is expressed with one or two nods. In conversation, they often touch one another. If you have a drink, maintain eye contact when clinking glasses.

BURMA/MYANMAR

If you must go to Burma, it is advisable to stick to designated tourist areas. Cycling and hitchhiking are strongly discouraged. It is not permitted to wear shorts or short skirts in religious buildings.

CAMBODIA

Always ask permission to take photographs of local people. Show extra courtesy towards monks.

CANADA

Remember that Canada is, by law, a bilingual country. French is the first language for about 25 per cent of the population and is the main language in Quebec. Smoking is banned in most public places including bars and restaurants.

CHILE

When meeting someone for the first time, the appropriate greeting is a firm handshake with direct eye contact. Close friends and relatives greet each other with a combination of a handshake and hug, with a kiss for women.

CHINA

Always use a person's proper title and expect a slight bow or handshake upon an introduction. Maintain distance when speaking, avoid open displays of affection, and never appear loud or aggressive. Tropical or lightweight clothing is acceptable in the summer in northern China and for most of the year in southern China. If you or your group are invited to meet a group of Chinese, they may greet you with applause; it is usual to clap your hands in return.

COLOMBIA

Colombians tend to be expressive with their hands and face when talking. Good manners are important to Colombians. In a group, it is considered impolite to take anything to eat without offering it to others first. Eating on the streets is frowned upon.

Costa Rica

Costa Ricans are some of the friendliest people you could meet. However, they are not used to seeing women travelling alone and local men may regard them as not spoken for, so can seem very forward and sexist. A traditional expression of interest is a hiss which can seem disconcerting for a stranger, but it can be ignored if unwelcome. When a couple – including just friends or travel companions – are out together, a woman should walk on the inside and the man next to the kerb, otherwise it may be taken as a sign that she is 'available'.

Cyprus

Visitors are given a warm and friendly welcome everywhere, and it is discourteous to refuse an offer of coffee or a cold drink. In Nicosia and Paphos, Western cultural values prevail but rural areas are very traditional. Travel across the Green Line into Turkish-controlled Northern Cyprus is restricted.

Czech Republic

Czechs do not visit one another unannounced. Czechs usually remove their shoes when entering a home and leave them by the door. Guests usually bring flowers.

Denmark

Although generally informal, Danes shake hands when introduced to strangers. When visiting, it is important to arrive on time. Bring a small gift for the host such as flowers, wine or chocolate. Danish is the official language but English is widely spoken and understood.

Dominica

It is an offence to wear camouflage-print clothing.

Dominican Republic

To Dominicans, privacy is unimportant. Hosts offer visitors something to drink and invite them to eat if it's nearly mealtime.

Ecuador

It is unwise to appear overly familiar with Ecuadorians. A handshake is acceptable when meeting for the first time. Women who are close friends may kiss each other in greeting, and men embrace. Many visitors have trouble breathing when they first arrive in Ecuador due to the high altitude, so it is advisable to relax and avoid exertion on your first day to give yourself time to acclimatize.

EGYPT

This is a Muslim country and the working week is Saturday to Thursday; Friday is a day of rest. Social engagements are usually held late in the day, so be prepared to sit down for dinner at 10.30 pm or later. English is widely spoken.

EL SALVADOR

Summer clothing is suitable all year round because of the warm climate. A brief, firm handshake is the usual formal greeting. It is impolite to point directly at people, but there is no problem about pointing to animals or objects.

FIJI

Introduce yourself with a handshake, a smile and raised eyebrows. When socializing, a drink of kava may be offered as a sign of goodwill. Kava is made from the root of a plant in the pepper family and is very potent. Refusal to drink may be taken as a discourtesy.

FINLAND

Taking a sauna is a national pastime, so take up an offer to join your host in the family's sauna as this represents an honour or a special occasion. At meals, it is usual for the guest of honour to offer a toast following the meal, so it is a good idea to save some wine until then. Silence is seen as part of social interaction and pauses in conversation are seen as friendly and appropriate, not awkward.

FRANCE

The French are very proud of their culture, heritage and way of life. They expect visitors to have some knowledge and appreciation of the French culture. Table manners are considered important. Fruit is peeled with a knife and eaten with a fork. It is polite to bring a gift to the host such as chocolate or flowers, but not wine unless it's high quality.

GERMANY
Remember that German people respect order and discipline.
Arrive on time if you are invited to a meal. When using the phone,
Germans generally avoid small talk, and get straight to the point.

GEORGIA
Georgian people are very friendly and hospitable and women
visitors are likely to be treated with flattery and a lot of
attention.

GREECE
If you want to say 'hello', don't wave your hand with an open
palm, instead raise your index finger with your palm closed.

GRENADA
Probably the friendliest people in the Caribbean. They always
offer guests some refreshment and it is considered impolite to
refuse. Grenadians have a passion for cricket; each town has a
local cricket team.

GUATEMALA
It is considered polite to speak softly, and the use of titles is
very important. Don't call out someone's name in public.
Instead, Guatemalans make a short hissing sound to get
someone's attention.

HONDURAS
Your host will almost certainly offer you some refreshments and
refusing is considered impolite. A handshake is an appropriate
greeting for men and urban women. In Honduras, individual
needs are considered more important than timetables, so being
late for social events is common.

HONG KONG
In Hong Kong, respect is fundamental even in a social meeting.
You must show respect to gain respect. Avoid the colours blue
and white as these represent death and mourning.

HUNGARY
When visiting a Hungarian home, bring a gift of flowers or sweets.
During a meal, hands but not elbows are kept on the table.

ICELAND

It is considered bad form to discuss the weather. There is a long tradition of dropping in rather than making appointments.

INDIA

If you are invited to a meal in India, you should offer a gift of flowers, sweets or fruit to your host. At some social gatherings, guests are adorned with garlands of flowers. It is customary to remove them and carry them over the arm as a sign of humility. Avoid discussing Kashmir or the problems of Pakistan and Afghanistan.

INDONESIA

Never touch another person's head, even to rustle a child's hair playfully, as the head is thought to be where the spirit resides. Handshaking is becoming more accepted. Avoid using your left hand to pass or receive anything, as it is considered unclean and will be taken as an insult.

IRELAND

The Irish always toast their visitors, and consider refusal to drink a bit of an insult. So if you must refuse, always say it's for health reasons. The Irish are famously not very time conscious. Avoid discussions about religion or politics.

ISRAEL

Israelis tend to be informal and use first names. Israelis love to visit friends and family and may even drop by unannounced. The main working week is Sunday to Thursday. On Friday, businesses close at 2 pm and stay closed all day Saturday. Hebrew is the official language but English is used all over.

ITALY

Meals in Italy are generally unhurried, and can last up to four hours. During the meal, it is impolite to put your hands in your lap, so keep them in view by resting your wrists – but not elbows – on the table.

JAMAICA

Good table manners are considered important even in casual social situations. English is the official language and Jamaicans generally like to have lively conversations. Cricket and soccer are very popular in Jamaica.

JAPAN

The Japanese are famously fastidious about social etiquette and good form, but have come to expect very poor standards from Westerners. You will make a good impression when you are invited into a Japanese home if you follow some basic customs, such as removing your shoes, but not having any holes in your socks. The famous greeting, the bow, is simple to carry out if you hold your arms straight down with your hands facing inwards against your legs, and bending with your back, not just your head. To show respect, go down lower than your host.

KAZAKHSTAN

Local people are very friendly and hospitable and welcome visitors. It is best not to wear shorts around town.

LAOS

Religious beliefs and practices should be respected; in practical terms this means do not pose for photographs in front of images of Buddha, or sit on the statues. Do not touch a person's head as this is where their spirit resides and is sacred.

LESOTHO

If you are going to stay in a rural village, introduce yourself to the chief.

MALAYSIA

It is considered rude to touch another person, although hand-shakes without gripping are becoming more common. You should particularly avoid patting children's heads as people believe the head is spiritually vulnerable. Kissing in public is not acceptable, and pointing a finger at someone is considered very rude. And don't use a finger gesture to call someone over to you – it's a sign adopted by prostitutes to entice clients. If you visit a Malaysian home or temple, take off your shoes at the entrance.

MALDIVES

A mainly Muslim nation living on more than 1,000 islands. Backpacking is not allowed.

MAURITIUS

When meeting for the first time, a handshake is usual. If you are invited into a family home, check if your host is wearing shoes; if he is not then take your shoes off as you enter. When you go to the bathroom, it is customary to put on a pair of slippers that you see beside the door.

MONGOLIA

Mongolians are friendly and hospitable people who welcome visitors. Avoid talking about death, divorce or accidents as it is considered a bad omen. The government tourist board urges visitors not to give money to beggars, but to donate to projects that help them instead.

MOROCCO

Men and boys selling trinkets or posing as guides can be a pest. But they leave you alone if you have a guide or can say a few words in Arabic to tell them to go away. Alcohol is tolerated in private bars out of sight of local people, such as on hotel rooftops.

NEPAL

The local people do not appreciate women wearing shorts while trekking. A skirt or trousers can be more practical anyway, especially as the weather is decidedly cooler the higher you get in the mountains. Women travelling alone in Nepal may now be accompanied by female porters.

NETHERLANDS

Narcotics are illegal throughout the country but smoking cannabis is permitted in licensed coffee shops in Amsterdam as the authorities believe people will then be less likely to go on to harder drugs. Buying and selling drugs elsewhere is forbidden.

NEW ZEALAND

If you are invited to a New Zealander's home for tea, bear in mind that this is their evening meal, dinner, and not an after-noon cup of tea. If you meet a Maori, the traditional greeting is to rub noses.

OMAN

Oman is more liberal than its neighbours in the Gulf, and has not long been open to foreigners. Men and women should dress conservatively, and non-Muslims are allowed inside mosques.

QATAR

Strict Muslim laws apply. Women may find they are not allowed in some restaurants.

ROMANIA

If you buy a bottle of soft drink at a street kiosk, you have only purchased the liquid and you are expected to drink it there and then and hand back the bottle.

RUSSIA

Russians are very proud of their cultural heritage and history and subsequently know a lot about it. They may seem surprised if guests from abroad are not able to talk about their own nation's great painters, writers or important historical facts.

ST KITTS AND NEVIS

Wearing camouflage-print clothing is banned.

SAMOA

Traditional Samoan society in both American Samoa and Western Samoa is very strict and the government tourist office issues a leaflet on dress and behaviour required of visitors. Swimming is not allowed on Sundays. Avoid walking or driving through villages during the period for evening prayers, which is 15 minutes between 6 pm and 7 pm marked by a bell or blowing a conch shell.

SAUDI ARABIA

Strict fundamentalist Muslim laws apply and alcohol is forbidden. Men and women are segregated and unaccompanied women cannot do very much on their own. Dress codes are enforced by officials or the police.

SENEGAL

If you visit a village, it is polite to introduce yourself to the head man or the schoolteacher.

SERBIA

Serbians shake hands a lot even when close friends meet casually. They rarely say please and thank you when buying things, but it is appreciated when visitors do. When having a drink, it is usual to clink glasses but take care to keep eye contact when doing so.

SINGAPORE

Chewing gum is banned, and dropping litter, spitting and failing to flush a public toilet are among numerous indiscretions that can incur an on-the-spot fine.

SRI LANKA

Hindu religious customs dominate culture. Arms and legs should be covered when visiting religious sites, and hats and shoes removed.

SUDAN

A strict Muslim country and while Western women are not obliged to wear the full-cover veil, some officials can make a fuss about insisting on it. Women tend not to be treated with much respect.

SWAZILAND

There is a traditional tribal culture. You must get the permission of the chief if you are going to stay in his village.

SYRIA

This is possibly the safest of the Middle East countries for visitors. The people are friendly and hospitable. Muslim customs apply and women are respected even if travelling alone.

TAIWAN

If you are in a cake shop, you may notice a tray of pastries on the counter. These are not for sale; they are a food offering reserved for the spirits of ancestors, so do not help yourself to them.

TIBET

These gregarious people will always welcome you. The traditional greeting is to stick out your tongue. The Tibetan Autonomous Region is now home to many Chinese. Tibetans love to receive a picture of their spiritual leader, His Holiness the Dalai Lama, who lives in exile, and the children appreciate pens and pencils from visitors, which are in short supply there.

THAILAND
Legs must be covered in holy places or the Royal Palace in Bangkok, and a sarong is not sufficient; women must wear a long skirt or trousers. If you are planning to visit temples, it may be worth taking along a pair of slip-on shoes that are easy to take off and put on. Mark your shoes with brightly-coloured sticky tape so you will be able to recognize them again among dozens or even hundreds of pairs at the doorway. The monarchy and religion are very important and criticism of either is not tolerated. Climbing or sitting on statues of Buddha is considered insulting.

UNITED ARAB EMIRATES
Possibly the most liberal of the Gulf states.

URUGUAY
Possibly the most European of the South American states in terms of lifestyle. Uruguayans are very hospitable and like to entertain visitors at home.

VIETNAM
Avoid wearing shorts, and remove your shoes when visiting Buddhist shrines. Do not touch anyone on the head. The authorities will seize anything they deem to be political, religious or pornographic.

YEMEN
Most Yemenis are friendly and welcoming. Western women cannot visit Yemen without a male escort, and should not look or smile at local men.

20
Environmental Issues

No matter where you go or how you travel, you will have an effect on the people you visit and their natural environment. Responsible travel is about being aware of the negative impact that this can have and, where possible, making a contribution to conserving natural resources and making a positive impact on people's lives.

Around 700 million people travel internationally each year and this is predicted to double by 2020. Eleven out of the world's twelve poorest countries are dependent on tourism for a significant part of their foreign exchange, local business earnings and jobs. Twelve per cent of all UK tourists now visit the developing world as part of their holiday.

Because of its enormous size, the travel and tourism industry often wreaks havoc on natural environments and precious cultural sites. Threats include increased development and infrastructure, greater local demand for material, food and water, and the growth of extractive industries. When planned well, local people can benefit from tourism, biodiversity and natural environments can be protected, and cultural and historic sites can remain intact.

Conducted properly, tourism can bring in much needed money to communities in less developed countries, and that provides them with incentives to preserve the natural environment that people like to visit. Villagers in remote areas have a chance to improve their standard of living by providing visitors with food, accommodation and support services. Responsible tourism means that local people can benefit rather than be exploited. They stand to earn a living from meeting visitors but this should not be at the cost of damage to the local environment.

Eco-tourism

Eco-tourism is a term that refers to responsible travel to areas where you can make a contribution to the conservation of the environment and the well-being of local people. Also known as green tourism and sustainable travel, it is one objective that is always worth setting as part of your adventures. Wherever possible, the places and people should benefit from your visit too. In some parts of the world, local communities are receiving training and support to establish and manage their own eco-tourism businesses.

Eco-tourism is also an opportunity for a learning experience for you. It's one thing to read about the rainforest, for example, but quite another to actually go there and see how people live. It doesn't mean that every journey has to be a field trip – it can be simply a journey of discovery and observation.

Programme for Belize (www.pfbelize.org), for example, is a non-profit organization that promotes the conservation of the natural resources of this small Central American country and organizes environmental education and research. The Rio Bravo Conservation Management Area is its flagship project, set in the sub-tropical forests of north-western Belize, about two-and-a-half hours away from Belize City. Its goal is to provide visitors with an enlightening but low-impact experience of the rainforest, and the money earned from encouraging responsible tourism goes towards conservation and the sustainable development of an area of great environmental importance. Another example of some good work being done to promote responsible travel is Wilderness Safaris based in Rivonia, South Africa, which manages 10,000 square kilometres of natural habitat in southern Africa. The company runs thirty-six lodges in six countries and provides visitors with information about conservation and sustainable management. It works with local communities to promote economic growth and provides a free one-week safari for underprivileged African children each year.

Eco-tourism is not limited to the sensitive areas of faraway places. Turismo da Natureza Portugal provides lodgings in Portuguese national protected areas and also promotes trade in traditional regional products. ATG Oxford uses ancient pilgrimage and farming paths as a basis for independent or guided walking tours through the Italian hinterland, including Tuscany and Umbria. Traditional agrarian village populations have benefited from increased business during the usual off-season. ATG Oxford is also instrumental in restoring centuries-old works of art and environments and helps local communities maintain their traditional lifestyles.

Specific Environmental Issues

Global tourism has increased through the development of air travel and providing for the influx of tourists and travellers has not always been done well. In popular resort areas like Hawaii and the coast of Brazil, overbuilt beachfront hotels have contributed to erosion and flooding and generated mountains of waste without adequate means of disposal. Pollution has made some local waters unsafe for fish or people.

Only one chance

Once an area has chosen the mass tourism option, it forever forfeits the chance to develop a more sustainable and eco-friendly tourism business. Some state and national governments have surrendered to the economic lure of mass tourism, choosing visitor volume over quality of experience, abandoning other conservation and social goals in the process. There are many examples around the world where tourism has spawned crime, drug use and prostitution. Many indigenous and rural community leaders often have good ideas and the best of intentions, but neither the political power nor the access to international markets to implement them.

Rainforest Alliance 2001

Another problem of increased travel to under-developed countries is that the benefits of tourism may bypass the local population. If tourists spend their money in Western-owned hotels, consuming imported food and drink, then the money may not reach the local economy. The jobs available to local people may be poorly paid and only provide insecure seasonal employment. Then there is pressure on land and scarce resources such as fresh water. Badly-planned development of visitor facilities does not help local people to prosper and can leave them worse off, facing loss of earnings from locally-grown food and higher prices for essentials as the cost of living goes up around them.

Water, and especially fresh water, is one of the most critical natural resources, especially in hot countries. The tourism industry generally overuses water resources for hotels, swimming pools, golf courses and personal use of water by tourists. This can result in water shortages and degradation of water supplies, as well as generating a greater volume of waste water which, without proper control, pollutes the earth, seas and lakes surrounding tourist attractions, further damaging the local environment.

The Rainforest Alliance, in a report in 2001, drew attention to the need for proper control of tourism, including much that calls itself eco-tourism.

Global-warming trends

One of the consequences of increased global travel is a rise in carbon dioxide emissions from aircraft into the atmosphere, which has direct implications for global warming. Global warming and climate change are predicted to have direct effects on the pattern of travel and tourism worldwide. Even a very small rise in the oceans can cause flooding and the erosion of coastal areas, which is having the knock-on effect of reducing the numbers of visitors. The Seychelles, for example, suffered the most extreme rainfall conditions for a century in 1997, causing extensive damage to housing and roads. A storm on Praslin Island in 2002 destroyed a large number of native trees, damaged infrastructure and paralysed tourism services with a resulting loss of income for the local community. A sea level rise in the Maldives is threatening coastal erosion and there are fears that a significant part of the land mass will disappear over the next 30 years and saltwater intrusion could make the islands uninhabitable.

Climate scientists say that most of the warming observed over the past 50 years is the result of human activities and the warmest years have occurred since 1983. It is noticeable in mountain regions, where it has become apparent that glaciers are melting at an alarming rate. Some people predict that half the glaciers in the Alps could disappear within the next 100 years and less reliable snow will have an effect on winter sport tourism and the economy of regions that depend on it. A report by scientists on the Inter-Governmental Panel on Climate Change has suggested that in the United States, the Glacier National Park in Montana will have no glaciers left by 2030. This warning could be a wake-up call to the United States government which has been reluctant to sign the Kyoto Protocol, a treaty aimed at reducing the problem of global warming from carbon emissions.

Protected areas such as national parks, wilderness reserves and coastal regions are at great risk from the rapid changes in the environment caused largely by humans. Global warming is likely to bring with it reduced rainfall in some areas, higher sea levels and storms.

The El Niño event in 1997–8 highlighted the potential for long-term damage to large sections of the world from natural climate phenomena. It crippled the fishing industry of Peru and caused mudslides, flooding and severe snowstorms. The predictions of weather experts are that its effects in future years could get worse as a result of global warming.

For example, when a natural area is transformed into miles of concrete and steel, tourism can be just as destructive as other economic activities such as slash-and-burn farming, unsustainable logging, oil drilling and mining. Tourism development requires new buildings and services such as hotels, parking space, restaurants and trails. Success and profit tend to breed more development which can very easily overwhelm a vulnerable natural area that is the very thing that attracts visitors. Tourism that is not managed properly causes pollution and erosion, disturbs wildlife, destroys plants, spoils scenery and can bring undesirable influences on once-isolated cultures and communities.

Coral Reefs

Fragile natural resources like coastlines can be destroyed by too many tourists or the uncontrolled development of modern hotel complexes, so the issue of balancing the need for generating income from visitors and preserving natural beauty is a fine one that now concerns governments and global bodies such as the United Nations. Coral reefs are fascinating natural structures that attract increasing numbers of visitors. They are colonies of tiny, soft-bodied animals, and grow about 2 cm per year in warm, shallow, ocean waters. They are the spawning grounds of many species of fish that can be commercially important to local people. Corals are sensitive to anything that changes the composition of the sea water in which they live; sediments and pollutants from human activities on the shore and excessive carbon dioxide from the air above are particularly harmful. In Central America, a scheme is being developed to engage local people in conserving an important coral reef by exploiting the positive opportunities provided by the interest and curiosity of visitors.

The Mesoamerican Reef is the world's second longest coral barrier, stretching about 1,000 km from the northern tip of the

Yucatan Peninsula in Mexico to the islands in Honduras Bay. It is home for more than fifty species of coral and 300 types of fish, but many of them are threatened by over-fishing. In Belize, more than 3,000 fishermen depend on the reef for their livelihood and they are being encouraged to turn their skills to protecting the coral reef through treating it as a visitor attraction and so earn more money than they made from fishing. Belize has designated ten sections of the reef as protected areas including the Bacalar Chico and Sapodilla Cayes Marine Reserves.

The Belizean fishermen are being retrained to manage conservation of the reef through funds that flow from carefully regulated nature tourism. They are beginning to act as tour guides for boat trips, diving and sea kayaking.

Treat reefs with care

Some tips from Jean-Michel Cousteau about enjoying a coral reef dive without causing harm.

- Make sure you're comfortable in the water; don't panic and break pieces of reef with your fins accidentally.
- Look but don't touch; avoid all contact with the bottom or marine life at all times.
- Don't kick sand in the reef's 'face' as you may choke the coral with a burst of sand.
- Anchor or tie your boat to established moorings; corals are not hitching posts!
- Leave it behind. As the underwater world recycles everything, you may disrupt the fragile ecosystem by taking shells from the sea or beach.
- Keep it clean and avoid polluting the ocean with your rubbish, oil or fuel.

Some fishermen are also helping in research studies of lobster, conch and commercial fish populations and others are allowed to continue their traditional fishing trade in strictly limited areas of the sea. The scheme is being observed by neighbouring countries as they too become aware that indiscriminate fishing is not sustainable and carefully regulated tourism is a real alternative source of earning potential for the long-term prosperity of a relatively poor region.

The authorities in the Caribbean have taken up the challenge to find a balance between encouraging visitors and taking care of the natural wonders of the islands. St Kitts and Nevis are among the Caribbean's finest destinations for eco-tourism. Both islands possess a remarkable range of unspoiled ecosystems, from coral reefs and windswept rocky coastlines to oceanic rainforests. A rugged hiking adventure up Mount Liamuiga on St Kitts takes you through the island's rainforest to the rim of a mile-wide crater of a dormant volcano. On Nevis, you can stroll along the east coast to learn about the island's ecology and archaeological history.

Mountain Environments

On the other side of the globe, attention has been focused on the mountain environment of the Himalaya where the influx of climbers and trekkers has put demands on local people as guides and porters. A different problem has arisen, with farmers from the valleys turning to servicing the mountain routes. It is a matter of worry to Tourism Concern, a London-based organization that campaigns for ethical and fair trade in tourism.

An example of one of its campaigns is to get a better deal for the working conditions of porters and guides on mountains around the world. The increase in the number of trekkers in Nepal has put an enormous strain on village communities and the overuse of wood for fuel has led to massive deforestation causing a terrible increase in soil erosion. And with so many people following well-worn tracks in the desire to visit the more remote mountain areas, such as the Solu Khumbu, the mountain paths are being widened causing further impact. Tourism Concern's website, at www.tourism-concern.org.uk, is full of ideas for developing a responsible approach to planning adventure travel and expeditions. When you are planning a trekking trip, it is a good idea to ask questions of your tour operator about how porters are treated and you could make the point that you don't want to exploit them unfairly. This does not mean that you should stop going on treks and expeditions to remote and high places, as they provide work and an income for local people. A responsible traveller should be concerned about their welfare and livelihood.

Advice for trekkers from Tourism Concern

If you're thinking of going trekking . . .

- Ask questions of tour operators.
- Let them know that it's important to you that your trip doesn't exploit porters.
- Ask them what policies they have on porters' working conditions – wages, loads, equipment – and what happens if porters have accidents or fall ill.
- Travel with an operator that has policies on porters.

While you're there, keep your eyes open . . .

- Take pictures of what you think might be bad practice – and good!
- What are the porters wearing – do they have adequate protective clothing?
- How big are the loads that the porters are carrying?
- What are the porters eating and where are they sleeping at night?

When you come back, act on what you saw . . .

- If you saw things that worried you about the way porters were treated, speak up. Tell your tour operator and tell Tourism Concern.
- And just as important, if the porters were treated fairly, let your tour operator know this was an important factor in an enjoyable trip.

If you know someone who's going trekking . . .

- Open their eyes to what's going on. Pass on this information, and get them involved.

Things You Can Do To Help

If you are planning your own adventure, there are a number of things you can do to be a responsible traveller yourself.

- Choose destinations that are not already over-crowded or over-developed.

- Plan to stay in environment-sensitive accommodation. Hotels in popular holiday resorts use up an excessive amount of local resources such as water and power to keep their guests comfortable, and import food products to satisfy foreign guests. Where this happens, it prevents local farmers from benefiting from the influx of visitors and is not eco-friendly or sustainable tourism.

- Make your arrangements through a responsible tour operator who is aware of environmental impacts and the need to make business contribute financially to conservation as well as profit. In Britain, www.responsibletravel.com, for example, makes this a condition for the small firms that they list as operators. Whoever you book with, tell them you want your trip to be low impact as far as the environment is concerned.

- Learn about the country's customs before travelling. Remember that you are a guest when you get there and behave accordingly. Try to include in your plans some cultural events such as music, so that local performers gain something from your visit in addition to providing you with entertainment.

- Prepare a few words of the local language and use them when meeting people. It helps if you invest in a phrase book. Speaking to local people in their own language, even if it's just a greeting, will show that you respect local culture.

- Think about supporting the local communities by buying gift items from local craft workers rather than mass-produced souvenirs that you will often see in hotels. This helps local communities to earn a living and keep cultural traditions alive. The Cofan peoples of the Amazon, for example, have been assisted to run an enterprise in their territory where they sustain a home-based craft industry and share their traditional knowledge of medicinal plants.

- Be prepared to pay a fair price for goods and services from local people, even though they may seem very cheap by Western standards.

Voluntary Environmental Work

A practical way that you can make a contribution to environmental protection as a traveller is to combine your zest for adventure with voluntary conservation work. One company which specializes in projects suitable for gap-year travel is the Expedition Company, near Taunton, Somerset. You can join a team expedition to the coast of Kenya and combine training for a diving qualification with some marine life survey work on fragile coral reefs. In Nicaragua, reforestation is vital to the future viability of the natural environment, and you could help in a campaign to plant thousands of trees and in cultivating a certain species which is ideal for the climate and soil composition.

The Earthwatch Institute (www.earthwatch.org) enlists volunteers without specific qualifications to join expeditions directed by scientists. One such expedition was to gather data on the expansion of the Gobi Desert in northern China, which is threatening the future of agriculture in the region. It combined an adventure in the footsteps of Marco Polo with collecting water samples for some very modern scientific research work. Maybe you are a hardy type and would like to face the Arctic in winter. Earthwatch volunteers help researchers measure snowpack thickness and collect winter-active insects from under the snow, as these are features relevant to understanding global warming.

Whatever your aims, there are operators based in the UK, usually the smaller specialist ones, that can help you to plan a positively responsible adventure by ensuring that local communities get some direct financial benefit from your visit. It has already been shown that if communities make money from nature tourism, they have more incentive to preserve the natural assets of their region because they can see them as the key to prosperity.

Environmental Bodies

No one advocates a total ban on travel to areas of natural beauty, though some restrictions are needed on access to delicate features such as coral reefs. The aim of international conservation bodies is to make travel and tourism benefit the localities through trade and education. The Pacific Asia Travel Association (PATA), for example, was founded over 50 years ago to promote responsible tourism and travel and has become influential in encouraging businesses and travellers to respect the environment which they seek to enjoy on visits. International travel to the Pacific Asia region has increased three-fold in the past decade from 25 million visitors a year to over 90 million. PATA helps communities to gain some economic prosperity from this growth, and even increased its marketing and promotional efforts in response to a downturn in travel as a result of more recent fears of terrorism, conflict and disease.

PATA has developed a website (www.travelwithpata.com) as a one-stop consumer source of authoritative information about travel in the region, which was hit hard by worldwide concern about SARS and bombings in Southeast Asia in 2003. PATA works mainly towards balancing growth in travel with conservation measures and has produced a code of conduct for travellers which contains a lot of common sense and should be at the forefront of any adventure or expedition plan.

Pacific Asia Travel Association Travellers' Code

Remember that travel is a passage through other people's lives and other people's places.

BE FLEXIBLE
Are you prepared to accept cultures and practices different from your own?

CHOOSE RESPONSIBILITY
Have you elected to support businesses that clearly and actively address the cultural and environmental concerns of the locale you are visiting?

DO YOUR HOMEWORK
Have you done any research about the people and places you plan to visit so you may avoid what may innocently offend them or harm their environment?

BE AWARE
Are you informed of the holidays, holy days and general religious and social customs of the places you visit?

SUPPORT LOCAL ENTERPRISE
Have you made a commitment to contribute to the local economy by using businesses that economically support the community you are visiting, eating in local restaurants and buying locally-made artisan crafts as remembrances of your trip?

BE RESPECTFUL AND OBSERVANT
Are you willing to respect local laws that may include restrictions of your usage of or access to places and things that may harm or otherwise erode the environment or alter or run counter to the places you visit?

The United Nations has long recognized the value of travel and tourism for developing countries and declared 2002 as the International Year of Eco-tourism as a way of fostering better understanding and awareness of the rich heritage of the environment and cultures in which different peoples live. It recognized that travel and tourism, if managed properly, can improve the living standards of local populations and support the conservation of natural ecosystems.

The World Tourism Organization puts into effect the UN's aims of encouraging responsible, sustainable travel and so stimulate prosperity while at the same time protecting the environment and cultural heritage of poorer nations around the world. There is an important role for governments in this process to gain the maximum benefit from foreign earnings and reducing the damage caused by unregulated tourism. As well as holding inter-governmental conferences and producing reports, the WTO is actively promoting travel opportunities through special projects such as the Silk Road and the Slave Route.

The WTO's Silk Road project aims to revitalize interest in the 12,000 km of ancient highways from Asia to Europe used by Marco Polo and the caravan traders who came after him. Sixteen countries are taking part in promoting the initiative to encourage travellers to explore, with familiarization trips and special events along the way from Japan, South Korea, North Korea, China, Kazakhstan, Kyrgyz Republic, Pakistan, Uzbekistan, Tajikistan, Turkmenistan, Iran, Azerbaijan, Turkey, Georgia, Greece and Egypt.

The Slave Route project was launched to boost cultural tourism to Western Africa and its immediate aims are to restore monuments and museums to encourage foreign visitors to learn about the history of West African countries. The project is to be expanded to include southern and east Africa and countries of the Caribbean.

Green Globe 21 is a worldwide certification scheme that demonstrates the environmental credentials of travel businesses to customers and the communities that benefit from the growth in global travel. It was created in response to the growth in demand for environmentally sensitive travel arrangements. A survey by Tearfund, one of the UK's leading relief and development agencies, showed that 85 per cent of tourists think it is very important not to damage the environment while on holiday, which is consistent with the results of a poll by the Travel Industry Association of America in 1997 which showed that 83 per cent of travellers are inclined to support 'green' travel companies. The Tearfund survey also revealed that more than 60 per cent of UK travellers were willing to pay extra for overseas travel if the money went towards the preservation of the local environment, and would pay up to £25 more to selected tourism operators to ensure commitment to environmental protection. Making informed, positive choices in favour of low-impact travel is one way that you can make a contribution to sustainable and environment-friendly global tourism. There is a growing number of tour operators that specialize in this field. Learning about eco-tourism could in itself be a theme of one of your adventures, or at least part of it, or you might be able to play some part in working to conserve an endangered habitat or supporting a local community initiative by your visit and by informing others about what you have seen and experienced when you return home.

21
Communications

It is hard to overstate the advances made in the way we communicate today in all walks of life. How this has changed the way we can approach adventure travel would leave someone like James Rennell Rodd dumbfounded if he saw how it could be done today. He was at the 'leading edge' of adventure in his day and was the first person to use communications (a Marconi radio wireless) on a crossing of the Sahara Desert. The supporting radio batteries alone made up a complete camel load, and now and again if the batteries bounced around on the camel's back and the acid leaked on to its skin, it would gallop off in any direction taking days to find, and creating (even for the 1920s) an unimagined impact on regular communication schedules.

Today you could make a similar journey with a SAT phone in your top pocket, and speak, send a text, or still or video images anywhere in the world in seconds. Rendell's radio kit weighed several hundred pounds; today it would weigh a few ounces, and in the next few years it will weigh nothing at all, being an integrated part of your environmentally protective clothing as part of your personal 'wearable communications' package.

Keeping in Touch

Why do we automatically have a need for access to any kind of communications on our adventures? The main reason is that communication in all its forms is so much a part of our daily lives. On adventures, communication equipment allows us on a regular basis to tell people we are safe, and that has to be common sense.

Nevertheless, there are still those who wish to recreate, or to experience, 'a true sense' of travel and these adventurers create scenarios or 'limitations' that cut them off from any external contact. It means they have taken complete control over their adventure and their lives, being completely self-reliant and self-supporting, cutting out any form of contact, and making the adventure one of complete commitment from start to finish.

Adventure of this kind is increasingly difficult to manufacture, as many far-flung communities have radio links to the outside world, even if it is just to call a doctor, and no aircraft or sea-going vessel is allowed by international law to be devoid of such equipment. Not using them could trigger a completely unnecessary search and rescue, which might take up valuable resources needed for a genuine call out. When planning, do make a conscious decision about communications, and make sure that friends and family know what it is. Establish a routine to be in touch with them and stick to it as much as possible.

Check the Options in Advance

As part of your plannings research check out the communications available in the countries you are visiting. Check out how reliable the national telephone system is. Does it only have a reliable infrastructure in the main conurbations, commercial and industrial areas only? What are the costs of using it? Does it shut down in remote areas at particular hours? Will the time difference affect when you call home? Some parts of the world have metered telephone booths where you can drop in. A member of staff will dial your number for you and charge you a dollar rate for the connection and duration of the call. These booths/businesses are usually well advertized (they will have ISDN and STD call centre somewhere on their window) and the service is honest, is usually working and is not expensive by Western standards.

Some Communication Options

Phone cards

One alternative is to take a pre-paid phone card, similar to the ones used by most Western military personnel who are issued with 20 minutes of free call time each month. They have the option to top up the time on their call card using their own credit cards, so extending their very cheap call time. This is now available to all of us who travel and it works by taking the cheapest possible routing for calls. The specialist operating companies like Telco and eKit card have negotiated 'off-peak routing times' with various national telephone companies across the world.

Quality is seldom affected; the old days of 'squelchy squishy' noises in the background have long gone. You operate the system by using a call back number and a PIN (personal identification number) that link you into the system. You can then dial the number you want. A recent advantage is the voice mail facility, where you can have messages left for you to collect when you dial in your PIN. The system is cost effective, secure, reliable and means you have less to carry.

Mobile phones

Another option is to take your mobile phone. Your network provider will have a partner network in most industrialized countries (check that coverage does not suffer from the same problem as landline coverage might – being intermittent or only in densely-populated areas). You will be able to connect just by switching on your phone as normal. If you do not have a roaming facility, ask your network provider to facilitate one before you leave on your trip, but do check the tariff. It may prove cheaper to change the SIM card to a local pay-as-you-go card and top up as necessary, emailing the new local number to friends and family. Do you need to take a mobile? It's just another possession to be responsible for and something else to lose. If a phone card will do, or the local system is good enough, it might be wiser to leave it at home.

SAT phones

When telecommunications for an adventure or expedition are a priority and reliability is essential from wherever you are in the world, satellite phones are your only real option. There are two favoured systems for the adventurer, Iridium and Thuraya.

Iridium provides a complete global coverage including the oceans, mountainous areas, airways and polar regions of the world. This is managed by a constellation of sixty-six low-Earth orbiting (LEO) satellites operated by Boeing Industries that are capable of covering remote areas where terrestrial communications are not available. LEO satellites were preferred in setting this system up, because the configuration offers a number of benefits. Unlike geosynchronous satellites, which hover above the equator at an altitude of 35,900 kilometres (22,300 miles), the satellites in the Iridium constellation are in polar orbits at an altitude of only 780 kilometres (485 miles). This orbital configuration provides no significant transmission delays, and lower transmitting power results in longer battery life – a vital aspect for anyone in a remote and difficult location.

Iridium has a track record of connecting people anywhere and vehicles just about everywhere, regardless of their location. You can send and receive voice messages and data at any time with the system and it has been used at both North and South Poles, as well as in the Himalayas and other normally difficult terrain, with outstanding clarity of reception and clear transmission. It has other uses too. In April 2003 the Iridum system was a key component in the location and successful rescue of Dr Ronald Shemenski from the South Pole.

Thuraya has an equally good reputation, however it must be said that they are not so focused on communications in difficult terrain; that still suits the Iridium system best. They have a very wide coverage encompassing Europe, north and central Africa, the Middle East, the CIS countries, Armenia, Azerbaijan, Belarus, Georgia, Kazakhstan, Kyrgyzstan, Moldova, Tajikistan, Turkmenistan, Ukraine, Uzbekistan and south Asia – more than enough for most adventures where the terrain is wild but not extreme. Users can benefit from continuous border-to-border coverage beyond boundaries of terrestrial systems and cellular networks. Another key benefit of this system is its dual service, enabling the user to access the GSM service at any time in local networks, yet being able to automatically switch on to satellite mode whenever out of local terrestrial reach. Thuraya handsets integrate satellite, GSM and location determination via Global Positioning System (GPS), and each handset offers voice, data, facsimile and messaging.

Global Positioning System (GPS)

A GPS communicates with satellite-based navigation systems that are made up of a network of twenty-four satellites placed in orbit by the US Department of Defence. GPS works in any weather conditions, anywhere in the world, 24 hours a day. It can fix your location or help you plan routes and journeys anywhere in the world and be accurate to a matter of metres. To use a GPS involves no subscription fees or set-up charges.

The GPS satellites circle the Earth twice a day in a very precise orbit and transmit a particular information signal. GPS receivers take this information and use triangulation to calculate the user's exact location. Essentially, the GPS receiver compares the time a signal was transmitted by a satellite with the time it was received. The time difference tells the GPS receiver how far away the satellite is. With these distance measurements from a few more satellites, the receiver can determine the user's position and display it on the unit's electronic map. A GPS receiver must be locked on to the signal of at least three satellites to calculate a 2D position (latitude and longitude) and track movement. With four satellites in view, the receiver can determine the user's 3D position (latitude, longitude and altitude). Once the user's position has been determined, the GPS unit can calculate other information, such as speed, bearing, track, trip distance, distance to destination, sunrise and sunset time and more.

Today's GPS receivers are extremely accurate, thanks to their parallel multi-channel design. In the same way as a SAT phone can have a secondary function as a GPS, some GPS receivers have a phone capability and much more. For example, the Garmin Rino (Radio Integrated Navigation Outdoors) 120 has a radio capability and enough memory to download detailed mapping. It can also coordinate and fix three other users' locations and update them all as they move. Most of the modern GPS can 'beam' your exact location to another user within a two-mile range using position reporting, an invaluable function in poor weather conditions. GPS today are tough, robust instruments and all the top brands make a variety of waterproof options.

While it is still advisable to take a map and compass on an adventure as a back up for any contingency, the GPS has become the preferred method of reading one's way across the most hostile of terrain. Check the classified ads in the papers and similar sites on the Internet for good second-hand GPS.

'Snail' mail

Before you set off, try to find out some information on the local postal system. You will inevitably have a use for it, if only to send home postcards. You might want to send home clothing and equipment you no longer require at the end of your trip. Or perhaps you have purchased something that is too heavy to carry. You may have been collating material (books, magazines, paper documents) to research back home for a project or post-graduate work. You need to know how the system works. (Will the stamps be steamed off for resale as soon as I am out of sight?)

If sending mail back home to your supporters, sponsors and newspapers, consider whether fax might be more reliable, quicker and more cost effective. If so, the phone booths already mentioned will be able to help.

Internet access

As 'sail gave way to steam', so the more traditional methods of communicating have given way to the Internet. Do bear in mind, however, that as fast and effective as the Internet is, there is no real substitute for the pleasure a handwritten letter can give the recipient from time to time, and a happy and enthusiastic-sounding voice at the other end of the phone can do the same. Remember that this can be made very cost effective over the net with compatible audio/voice systems, should you be able to use them.

By far the most practical way to use the Internet is to set up a free service email account. Do this before you go, and get conversant with its potential, if you have the time. The advantage of this is that you can access your mail from just about anywhere. Using cyber cafes or some of the 'phone home' booths is usually very inexpensive, and a great advantage to the free service route is that you do not need to take a laptop or notebook computer. It is also something less to lose, have stolen, or have hassle with 'dutiable or restricted

Free service accounts

If using a free service account, do remember not to become a dormant user. All of the free servers have a regular clear out of addresses that are not getting used. The usual time for making your email address dormant is about 90 days, so for most people away from home this should not happen.

Check out bulletin boards, news groups and discussion forums that are pertinent to your pre-departure plans and again regularly while you are away. There is nothing like learning from someone else's recent and up-to-date experience. There may be some good recommendations and reviews of places that you will never have heard of, and they could make your adventure just that little bit more special.

items' at customs or border crossings. If equipment and services of any kind are there 'in country' and are reasonably reliable, it makes sense to use them to give yourself greater flexibility.

It might be useful to warn friends and family of your departure plans by using the free service email before you go. This ensures that they have a log of your plan, timings and intentions and that they have your new email address.

There are plenty of free services for you to choose from. Using a well-known service like Hotmail, Lycos or Yahoo is most common. They seldom have technical problems and are fast to access. Do remember that the speed of access might vary with the sophistication (or lack of it) of the national phone system, and the rate of the modem the computer is using. Using any of the various Internet directories of cyber cafes, you can look up the different places that Internet access will be available to you. You could pre-plan times of the week to 'hit' these locations to pick up and send your email. These days there are cyber cafes in the most unlikely places. You can now send an email from a cafe in a tent at Everest Base Camp at 18,300 feet!

PALM or WAP?

For those of you who do want to have mobile Internet communications, the new generation of palmtops are likely to be the answer. They will seamlessly integrate with Microsoft, Lotus and Corel desktop applications. Most have a flexible database for personal records, a jotter including an embedded sketching facility, a voice memo recorder, an alarm clock and they will send and receive email messages using your normal Internet service provider (ISP).

You can also have an infrared travel modem installed in some of the palms and they can then use a GSM digital phone as the 'slave' to connect you.

A WAP phone which will connect to the low-level orbital satellite system might be the answer for some of your destinations, but you must prioritize the use you will have. Is it voice communication you require most, with an occasional but slowish connection to the Internet? If this were not the case a palm or small notebook would probably suit you best and the 'ether time' will likely be more cost effective.

Communicating images

Digital cameras are now serious rivals to more normal analogue (film-loaded) cameras and they have several advantages besides the fact that prices have dramatically fallen and the adventure traveller can now buy a very handy camera for well under £40.

Analogue cameras use film which comes in 12, 24 or 36 exposure, is housed in a bulky cassette, can be effected by extremes of temperature (the feed lip can snap in intense cold), can be fiddly to load in awkward circumstances – with wet, numb or sweaty hands, or in a canoe, up a cliff or in a moving vehicle – and the film can be scratched or damaged with dust or grit if the environment is not ideal. Once finished, the film is developed. If you wanted to 'wire' an image from the film, you would need to process it, scan it into a computer and then send it in a suitable format as an attached file by email. This could be expensive depending on the size of the file and speed of the modem.

The good news with a digital camera is that it has no film, but light-sensitive cells, which are often made from crystalline silicon. The digital camera will either have a small amount of built-in computer-like memory for storing the images, or will utilize removable memory cards. It is important to bear in mind that the greater the pixel resolution, i.e. the number of light-sensitive cells, the better the picture quality. Also digital cameras generally have to use longer exposure times or larger aperture sizes. For the adventurous traveller, the advantages are obvious, as pictures can be viewed immediately, unwanted compositions can be discarded, the memory cards can be removed and downloaded on to a computer to be stored, edited or printed and the images can then be deleted from the camera or memory card, freeing up storage space.

For the weight-conscious adventurer, the SIPIX Blink Digital Camera should be seriously considered. It stores 100 640 x 480 (0.3 megapixel images) or 400 320 x 240 images and only uses a single AAA battery (although the images will be lost if the battery is removed before they have been downloaded). The SIPIX can also store short motion clips and is only the size of a matchbox. Digital video is based on the same principles and many cameras today are capable of video imaging.

High-frequency transceivers

There will be occasions when radio is still the most appropriate form of communication, especially on scientific expeditions that are field bound for long periods of time. Local government regulations might insist upon it and not allow any other form of communication. There may be a need to keep connection time costs to a minimum, and with such transceivers the only extra cost besides the purchase or hire of the equipment is likely to be an operating licence applied for from the correct government department, and managed on similar lines to a standard UK television and radio licence. HF has a distinct advantage here as every other type of communication mentioned so far has a cost implication every time it is used. HF suits a multi-station tasking requirement for expeditions where possibly weight or load carrying may not be so crucial.

The Australians (used to covering vast distances by radio) have a radio set called the HF-90 and it is one of the most versatile HF transceivers available anywhere suited to civilian applications. It has reliable communications up to distances of 3,0000 km and is currently in use in over seventy-five countries worldwide, which means that spares are in good supply. This rugged all-purpose HF SSB transceiver is designed for backpack use, vehicles and for fixed-base station applications.

Power sources

Remember, too, that your communications will only be viable with a regular source of power. How will you achieve this?

MOBILE POWER

Mobile phones have been limited in their use even on short-term adventures where a plug-in source of power, like a cigarette lighter in a vehicle, was not available. Recently, however, a small 'snap in' hand-cranking generator has been designed that takes about three minutes to fully charge a standard-size mobile phone battery and weighs next to nothing.

SOLAR POWER

Portable solar panel technology is now very advanced. It is light-weight and even works on cloudy days. This could be the answer for notebook and laptop computers when away from all other sources.

GENERATORS

Petrol or diesel generators (depending on the altitude) are reliable, heavy (as is the fuel to run them, as well as being smelly and polluting), fast, noisy and efficient. Some vehicles will have gener-ating capabilities so check this with the supplier or manufacturer.

When on the move it is an extremely compact and light-weight unit, and has only essential controls to ensure ease of operation. It has a capacity for up to 255 programmed channels. It can operate at a selected power level of up to 50 watts, and has very low battery consumption. The reception is excellent even in the most crowded radio environments. Remember that you will need to use a set form of radio etiquette, and to designate station codes and identifications.

If you need to buy equipment like this in advance, consider checking out a government surplus store to see if there is any second-hand equipment that will meet your communicating needs at a fraction of the cost of buying new equipment.

Consider the Impact on Others

Always consider your need to communicate and the various levels that are necessary. Look closely at the 'needs' rather than the 'wants'. Look at the availability of producing power to sustain your communications, while you (hopefully) show concern for the environmental impact and any noise pollution you will create in remote locations and fragile ecosystems.

Whatever form of communication you use, remember it uses power, and generating the power can have an enormous impact on the environment and the people around you. Be responsible. Use sustainable energy sources or think twice about whether your use of electronic devices is a necessity in the circumstances.

PART III
GAZETTEER

Compiled by Nigel Gifford and David Browne

This section of the book provides you with a set of resources and contacts for planning your adventure and researching the places you would like to visit. It has information on where to get advice and where to obtain products and services that you will need for a safe but exciting and purposeful journey, whether it's an expedition, a field trip or an adventure off the beaten track away from the more usual holiday destinations. The lists are not exhaustive; there may be other organizations and businesses that could be useful to you. The Internet is a vast source of information and so web addresses are included along with postal addresses and phone numbers.

Contents

Adventure Travel Organizers

It would be impossible to list every company in the world that organizes adventure and discovery tours to remote places off the beaten track. This list is a selection of businesses that organize tours on the principles of responsible tourism and engage local companies and guides in the locations you will be visiting. Making your arrangements through these companies ensures that the local economy benefits from your visit and you get the help and assistance from local people who know and love their country and its natural assets. The ground agents are chosen for their knowledge and high standards and for their understanding of the ideals of eco-tourism, which benefits the local community and helps to conserve the natural environment.

Active Africa Adventures & Touring
PO Box 30993
Tokai, 7966
Cape Town
South Africa
www.active-africa.com
Email: info@activeafrica.co.za
Tel: +27 21 788 8750

Adventure Alternative
31 Myrtledene Road
Belfast BT8 6GQ
www.adventurealternative.com
Email: office@adventure
alternative.com
Tel: 02890 701476
Personal adventure tour and expedition planning service, with expert guidance and leadership and advice on logistics and routes. Wide range of escorted adventure trips and expeditions.

Adventure Extreme ATI Ltd
Victoria Cottage
Tomintoul AB37 9ET
www.adventure-ext.demon.co.uk
Email: trips@adventure-x.com
Tel: 07092 283020
Scheduled and tailor-made mountain expeditions and paragliding courses.

Adventure Overland
9 Ridge Road
Mitcham
Surrey CR4 2ET
www.adventureoverland.com
Email: info@adventureoverland.com
Tel: 020 8640 8105
Overland low-impact adventures for small groups and individuals with local guides and family-run accommodation in central Asia.

Adventure Peaks Ltd
3 Beechwood Close
Bowness-on-Windermere
Cumbria LA23 3AB
www.adventurepeaks.com
Tel: 01539 447301
Expedition company providing worldwide mountaineering expeditions and courses.

Africa & Asia Venture (AV)
10 Market Place
Devizes
Wiltshire SN10 1HT
www.aventure.co.uk
Email: av@aventure.co.uk
Tel: 01380 729009
Adventure travel through conservation work, teaching and sports coaching in Africa, Asia and Mexico, and charity fundraising. A founder member of the Year Out Group, promoting the benefits of well-structured gap-year programmes.

African Pride
Box Tree House
Northminster Business Park
York YO26 2QU
Tel: 01904 781500
www.african-pride.co.uk
Email: info@africa-pride.co.uk
Tailored bespoke adventures to
southern and East Africa,
including village and cultural
tours, white-water rafting and
mountain biking.

African Trails
3 Conway Avenue
Preston
Lancashire PR1 9TR
www.africantrails.co.uk
Email: web@africantrails.co.uk
Tel: 01772 330907
Overland driving adventures in
fully equipped trucks.

Amazon Explorama Lodges
Explorama Lodges
Box 446
Iquitos
Peru
www.explorama.com
Email: amazon@explorama.com
Tel: 00 51 65 25 2530
Small group adventures in the
region of the Upper Amazon, with
tours escorted by multilingual
naturalists exploring the wildlife,
including excursions to the
Canopy Walkway, a 500-metre
rope bridge in the rainforest of
Iquitos, Peru.

Amazonas Explorer
PO Box 722
Cusco
Peru
www.amazonas-explorer.com
Email: sales@amazonas-
explorer.com
Tel (UK brochure line):
01437 891743
Small group adventures and
expeditions in Peru and Bolivia.

Andean Trails
The Clockhouse
Bonnington Mill Business Centre
72 Newhaven Road
Edinburgh EH6 5QG
www.andeantrails.co.uk
Email: info@andeantrails.co.uk
Tel: 0131 467 7086
Adventure tour operator for
challenging activity, adventure
and expeditions in South America,
including climbing Cotopaxi or
Chimborazo in Ecuador, trekking
in Peru or Patagonia jungle
expeditions in the Amazon region
of Bolivia to the Madidi National
Park.

Andes
37a St Andrew Street
Castle Douglas
DG7 1EN
www.andes.org.uk
Email: john@andes.org.uk
Tel: 01556 503929
Specialist operator of trekking,
climbing, mountaineering, skiing
and biking expeditions to South
America. Andes also publish
climbing and trekking guidebooks
to the Andes.

Archipelago Azores Ltd
48 Main Street
Keswick
Cumbria CA12 5JJ
www.azoreschoice.com
Email: info@azoreschoice.com
Tel: 01768 775672
Tailor-made adventures on the
Azores archipelago, a group of
nine volcanic islands in the mid-
Atlantic. This is the only UK tour
operator specializing in the
Azores.

Arcturus Expeditions Ltd
PO Box 850
Gartocharn
Alexandria
Dunbartonshire G83 8RL
www.arcturusexpeditions.co.uk

Email: info@arcturusexpeditions.
co.uk
Tel: 01389 830204
Small travel company specializing
in Polar tours with Kathleen and
Neville Cartwright and Robert
Burton, with the emphasis on
enjoying wildlife and scenery.
Winner of a WWF award for
work in linking tourism and
conservation in the Arctic.

Artro Adventure
Gilfach Goch
Llanbedr
Gwynedd LL45 2LT
www.artroadventure.co.uk
Email: mail@artroadventure.co.uk
Tel: 01341 241275
Adventure in Snowdonia, north
Wales, and in the mountains of
Sierra Mantiqueira in Brazil.

Audley Travel Ltd
6 Willows Gate
Stratton Audley
Oxfordshire OX27 9AU
www.audleytravel.com
Email: mail@audleytravel.com
Tel: 01869 276200
Tailor-made adventures and
escorted group tours to South
America, north and central Asia,
and the Far East.

Austral Tours Ltd
20 Upper Tachbrook Street
London SW1V 1SH
www.latinamerica.co.uk
Email: info@latinamerica.co.uk
Tel: 020 7233 5384
Personalized adventure planning
service for independent travellers
to South America and special
interest holidays including a
multi-activity break in the Chilean
lake district.

Avian Adventures
49 Sandy Road
Norton
Stourbridge

West Midlands DY8 3AJ
www.avianadventures.co.uk
Email: aviantours@argonet.co.uk
Tel: 01384 372013
Adventures based on bird-watching
tours worldwide, including
Kwazululand, Ecuador, Guyana
and Guatemala, also Australia,
Alaska and India.

Baobab Travel
Old Fallings Hall
Old Fallings Lane
Wolverhampton WV10 8BL
www.baobabtravel.com
Email: info@baobabtravel.com
Tel: 01902 558316
Tailor-made eco-tourism
adventures to remote locations,
avoiding resorts created for
mass tourism, in Egypt, South
Africa and Tanzania.

Barefoot Traveller
204 King Street
London W6 0RA
www.barefoot-traveller.com
Email: dive@barefoot-traveller.com
Tel: 020 8741 4319
Tailor-made marine adventures
for divers of all abilities, to the
Caribbean, the Indian Ocean and
Thailand.

Biosphere Expeditions
Sprat's Water
Nr Carlton Colville
The Broads National Park
Suffolk NR33 8BP
www.biosphere-expeditions.org
Email: info@biosphere-
expeditions.org
Tel: 01502 583085
Not-for-profit wildlife conservation
adventures lasting from two weeks
to several months, alongside teams
of local researchers. No special
skills required. The projects are
not safaris or package holidays,
and involve work that will
contribute to research and care
of the environment.

Blue Dog Adventures
Amwell Farmhouse
Nomansland
Wheathampstead
St Albans
Hertfordshire AL4 8EJ
www.bluedogadventures.com
Email: info@bluedogadventures.com
Tel: 01582 831302
Blue Dog Adventures include horse riding treks in Romania and South Africa, scuba diving and crewing the *Empire Sandy* which is part of the EARTHSHIP programme. EARTHSHIP is a Caribbean tall-ship eco-adventure that lets you join ongoing environmental initiatives in the Grenadine Islands, supporting the valuable efforts of environmental research and protection.

Blue Ventures
52 Avenue Road
London N6 5DR
www.blueventures.org
Email: enquiries@blueventures.org
Blue Ventures is an award-winning, UK-based, not-for-profit, organization dedicated to facilitating projects that enhance global coral reef conservation and research. Blue Ventures has coordinated marine projects in Madagascar, Tanzania, New Zealand, South Africa and the Comoros Islands. Blue Ventures coordinates teams of marine scientists and volunteers, working with local biologists, marine institutes and communities whose livelihoods depend on coral reefs.

Brathay Exploration Group
Brathay Hall
Ambleside
Cumbria LA22 0HP
www.brathayexploration.org.uk
Email: admin@brathayexploration.org.uk
Tel: 01539 433942
The highly respected Brathay Exploration Group has been leading non-profit-making youth expeditions for 55 years and has an RGS gold medal to its credit.

British Schools Exploring Society (BSES)
The Royal Geographical Society
1 Kensington Gore
London SW7 2AR
www.bses.org.uk
Email: bses@rgs.org
Tel: 020 7591 3141
Youth development charity devoted to taking young people to unusual places to learn about some of the most fragile and remote environments on Earth. The adventures are challenging and fun and are organized with in-country organizations, UK schools and colleges and charities. The projects last from four to twelve weeks in wild and trackless regions.

Bufo Ventures Ltd
3 Elim Grove
Windermere
Cumbria LA23 2JN
www.bufoventures.co.uk
Email: sherpa@bufoventures.co.uk
Tel: 01539 445445
Tailor-made trekking holidays and expeditions in Nepal for groups and individuals. Camping and tea-shop treks can be arranged as well as climbing expeditions. The company is linked to the Highland Sherpa trekking agency based in Kathmandu.

Canary Nature
St Martins House
59 St Martins Lane
Covent Garden
London WC2H 4JS
www.canarynature.com
Email: ed.bentham@canarynature.com

Educational group travels and special interest activities, including whale watching in the Canary Islands. Supports the Atlantic Whale Foundation.

Caravanserai Tours
1–3 Love Lane
Woolwich
London SE18 6QT
www.caravanserai-tours.com
Email: info@caravanserai-tours.com
Tel: 020 8855 6373
Journeys of inspiration and discovery in Libya and Iran, including archaeology and desert exploration.

Classic Journeys
33 High Street
Tibshelf
Alfreton
Derbyshire DE55 5NX
www.classicjourneys.co.uk
Email: enquiry@classicjourneys.co.uk
Tel: 01773 873497
Adventure holidays throughout the Himalayas, Nepal, India, Tibet, Bhutan, Sri Lanka, Morocco and Peru. From easy two-week introductory treks and wildlife journeys to more demanding four-week treks and climbing holidays.

Community Action Treks
Warwick Mill
Warwick Bridge
Carlisle
Cumbria CA4 8RR
www.catreks.com
Email: info@catreks.com
Tel: 01228 564488
Travel company headed by mountaineer Doug Scott and trek leader Jeff Frew, specializing in trekking and climbing in the Himalaya and other mountain regions. The company is the fundraising arm of Community Action Nepal and all profits go to fund community

development projects in the country, including schools, health centres and clean water supplies.

Condor Journeys and Adventures
2 Ferry Bank
Colintraive
Argyll PA22 3AR
www.condorjourneys-adventures.com
Email: danielle@condorjourneys-adventures.com
Tel: 01700 841318
Independent and small-group adventures off the beaten track in South America.

Coral Cay Conservation
The Tower, 13th Floor
125 High Street
Colliers Wood
London SW19 2JG
www.coralcay.org
Email: info@coralcay.org
Tel: 0870 750 0668
Adventures based on reef and rainforest conservation expeditions in Mexico, Fiji, Malaysia and the Philippines.

Crusader Travel
57 Church Street
Twickenham TW1 3NR
www.crusadertravel.com
Email: info@crusadertravel.com
Tel: 020 8744 0474
Specialists in diving adventures.

CycleActive
8 Low Mill
Langwathby
Penrith
Cumbria CA10 1NQ
www.cycleactive.co.uk
Email: sales@cycleactive.co.uk
Tel: 01768 881111
Mountain biking and activity holidays worldwide.

Discover Adventure
Throope Down House
Blandford Road

Coombe Bissett
Salisbury SP5 4LN
www.discoveradventure.co.uk
Tel: 01722 718444
Trekking and cycling adventures
and charity challenge projects in
Iceland, Morocco, Tanzania,
Nepal, Peru and other locations
around the world, with experi-
enced expedition leaders.

Discovery Initiatives
The Travel House
51 Castle Street
Cirencester
Gloucestershire GL7 1QD
www.discoveryinitiatives.com
Email: enquiry@discoveryinitiatives.
com
Tel: 01285 643333
Inspirational ecology journeys
committed to conservation of
endangered habitats, including
surveys of orang-utan, snow
leopards of northern India and
wolves, bears and eagles in
Slovakia.

Dragoman
Camp Green
Debenham
Stowmarket
Suffolk IP14 6LA
www.dragoman.com
Email: info@dragoman.co.uk
Tel: 01728 861133
Dragoman have 20 years of
experience and are the leading
overland adventure operator.
Committed to responsible
tourism, Dragoman organize
rafting on the Zambezi, hiking
the Inca Trail or trekking up
Kilimanjaro.

Drive Africa
PO Box 26705
London SW12 8WG
www.driveafrica.com
Email: mail@driveafrica.com
Tel: 020 8675 3974
Overland driving expeditions in

Africa on responsible tourism
principles.

Eco Resorts Kenya
PO Box 120
Watamu
Kenya
www.eco-resorts.com
Email: info@eco-resorts.com
Adventures and wildlife expeditions in Kenya and Tanzania
with a web page devoted to
information and discussion
about eco-tourism ideals.

Encounter Overland
2002 Camp Green
Debenham
Stowmarket
Suffolk IP14 6LA
www.encounter.co.uk
Tel: 01728 862222
Active adventure holidays and
overland expeditions through
South America, Africa and Asia,
driving, biking, trekking, rafting.

Ecovolunteer Network
www.ecovolunteer.org
Adventures through working on
conservation projects.

Exodus
Grange Mills
Weir Road
London SW12 0NE
www.exodus.co.uk
Email: info@exodus.co.uk
Tel: 020 8675 5550
Walking and trekking on classic
routes including the Inca Trail,
high-attitude treks to Everest Base
Camp, and Kilimanjaro; also
overland driving across Africa, the
Andes and Australia.

Expedicio Studio Kit
Elem utca 5–7
Budapest
1045
Hungary
www.expedicio.on.hu
Email: expedicico@hu.inter.net

Tel: +36 1 370 0082
Equipment supply, insurance
service, expedition advice, expedi-
tion tours to Romania, Serbia and
Montenegro, Bosnia, North
Africa, Iran and Pakistan.

The Expedition Company Ltd
PO Box 17
Wiveliscombe
Taunton TA4 2YL
www.expedition.co.uk
E-mail: info@expedition.co.uk
Tel: 01984 624780
Adventurous challenges that stretch
you mentally and physically, with a
sense of responsibility to maintain
and improve the natural environ-
ment of the locations visited.

Expedition World
Hollycroft Farm
Colworth
Chichester
West Sussex PO20 2DU
www.expeditionworld.com
Email: sianpj@hotmail.com
Tel: 01243 789264
Overland driving across the
Sahara and to Kathmandu and
India.

Explore Worldwide Ltd
1 Frederick Street
Aldershot
Hampshire GU11 1LQ
www.exploreworldwide.com
Email: info@exploreworldwide.com
Tel: 01252 760000
Adventure tours and holidays
worldwide, supporting carbon-
balanced travel by contributing to
Climate Care.

Explorers Tours
223 Coppermill Road
Wraysbury TW19 5NW
www.explorers.co.uk
Email: dive@explorers.co.uk
Tel: 01753 681999
Specialists in diving adventure
holidays for all levels of experience, and astronomy tours
following solar eclipses.

Far Frontiers Ltd
The Pound
Ampney Crucis,
Gloucestershire GL7 5SA
www.farfrontiers.com
Email: info@farfrontiers.com
Tel: 01285 850926
Specialists in personal travel
planning, including tailor-made
adventurous trips and escorted
journeys worldwide.

First 48 Ltd
PO Box 150
Pudsey
West Yorkshire LS28 5GY
www.first48.com
Email: tours@first48.com
Tel: 0845 130 4849/0700
423 8368
Adventure travel in central Asia
and the Middle East.

Footloose Adventure Travel
3 Springs Pavement
Ilkey LS29 8HD
West Yorkshire
www.footlooseadventure.co.uk/
Email: info@footlooseadventure.
co.uk
Tel: 01943 604030
Adventure trekking, independent
travel and tailor-made trips, with
planning advice and arrangements
for contact with guides and
companies in the locality you
intend to visit. Footloose is
committed to responsible tourism
and supports Climate Care with a
financial contribution to counteract carbon emissions from
flights.

Friendly Islands Kayak Company
Private Bag 10
Neiafu
Vava'u
Tonga
www.fikco.com

Email: tours@fikco.com
Adventure travel to the Kingdom of Tonga in the South Pacific.

Frontier
50–52 Rivington Street
London EC2A 3QP
www.frontier.ac.uk
Email: becky@frontier.ac.uk
Tel: 020 7613 2422
Conservation volunteer adventures to Madagascar, Nicaragua and Tanzania.

Frontier Canada
6 Sydenham Avenue
London SE26 6UH
www.frontiercanada.co.uk
Email: info@frontier-travel.co.uk
Tel: 020 8776 8709
Tailor-made visits to Canada for hiking, dog-sledding, kayaking and rafting.

Galapagos Adventure Tours
79 Maltings Place
169 Tower Bridge Road,
London SE1 3LJ
www.galapagos.co.uk
Tel: 020 7407 1478
Small-group escorted adventure tours to Ecuador and the Galapagos Islands.

Gecko Travel
94 Old Manor Way
Portsmouth
Hampshire PO6 2NL
www.geckotravel.com
Email: frontdesk@geckotravel.com
Tel: 0239 225 8859
Independent adventures to Thailand, Laos, Cambodia, Vietnam and Malaysia, including scheduled or tailor-made itineraries.

Geodyssey
116 Tollington Park
London N4 3RB
www.geodyssey.co.uk
Email: info@geodyssey.co.uk
Tel: 020 7281 7788

Specialists in all types of travel to Venezuela, but covering also Costa Rica and Trinidad and Tobago.

Global Vision International
Amwell Farmhouse
Nomansland
Wheathampstead
Hertfordshire AL4 8ES
www.gvi.co.uk
Email: info@gvi.co.uk
Tel: 01582 831300
Global Vision International offers the chance to work alongside carefully selected partner organizations including the Diane Fossey Gorilla Fund, Rainforest Concern and the South Africa National Parks Board. You can join any of 20 expeditions in 15 countries including marine mammal expeditions in Mexico and survey expeditions in the Amazon jungle. No experience is necessary as full training is given.

Greenforce
11–15 Betterton Street
Covent Garden
London WC2H 9BP
www.greenforce.org
Email: info@greenforce.org
Tel: 0870 770 2646
Wildlife conservation expeditions for volunteers to be the eyes and ears of a research team in regions where few tourists have ever been.

Greentours
Leigh Cottage
Gauledge Lane
Longnor
Buxton
Derbyshire SK17 0PA
www.greentours.co.uk
Tel: 01298 83563
Wildlife and natural history small-group tours all over the world, from alpine flora to rainforests and whale-watching. A proportion

of company profits goes to conservation projects and a contribution is made to Climate Care to counteract the CO_2 produced by your flight.

Guerba
Wessex House
40 Station Road
Westbury
Wiltshire BA13 3JN
www.guerba.co.uk
Email: info@guerba.co.uk
Tel: 01373 858956
Adventure and discovery holidays to Africa, Latin America, Asia including the Himalayas, and Europe. Guerba makes a contribution to C-Level for carbon dioxide produced in travel flights.

High & Wild
1 Heritage Courtyard
Sadler Street
Wells BA5 2RR
www.highandwild.co.uk
Email: adventures@highandwild.co.uk
Tel: 01749 671777
Tailor-made adventures and journeys of discovery to wilderness, jungle, Himalayas and Polar regions. High & Wild are committed to Green Globe 21 principles of sustainable tourism, from a base in Wells, High & Wild undertake all the planning, in-country travel requirements, including vehicles, trains, camels and elephants, all logistics including porters, guides and interpreters, accommodation bookings and political and geographical risk assessment.

High Places Ltd
Globe Centre
Penistone Road
Sheffield
South Yorkshire S6 3AE
www.highplaces.co.uk
Email: treks@highplaces.co.uk
Tel: 0114 275 7500

Independent family-run mountain travel company, organizing informal treks, hikes, climbs and ski-tours in high places worldwide.

Himalayan Kingdoms Ltd
Old Crown House
18 Market Street
Wotton-under-Edge
Gloucestershire GL12 7AE
www.himalayankingdoms.com
Email: info@himalyankingdoms.com
Tel: 0845 330 8579

Hinterland Travel
12 The Enterdent
Godstone
Surrey RH9 8EG
Email: hinterland@tinyworld.co.uk
Tel: 01883 743584
Overland adventure travel specialist with trips to Mesopotamia in Iraq and to Afghanistan.

Intrepid Travel
Unit 202
Buspace Studios
Conlan Street
London W10 5AP
www.intrepidtravel.com
Email: uk@intrepidtravel.com
Tel: 020 8960 6333
A company dedicated to the preservation of Asia's unique environment and diverse cultures, through responsible travel and fair trade.

Jagged Globe
The Foundry Studios
45 Mowbray Street
Sheffield
South Yorkshire S3 8EN
www.jagged-globe.co.uk
Email: climb@jagged-globe.co.uk
Tel: 0845 345 8848
One of the UK's leading mountaineering companies, offering a wide range of expeditions and training courses.

Journey Latin America
12/13 Heathfield Terrace
Chiswick
London W4 4JE
www.journeylatinamerica.co.uk
Email: adventure@journeylatin
america.co.uk
Tel: 020 8747 8315
also
12 St Ann's Square, 2nd Floor
Manchester M2 7HW
Email: sales@jlamanchester.co.uk
Tel: 0161 832 1441

Journeymen
The Hollow
Sutton Waldron
Blandford
Dorset DT11 8NP
www.journeymen.co.uk
Email: john.burton@journeymen.
co.uk
Trekking, cycle and rafting
adventure in Nepal. They
specialize in fully accompanied
tours in the Annapurna region as
well as visiting Kathmandu and
Pokhara.

Karakorum Expeditions
Jiguur Grand Hotel
Transport Street
PO Box 542
Ulaanbaatar-46
Mongolia
www.gomongolia.com
Email: info@gomongolia.com
Tel: +976 11 315655
Adventures in Mongolia.

KE Adventure Travel
32 Lake Road
Keswick
Cumbria CA12 5DQ
www.keadventure.co.uk
Email: info@keadventure.co.uk
Tel: 01768 773966
Adventure in Nepal, Tibet,
Pakistan, China, Mongolia,
Bhutan, India, Ecuador, Peru,
Bolivia, Chile and Africa.

Kerala Connections Ltd
School House Lane
Horsmonden
Kent TN12 8BP
www.keralaconnect.co.uk
Email: info@keralaconnect.co.uk
Tel: 01892 722440
Independent tour operator special-
izing in personalized planning of
adventure holidays in Kerala and
south India.

Kumuka
40 Earls Court Road
London W8 6EJ
www.kumuka.com
Email: enquiries@kumuka.com
Tel: 020 7937 8855
Independent adventure tour
operator committed to responsible
tourism. Tours range from four
days to 35 weeks and the
company covers 54 countries.

Last Frontiers
Fleet Marston Farm
Aylesbury
Buckinghamshire HP18 0QT
www.lastfrontiers.com
Tel: 01296 653000
Small specialist tour operator
offering tailor-made travel to
Latin America and Antarctica.

Magic Carpet Travel Ltd
1 Field House Close
Ascot
Berkshire SL5 9LT
www.magiccarpettravel.co.uk
Email: info@magiccarpettravel.
co.uk
Tel: 01344 622832
Independent and small-group
adventure tours of Iran, including
skiing and horse riding in the
Turkoman Steppes.

Magic Globe Travel Network
Flat 3
35 Eccleston Square
London SW1V 1PB
www.magicglobe.co.uk

Email: info@magiclobe.com
Tel: 0870 0110270
Adventure holidays in Latin
America and East Africa.

Magic of Bolivia Ltd
182 Westbourne Grove
London W11 2RH
www.bolivia.co.uk
Email: zoe@bolivia.co.uk
Tel: 020 7221 7310

Make A Difference Adventures Ltd
24 Ringwood Road
Farnborough
Hampshire GU14 8BG
www.mad-adventures.com
Email: info@mad-adventures.com
Tel: 0845 122 1304
Make A Difference Adventures is
a small eco-friendly and responsible adventure travel company
with a difference in that each of
their trips supports a local
community project. A percentage
of each trip price is donated to
the linked project and clients are
also offered the opportunity to
spend a little time meeting and
assisting the people who benefit
from their holiday. MAD is not
about charity and clients don't
have to raise any sponsorship
money or be able to commit to
months working abroad.

Mountain Dream Ltd
2 Kirkhouses
Great Salkeld
Penrith
Cumbria CA11 9NA
www.mountaindream.co.uk
Tel: 01768 210969

Mountain Nomad
www.mountainnomad.co.uk
Email: adventures@mountain
nomad.co.uk
Tel: 01484 850061
Individually planned mountain
trek adventures on responsible
tourism principles with local

guides and porters paid a wage
and properly equipped and
insured. Destinations include
Nepal, Tibet, India, Sikkim,
Bhutan and Tanzania.

Mountain Tracks Ltd
3 Broomhill Road
London SW18 4JQ
www.mountaintracks.co.uk
Email: info@mountaintracks.co.uk
Tel: 020 8877 5773
Mountain Tracks specialize in
mountain adventures and organize
guided skiing, trekking and mountaineering trips worldwide in
small groups that ensure you
benefit from the knowledge,
expertise and enthusiasm of their
highly respected guides.

Mountain Travel Sobek UK
67 Verney Avenue
High Wycombe
Bucks HP12 3ND
www.mtsobek.com/
Email: info@mtsobek.com
Tel: 01494 448901

MustGo Travel
Mercantile Chambers
53 Bothwell Street
Glasgow G2 6TS
www.mustgo.com/
Email: feedback@mustgo.com
Adventure and cultural travel.

**Muir's Tours (Nepal Kingdom
Foundation)**
Nepal House
97a Swansea Road
Reading
Berkshire RG1 8HA
www.nkf-mt.org.uk
Email: info@nkf-mt.org.uk
Tel: 0118 950 2281
Fair trade, eco-friendly adventure
travel in small groups. A non-profit
travel organizer owned by The
Nepal Kingdom Foundation, which
works in close partnership with
local communities who benefit

from the money made from trading in tour organizing.

Nature Trek
Cheriton Hill
Cheriton
Alresford
Hampshire SO24 0NG
www.naturetrek.co.uk
Email: info@naturetrek.co.uk
Tel: 01962 733051

Nomad African Travel
Smugglers Cottage
Church Road
Westbourne
Emsworth
Hampshire PO10 8UA
www.nomadafricantravel.co.uk
Email: info@nomadfricantravel.
co.uk
Tel: 01243 373929

Nomadic Expeditions Ltd
26 Matthews Green Road
Wokingham
Berkshire RG41 1JU
www.nomadic.co.uk
Email: info@nomadic.co.uk
Tel: 0870 220 1718
Nomadic expeditions in Morocco and west Africa, driving overland in a 4 × 4 truck.

Oasis Overland Ltd
The Marsh
Henstridge
Somerset BA8 0TF
www.oasisoverland.co.uk
Email: info@oasisoverland.co.uk
Tel: 01963 363400

Oksana Travel
98b Water Lane
Wilmslow
Cheshire SK9 5BB
www.oksana.co.uk
Email: trips@oksana.co.uk
Tel: 01625 530035
Tailor-made wildlife and discovery adventures on the principles of responsible tourism.

Operation Wallacea
Hope House
Old Bolingbroke
Spilsby
Lincolnshire PE23 4EX
www.opwall.com
Email: info@opwall.com
Tel: 01790 763194
Scientific and conservation expeditions to Indonesia and Cuba including forest and marine study tours.

The Oriental Caravan
www.theorientalcaravan.com
Email:
info@theorientalcaravan.com
Tel: 020 7582 0716
Small group adventures in Bhutan, Mongolia, Tibet, China and Japan.

Outreach International
Bartlett's Farm
Hayes Road
Compton Dundon
Somerset TA11 6PF
www.outreachinternational.co.uk
Email: info@outreachinternational.
co.uk
Tel: 01458 274957
Gap-year travel projects of three- to nine-months duration in Mexico, Ecuador and Cambodia, and cross-culture exchanges.

Overland Club
2 The Gabbles
Sedgefield
County Durham TS21 3EU
www.overlandclub.com
Email: info@overlandclub.com
Tel: 01740 623633
Budget overland adventures around the world.

Paddy's Treks and Tours
A-1/229, 2nd Floor
Safdarjung Enclave
New Delhi – 110 029
India
www.microvac.com/paddystours/

Email: paddystours@mantraonline.
com
Tel: 0091 11 616 4284
Individual trekking tours, organized
by a team of in-country experts, to
the Himalayas, Rajasthan, Bhutan
and all over India.

Palanquin Travels
42 High Street
Wanstead
London E11 2RJ
www.palanquin.co.uk
Email: info@palanquintravels.com
Tel: 020 7724 6022 and 01937
587182
Palanquin Travels was set up by a
group of professional travellers,
explorers and mountain leaders
with specialist knowledge of
India. Nepal and Tibet who plan
small-group adventures on the
principles of responsible tourism,
and contribute to the local
economies of the people who live
in remote places. Palanquin also
helps volunteers to find work
placements, particularly if you
have teaching or medical qualifications.

Papua New Guinea Tours
PO Box 371
Mount Hagen
Papua New Guinea
www.pngtours.com
Email: travel@pngtours.com

Peregrine Adventures/Gecko's
First Floor
8 Clerewater Place
Lower Way
Thatcham
Berkshire RG19 3RF
www.peregrineadventures.com
Email: sales@peregrineadventures.
com
Tel: 01635 872300
Peregrine provides adventure
holidays that focus in depth on
the culture, history, wildlife,
wilderness and landscapes of
some of the most spectacular and
remote parts of the planet. There's
an element of participation and an
emphasis on the outdoors, with a
range of accommodation from
comfortable hotels to tribal huts.

Peregrine Holidays
Andrew Brock Travel Ltd
29a Main Street
Lyddington
Oakham
Rutland LE15 9LR
www.peregrineholidays.co.uk
Email: webmail@peregrineholidays.
co.uk
Tel: 01572 821330

Persian Voyages
12d Rothes Road
Dorking
Surrey RH4 1JN
www.persianvoyages.com
Email: info@persianvoyages.com
Tel: 01306 885894
Tailor-made, small-group tours
and independent travel to Iran,
organized by a team that is well
informed about archaeological
sites, Islamic monuments, mountain terrain and desert and forests
bordering the Caspian Sea.

Pura Aventura
18 Bond Street
Brighton
Sussex BN1 1RD
www.pura-aventura.com
Email: info@pura-aventura.com
Tel: 01273 676712
For adventurous travellers who
don't want to rough it, but use
small locally owned hotels.

Pyrenean Mountain Tours
2 Rectory Cottages
Rectory Lane
Tadley
Hampshire RG26 5RS
www.pyrenees.co.uk
Email: pmtfrance@aol.com
Tel: 01635 297209

Quark Expeditions
19A Crendon Street
High Wycombe
Buckinghamshire HP13 6LJ
www.quarkexpeditions.com
Tel: 01494 464080

Quest Overseas
32 Clapham Mansions
Nightingale Lane
London SW4 9AQ
www.questoverseas.com
Email: emailingyou@questoverseas.com
Tel: 020 8673 3313
Specialists in worthwhile projects and expeditions to Africa and South America, especially for gap-year ventures. Projects include animal sanctuary work, helping children and building schools.

Rainbow Tours
64 Essex Road
London N1 8LR
www.rainbowtours.co.uk
Email: info@rainbowtours.co.uk
Tel: 020 7226 1004

Raleigh International
27 Parsons Green Lane
London SW6 4HZ
www.raleigh.org.uk
Email: international@raleigh.org.uk
Tel: 020 7371 8585

Real Africa
www.realafrica.net
Email: paul@realafrica.net
Tel: 01462 812638
Garden guest house holidays in West Africa.

Red Spokes Cycling Adventures
29 Northfield Road
Stamford Hill
London N16 5RL
www.redspokes.co.uk
Email: office@redspokes.co.uk
Tel: 020 7502 7252

Reef and Rainforest Tours Ltd
1 The Plains
Totnes
Devon TQ9 5DR
www.reefandrainforest.co.uk
Email: mail@reefandrainforest.co.uk
Tel: 01803 866965

Responsible Travel
www.responsibletravel.com
Email: info@responsibletravel.com
Brighton-based online marketplace and forum for environment-friendly, responsible travel opportunities, supported by Anita Roddick, founder of Body Shop.

Round Oz
Australia
www.roundoz.com.au
Email: info@roundoz.com.au
Tel: +61 36458 1430

The Russian Experience
Research House
Fraser Road
Perivale
Middlesex UB6 7AQ
www.trans-siberian.co.uk
Email: info@trans-siberian.co.uk
Tel: 020 8566 8846

Sabre Adventures
Bettencourt House
276 Horton Road
Datchet
Berkshire SL3 9HN
www.sabreadventures.co.uk
Email: info@sabreadventures.co.uk
Tel: 01753 585123
Sabre run expeditions that combine project work with frontier overland adventure. Short, project-based expeditions require your involvement in community building work for schools and medical clinics in Africa.

Sherpa Expeditions
131a Heston Road
Hounslow TW5 0RF
www.sherpaexpeditions.com

Email: sales@sherpa-walking-
holidays.co.uk
Tel: 020 8577 2717

Silk Road Tours
371 Kensington High Street
London W14 8QZ
www.silkroadtours.co.uk
Email: sales@silkroadtours.co.uk
Tel: 020 7371 3131

Simply Tanzania Tour Company
54 Cotesbach Road
London E5 9QJ
www.simplytanzania.co.uk
Email: enquiries@simplytanzania.
co.uk
Tel: 020 8986 0615

South American Experience
47 Causton Street
London SW1P 4AT
www.southamericanexperience.
co.uk
Email: info@southamerican
experience.co.uk
Tel: 020 7976 5511
Tailor-made responsible travel to
Cuba, Mexico, Central and South
America, the Falkland Islands and
Antarctica. The company supports
Climate Care and has a network
of English-speaking guides in the
locations.

Specialist Trekking
www.specialisttrekking.co.uk
Tel: 01228 562305
Small-group trekking expeditions
to Nepal, Bhutan and Tibet.

Spirit of Adventure
Powdermits
Princetown
Yelverton
Devon PL20 6SP
www.spirit-of-adventure.com/
Email: martin@spirit-of-adventure.
com
Tel: 01822 880277
Worldwide activity and adventure
journeys from a company based

in the Dartmoor National Park,
including tailor-made expeditions.

Stonebee
Stoneridge House
Fields Road
Chedworth
Gloucestershire GL54 4NQ
www.stonebee.com
Email: mail@stonebee.com
Tel: 01285 720792
Adventures to the North Pole with
explorers Richard Weber and Mik-
hail Malakhov and their team, from
the Norwegian island of Svalbard
and the Ice Station Borneo floating
airstrip and base camp.

**Storm Chasing Adventure
Tours Inc.**
56750 Lunar Drive
Sunriver
OR 97707
USA
www.stormchasing.com/
Email: Todd@stormchasing.com
Organizers of severe weather
adventure tours in Tornado Alley.

Symbiosis Travel
Studio 1B
101 Farm Lane
London SW6 1QJ
www.symbiosis-travel.com
Tel: 0845 123 2844
Small-group and tailor-made trekking and cycling adventures and
cultural tours in Southeast Asia;
also responsible diving expeditions
in sensitive marine environments.

Tangent Expeditions
3 Millbeck
New Hutton
Kendal
Cumbria LA8 0BD
www.tangent-expeditions.co.uk
Email: paul@tangent-expeditions.
co.uk
Tel: 01539 737757
Arctic mountaineering, ski-touring
and dog sledding adventures.

Terra Firma Travel
Eunant
Lake Vymwy
Powys SY10 0NF
www.terrafirmatravel.com
Email: info@terrafirmatravel.com
Tel: 01691 870321
Low-impact, tailor-made trekking
adventures in the world's moun-
tain regions, with concern for the
environment and local communi-
ties, in Nepal, Annapurna,
Karakoram, South America and
Europe.

Tim Best Travel
68 Old Brompton Road
London SW7 3LQ
www.timbesttravel.com/
Email: info@timbesttravel.com
Tel: 020 7591 0300
Expeditions and adventure trips in
Africa and Latin America.

Trailmasters International Ltd
PO Box 4
Llanfyllin SY22 5WA
www.trailmasters.com
Email: info@trailmasters.com
Tel: 01691 649194
Off-road, self-drive adventure
tours across the Atlas
Mountains of Morocco, the
Sahara Desert and the Atlantic
coast.

TransIndus Ltd
11 The Pavement
Popes Lane
London W5 4NG
www.transindus.co.uk
Email: enquires@transindus.co.uk
Tel: 020 8566 2729

Trek America
4 Waterperry Court
Middleton Road
Banbury
Oxfordshire OX16 4QB
www.trekamerica.co.uk
Email: sales@trekamerica.co.uk
Tel: 0870 444 8735

Camping and adventure tours of
North America including Mexico.

Tribes Travel
www.tribes.co.uk
Email: web@tribes.co.uk
Tel: 01728 685971
A Fair Trade travel company
specializing in tailor-made
trekking adventures on the
principles of responsible travel.

Trips Worldwide Ltd
14 Frederick Place
Clifton
Bristol BS8 1AS
www.tripsworldwide.co.uk
Email: info@tripsworldwide.co.uk
Tel: 0117 311 4400
Tailor-made, responsible travel
holidays to Latin America and the
Caribbean.

Truck Africa
Wissett Place
Norwich Road
Halesworth
Suffolk IP19 8HY
www.truckafrica.com
Email: sales@truckafrica.com
Tel: 01509 881509
Serious overland expeditions
across Africa.

Visit Vietnam
Tennyson Travel
30–32 Fulham High Street
London SW6 3LQ
www.visitvietnam.co.uk
Email: tennyson@visitvietnam.co.uk
Tel: 020 7736 4347
Small-group and independent
travel to Vietnam, including
eco-tours, trekking, cycling and
train travel.

Voyage Concepts
81–83 Victoria Road
Surbiton
Surrey KT6 4NS
www.voyageconcepts.co.uk
Email: info@voyageconcepts.co.uk

Tel: 020 8399 9090
Voyage Discovery opens doors for
those who want to take that next
step on the travel ladder. Often
this involves remote locations and
physically demanding activities.
You will be rewarded with a
unique journey.

Wagon Trails
3 Conway Avenue
Preston
Lancashire PR1 9TR
www.wagontrails.co.uk
Email: web@wagontrails.co.uk
Tel: 01772 336624
Small-group adventures in
Southern Africa from three days
to 36 days.

Walks Worldwide
Kings Arms Building
15 Main Street
High Bentham
Lancaster LA2 7LG
www.walksworldwide.com
Email: sales@walksworldwide.com
Tel: 01524 262255
Specialist travel company
offering walking holidays to suit
the needs of active people,
following famous routes such as
the Inca Trail or the Tour of
Mont Blanc, cultural trekking in
the Atlas Mountains of Morocco
or among the hill tribes of
Vietnam.

Whitts Adventures
Mile 131.5
Denali Hwy, Box 114
Cantwell
Alaska
99729-0114
United States
www.whittsadventures.com
Email:
whittsadventures@lycos.com
Tel: 001 907 768 2662
Experts in adventure exploration
of Alaska.

Wild Horizons
Innovation Centre
University of Wales Swansea
Swansea SA2 8PP
www.wildhorizons.org
Tel: 01656 880480
Wildlife and polar adventures
and humpback whale research
expeditions.

WildWings/WildOceans
Tel: 0117 965 8333
WildWings is a specialist tour
operator and independent travel
agency. Tour programmes include
whale watching and expedition
cruises to the polar regions. UK
agents for Ecovolunteers, working
conservation holidays and for
Deep Sea Exploration, and for
Space Travel including flight
adventures.

World Expeditions
3 Northfields Prospect
Putney Bridge Road
London SW18 1PE
www.worldexpeditions.co.uk
Email: enquires@worldexpeditions.
co.uk
Tel: 020 8870 2600
Responsible adventure travel
worldwide, including the
Himalayas and South America
tours.

**Yorkshire Schools Exploring
Society**
1A Garnett Street
Otley
West Yorkshire LS21 1AL
www.leeds.ac.uk/sports_science/yses/
Email: admin@yses.freeserve.co.uk
Tel: 01943 468049

Charity Fundraising Adventures and Expeditions

Across the Divide Expeditions
Jubilee House
Fore Street
Thorncombe
Chard
Somerset TA20 4PP
www.atd-expeditions.co.uk
Email: events@acrossthe
divide.com
Tel: 01460 30456
ATD has a wealth of experience in organizing trekking and adventure events for charity challenges, including the Inca Trail for Cancer Research UK and mountain bike events for Mencap. All their events have full medical back-up teams.

Assin Endwa Trust UK
184 Maldon Road
Chelmsford
Essex CM2 7DG
www.endwa.org.uk
Email: volunteer@endwa.org.uk
Tel: 01245 475920
A project begun by a group of young people looking for something memorable to do in a gap year, which is helping a village in Ghana to improve its schools and health centre, by sponsored voluntary work placements.

Care International UK
10–13 Rushworth Street
London SE1 0RB
www.careinternational.org.uk
Email: info@ciuk.org
Tel: 020 7934 9334
Mountain challenges for fundraising, environmental awareness and corporate team-building.

Charity Challenge
Head Office
7th Floor, Northway House

1379 High Road
London N20 9LP
www.charitychallenge.com
Tel: 020 8557 0000
Sponsored expeditions and adventures to raise funds for a wide range of charities; includes an online giving facility that enables sponsors to pledge donations by credit card direct to the charity. The Charity Challenge website is a good starting point for discussing ideas about embarking on an adventure or expedition with the purpose of raising funds and helping under-privileged people.

The Jubilee Sailing Trust
Hazel Road
Woolston
Southampton
Hampshire SO19 7GB
www.jst.org.uk
Email: info@jst.org.uk
Tel: 023 8044 9108
World leaders in integrated adventure sailing for able-bodied and disabled people on two specially designed tall ships, the *Lord Nelson* and *Tenacious*. All participants take part in running the ship under the supervision of a permanent crew.

Mencap
123 Golden Lane
London EC1Y 0RT
www.mencap.org.uk
Email:
information@mencap.org.uk
Tel: 020 7454 0454
also
Segal House
4 Annadale Avenue
Belfast BT7 3JH
Email: mencapni@mencap.org.uk
Tel: 02890 691351
also
31 Lambourne Crescent
Cardiff Business Park

Llanishen
Cardiff CF14 5GF
Tel: 02920 747588
Email: information.wales@mencap.org.uk
Overseas sponsored bike rides, treks and voluntary work project holidays to raise funds for Mencap's work with people with learning disabilities.

Raleigh International
27 Parsons Green Lane
London SW6 4HZ
www.raleighinternational.org
Email: volunteer@raleigh.org.uk
Tel: 020 7371 8585
Raleigh International is a development charity which inspires young people aged 17 to 25 to discover their full potential by working together on challenging environmental and community projects around the world. Three-month expeditions are part of a longer programme of training weekends and workshops prior to expedition, concentrating on personal development, cultural awareness, global issues and preparing for expedition life. Raleigh International runs eleven expeditions a year to Chile. Costa Rica and Nicaragua, Ghana, Namibia and Sabah-Borneo.

UCA (Union de Co-operativas Agricolas)
www.arrakis.es/~barneo
Email: maggiejo.stjohn@btinternet.com
This voluntary project offers an opportunity to live and work with one of the communities on the beautiful Miraflor nature reserve in Nicaragua. By teaching English you can make a valuable contribution to this coffee-growing region's conservation and revitalization programmes in areas such as eco-tourism, youth development and organic farming.

Demand for English is high: it enables them to share their special way of life and hospitality with all visitors, and enhances young people's skills. Maggie Jo St John is the UK coordinator.

Gap-year Travel Projects

Adventure Jobs
www.adventurejobs.co.uk
An online directory of employment opportunities for anyone seeking paid or voluntary employment in the adventure activity industry. Jobs for trainee and qualified Activity Instructors. Group Leaders and Support Staff are available for seasonal positions lasting anything from three to twelve months in all regions of the UK and abroad. Many of the positions at residential centres offer full board accommodation as well as a competitive wage and free training.

AFS Intercultural Programmes
www.afsuk.org
An international, voluntary not-for-profit organization that provides intercultural learning opportunities to help people develop the knowledge, skills and understanding needed to create a more just and peaceful world.

Africa & Asia Venture
www.aventure.co.uk
Email: av@aventure.co.uk
AV still has challenging opportunities for 18–23 year olds in rural schools and in conservation or community projects in Africa, India, Nepal and Mexico for 4–5 months including an exciting safari. Also shorter vacation expeditions including voluntary work in Kenya.

African Conservation Experience
PO Box 9706
Solihull B91 3FF
West Midlands
www.conservationafrica.net
Email: info@conservationafrica.net
Tel: 0870 2415816
Arranges for young people to work on nature reserves in southern Africa, playing an active role in conservation and the maintenance of the environment – working closely with rangers and conservationists.

Alliances Abroad
www.alliancesabroad.com
Customized programmes for individuals and groups who want to learn about other cultures by teaching, interning, volunteering or working abroad.

Blue Dog Adventures
www.bluedogadventures.com
Email: info@bluedogadventures.com
Adventure training and equestrian experiences worldwide over one to six months. The programmes include white-water raft guiding, leading horseback safaris, mastering scuba diving, or survival in the African bush.

BSES Expeditions
www.bses.org.uk
Challenging expeditions to wilderness areas throughout the world. From tracking river dolphins in the Amazon to avoiding polar bears in the Arctic Circle, you can choose from a range of exciting destinations. Expeditions may last from four to six weeks during the summer holidays, to a longer gap-year expedition any time of year.

Camps International
www.campsinternational.com
Email: info@campsinternational.com

Camps and lodges based in wild bush and the Indian Ocean coastline of East Africa. Projects are community and wildlife orientated and adventures range from mountains to scuba diving.

CCUSA
www.ccusa.com
Email: unitedkingdom@ccusa.com
A company that has given over 100,000 young people the opportunity to work and travel in America, Australia, New Zealand, Brazil and Russia.

CESA Languages Abroad
www.cesalanguages.com
Email: info@cesalanguages.com
Language courses including French in Guadeloupe and Spanish in Ecuador.

Challenge UK
www.challengeuk.com
Specialists in educational and cultural exchange programmes. Spend a year or a term at an American high school or learn French in France.

Changing Worlds
www.changingworlds.co.uk
Exciting, worthwhile and challenging paid and voluntary work placements worldwide. Opportunities last from three to six months and departures take place all year round.

Coral Cay Conservation Expeditions
www.coralcay.org
Conservation volunteer work on reef and rainforest projects in Fiji, Honduras, Malaysia and the Philippines. You can take an active part in protecting and managing threatened marine and forest environments through scientific surveys and local community work.

Eco Africa Experience
www.ecoafricaexperience.com
Email: info@ecoafricaexperience.
com
Conservation opportunities to
work on some of southern
Africa's game reserves or leading
marine ocean research projects.
You could be involved in projects
like anti-poaching patrols, moni-
toring and counting of wildlife,
darting and animal capture, bush
rehabilitation, and the day-to-day
maintenance of the reserve.

**EF International Language
Schools**
www.ef.com
Email: efedtours@ef.com
You can travel, learn a language
and make friends from all over
the world for part of your gap
year. Chinese, French, Spanish,
Italian, German or Russian
language tuition and TEFL
qualifications.

Encounter Overland
www.encounter.co.uk

Euro Academy
www.euroacademy.co.uk
Learn or improve your language
skills with a course or work
placement in the cultural capitals
of Europe or South America.

Frontier
www.frontier.ac.uk
Email: becky@frontier.ac.uk
You could boost your CV with
a BTEC diploma in Tropical
Habitat Conservation on a
conservation expedition. Help
save endangered wildlife and
habitats, and enable local communities to manage the use of
natural resources. Expeditions
over four to 20 weeks to the
Andaman Islands, Madagascar,
Nicaragua, Tanzania and
Vietnam.

GAP Activity Projects
www.gap.org.uk
Email: volunteer@gap.org.uk
Voluntary work placements including teaching English, classroom
assistance, caring, conservation,
outdoor and medical work in
thirty-two countries. On your
return, you can keep in touch
through their Alumni Club and
join their Business Partner Scheme
for help with graduate recruitment.

Gap Challenge
www.gap-challenge.co.uk
Voluntary and paid placements in
some of the most remote and
culturally diverse places on Earth,
from conservation projects in Peru
to ski instructor programmes in
Canada.

Gap Sports Abroad (GSA)
www.gapsportsabroad.co.uk
Email: info@gapsportsabroad.co.uk
Leading the way in sports
coaching placements in football,
basketball and tennis. GSA also
offers teaching, art & design,
media, sports psychology, physio-
therapy and medical placements.

GapWork.com
www.gapwork.com
Email: info@gapwork.com
Online information about gap-
year opportunities.

GapYear.com
www.gapyear.com
Online directory of gap-year
placements including a 'clearing'
facility for late-notice applications. The website has ideas and
advice on everything from
packing a backpack to fundraising
techniques.

Global Vision International
www.gvi.co.uk
Email: info@gvi.co.uk
Adventure in fifteen countries,

including marine expeditions in Mexico, wildlife survey expeditions in the Amazon and helping street children projects in Guatemala, ranging from four weeks to 12 months. No previous experience is needed as full training is given.

Greenforce
www.greenforce.org
Email: info@greenforce.org
Wildlife research projects lasting four to 10 weeks, such as learning to track elephants in Africa, jaguars in the Amazon or discovering the coral reefs of Borneo, Fiji and the Bahamas and conserving endangered habitats in Peru and Zambia.

i-to-i
www.i-to-i.com
Email: info@i-to-i.com
Project-based adventure placements from four to 24 weeks in 20 countries including conservation work in South African lion parks, Buddhist monasteries in Nepal and teaching in Thailand. Full training and back-up provided. You can train for a qualification in teaching English (TEFL).

ICE (The International Centre of Excellence for Snowsport Instructors)
www.icesi.org
The company delivers 10-week gap-year ski courses in Val d'Isere, France, which cover first aid, mountain awareness and safety, as well as all aspects of skiing. The course results in a British Association of Snowsports Instructors qualification, which means successful students can teach skiing worldwide. The course includes accommodation, lift pass, full board, membership of BASI and all training fees.

The Jubilee Sailing Trust
www.jst.org.uk
Email: info@jst.org.uk
Tall-ship sailing adventures for all abilities from complete novice to accomplished sailor, including people with a disability. The fun and challenge of crewing a tall ship is unmatched by anything else.

Karen Hilltribes Trust
www.karenhilltribes.org.uk
Email: penelope@karenhilltribes.org.uk
Opportunities for people aged 18 or over to carry out long-term voluntary work (minimum six months) among upland communities in Thailand, working as classroom assistants and on water projects alongside the villagers.

The Leap
www.theleap.co.uk
Email: info@theleap.co.uk
Three-month voluntary work placements combining conservation and community issues in game reserves and coastal locations throughout Africa and Asia. You can assist in eco-tourism and conservation for the protection, survival and management of wildlife, tribal people and environments.

Madventurer
www.madventurer.com
Email: team@madventurer.com
Programmes combine overland travel with development projects in rural village communities. Madventurers take part in building, teaching, coaching and environmental projects before departing on overland tours. Projects are available throughout the year in Kenya, Uganda, Tanzania, Ghana, Togo, Peru and Chile.

NonStopSki
www.nonstopski.com
Email: info@nonstopski.com
Ski and snowboard instructor courses in Fernie, British Columbia, Canada, training to become a fully-qualified ski or snowboard instructor.

Peak Leaders UK Ltd
Email: info@peakleaders.co.uk
Gap-year training adventures in the mountains of Canada and Argentina and also in the jungles of Indonesia with courses in expedition safety, leading to internationally recognized qualifications.

PGL
www.pgl.co.uk/people
Email: head-officepeople@pgl.co.uk
A wide range of opportunities for gap-year projects working with young people in adventure holiday camps.

POD (Personal Overseas Development)
www.thepodsite.co.uk
Email: info@thepodsite.co.uk
Gap-year programmes to develop new skills in Tanzania, Peru and Thailand from two to six months, teaching English, helping in orphanages, or becoming a diving instructor. All projects include full training, in-country support and adventure activities.

Project Trust
www.projecttrust.org.uk
Email: info@projecttrust.org.uk
Twelve-month and eight-month projects including teaching, caring, conservation, medical and outdoor education pursuits in twenty-five countries. All volunteers attend a five-day selection course and a five-day training course on the Isle of Coll. The Project Trust package includes full training, debriefing, accommodation, food, flights, medical insurance, full back-up and support.

Quest Overseas
www.questoverseas.com
Email: emailingyou@questoverseas.com
Gapyear Quest is a three-month programme in South America or Africa combining a worthwhile project and a challenging expedition. Their long-term projects involve constructing schools, helping shanty town kids, rehabilitating animals, working in game reserves or in the depths of the Amazon Basin.

Raleigh International
www.raleigh.org.uk
Email: volunteer@raleigh.org.uk
Challenging and sustainable projects in some of the most remote and beautiful places around the world on a 10-week expedition to Ghana, Namibia. Costa Rica and Nicaragua, Chile or Malaysia.

Ski Le Gap
www.skilegap.com
Email: info@skilegap.com
Ski and snowboarding instructor courses. Spend three months skiing/boarding with qualified instructors and gain qualifications yourself. You can achieve your instructor's certification in one month and teach for the season.

Student Partnership Worldwide
www.spw.org
Email: spwuk@gn.apc.org
Opportunities to help in projects that tackle health and environmental threats in rural Africa and Asia.

Teaching & Projects Abroad
Gerrard House
Rustington
West Sussex BN16 1AW

www.teaching-abroad.co.uk
Email: info@teaching-abroad.co.uk
Tel: 01903 859911
Gap-year programmes in 15 different countries. You can join them for a month or the whole year. The local staff will take care of all the arrangements and you will be free to contribute your skills where they are needed.

Travellers Contact Point
2–6 Inverness Terrace
Bayswater
London W2 3HX
Email: enquiries@travellersuk.com
Tel: 020 7243 7887
Open Mon – Fri
also
7th Floor, Dymocks Building
428 George Street
Sydney NSW 2000
Australia
Email: info@travellers.com.au
also
Ground Floor, Dingwall Building
87 Queen Street
Auckland, New Zealand
www.travellers.com.au
Email: info@travellersnz.com
Travellers Contact Point is a one-stop shop for independent and working holiday travellers, where you can book your travel, find a job, locate accommodation, check your email and learn all the latest travel tips.

Travellers Worldwide
www.travellersworldwide.com
Email: info@travellersworldwide.com
Programmes include teaching, conservation and work placements in Asia, Africa and Europe. Flexible programmes are tailored to individual requirements.

Trekforce Expeditions
www.trekforce.org.uk
Email: info@trekforce.org.uk
Two- to five-month intrepid expeditions to the jungles and rainforests of Central and South America or East Malaysia, working on conservation, scientific or community projects. Longer programmes combine project work, learning a new language and teaching.

VentureCo Worldwide
The Ironyard
64–66 The Market Place
Warwick CV34 4SD
www.ventureco-worldwide.com
Email: mail@ventureco-worldwide.com
Tel: 01926 411122
Worldwide programme for the gap-year adventure including projects and adventures in South and Central America, India and Nepal.

Visit Oz
www.visitoz.org
Email: info@visitoz.org
Agricultural and hospitality training for backpackers with working holiday visas coupled with guaranteed well-paid jobs for the rest of their stay.

Whizz-kidz
www.whizz-kidz.org.uk
Email: info@whizz-kids.org.uk
Fundraising expeditions to places like Everest and Mount Kilimanjaro, aiming to improve the quality of life of disabled children and young people in the UK by providing customized mobility equipment which is not available on the NHS.

The Year Out Group
Queensfield
28 Kings Road
Easterton
Wiltshire SN10 4PX
www.yearoutgroup.org/index.htm
Email: info@yearoutgroup.org
Tel: 07980 395789

An association of organizations to promote the concept and benefits of well-structured year-out or gap-year programmes, to promote good practice and to help young people and their advisers in selecting suitable and worthwhile projects. The projects are educational in a broad sense and include cultural courses and exchanges, expeditions, volunteer work, structured voluntary work placements and independent travel. The Year Out Group aims to provide accurate, impartial information about structured gap-year opportunities and their website includes a list of organizations and projects.

Expedition Planning Advice

Royal Geographical Society with the Institute of British Geographers (RGS-IBG)
1 Kensington Gore
London SW7 2AR
www.rgs.org
Email: info@rgs.org
Tel: 020 7591 3000
For advice on a serious expedition for research or exploration purposes, your first contact should be with the Royal Geographical Society (with the Institute of Geographers). It supports research, education and training as well as a wider understanding and appreciation of geography, society and the environment. The RGS-IBG is one of the largest geographical societies in the world and has been active in encouraging and supporting explorers since 1830. The Society is based in a listed building set in its own grounds close to Hyde Park in London, where there is a library, map room and picture collection.

It now has funding from the National Lottery for a project called Unlocking the Archives, to make its immense collection of materials more accessible to the public. There are over 500,000 heritage items including maps, photographs, artefacts, books and manuscripts that trace the history of British exploration in the nineteenth and twentieth centuries. The RGS-IBG continues to support explorers with grants from its own resources.

The RGS headquarters also host a number of organizations that organize or support adventure or exploration projects.

British Schools Exploring Society (BSES)
www.bses.org.uk
Email: bses@orgs.org
A charity founded by Commander Murray Levick who was a member of Scott's Antarctic Expedition of 1910, the BSES provides opportunities for young people to take part in projects of exploration led by experts to remote places. To be eligible you must be aged between 16 and 20 at the time of the expedition and in full-time education (but including gap-year students). Recent young explorer expeditions have been to Lesotho, a land-locked country surrounded by South Africa, Alaska, southern Chile and the Falkland Islands in the footsteps of Shackleton, and the Amazonas region of Brazil.

Young Explorers Trust (The Association of British Youth Exploration Societies)
1 Kensington Gore
London SW7 2AR
www.theyet.org
Email: info@theyet.org
Tel: 020 7591 3141

A forum for societies and individuals to exchange information and advice on expeditions and exploring for young people. Yet promotes safe and responsible expeditions to give young people the chance to take part in exploration, discovery and challenging adventures. YET does not run expeditions, but provides advice to leaders.

Expedition Advisory Centre
Royal Geographical Society
1 Kensington Gore
London SW7 2AR
www.rgs.org
Email: info@rgs.org
Tel: 020 7591 3030
Information, advice and a training service for expedition planning. The Centre also publishes the *Expedition Planner's Handbook and Directory*.

Royal Scottish Geographical Society
Graham Hills Building
University of Strathclyde
40 George Street
Glasgow G1 1QE
www.geo.ed.ac.uk/~rsgs/
Email: rsgs@strath.ac.uk
Tel: 0141 552 3330
The Scottish affiliate of the RGS.

Scientific Exploration Society
Expedition Base
Motcombe
Shaftesbury
Dorset SP7 9PB
www.ses-explore.org
Email: base@ses-explore.org
Tel: 01747 853353
The home base of the famous British explorer John Blashford-Snell, the SES organizes its own expeditions and training and also advises and supports others.

The Jubilee Sailing Trust
Hazel Road
Woolston
Southampton SO19 7GB
www.jst.org.uk
Email: info@jst.org.uk
Tel: 023 804 49108
Britain's premier sail training resource and contact point for adventures on traditional-style tall ships.

The Explorers Club
46 East 70th Street
New York, NY 10021
www.british-explorers.org
Email: barrymoss@british-explorers.org
Tel: 212 628 8383
An international professional society for explorers and scientists, with a British section or Chapter, the Explorers Club is dedicated to the advancement of scientific exploration and field research. It provides expedition planning assistance, help on research funding, educational lectures and publications and exciting adventure travel opportunities.

South American Explorers Club
Av. Portugal 146, Brena
Postal Casilla 3714
Lima 100, Peru
Tel: 001 425 0142
also
Jorge Washington 311 y L. Plaza
Postal Apartado 21–431
Quito
Ecuador
www.samexplo.org
A club to promote travel and sporting aspects of exploration. Publications include *The South American Explorer* magazine. They have a clubhouse, with reading rooms, maps and guidebooks, at the address in Lima which you may visit at any time.

Expedition Organizers

Some of the organizations offer a first-time expedition experience, while others are looking for leaders or contributors with skills to work on environmental or community projects in the course of their journey. It is important to look in detail at the information about any that take your interest, to check whether you would be eligible. Some are voluntary bodies or charities with a main aim of doing a work project, while others have an educational or discovery aim though not at the level of conducting university-style scientific research. A few are commercial companies in the travel business who offer unusual adventure opportunities that you would not find in your local travel agent's brochures, which can be a good way to get into adventure travel at whatever age you start. At the very least, a search through this list should give you some ideas for setting your aim for an adventure of your own.

For the more extreme expeditions, to the polar regions for example or any involving technical mountaineering, it will be expected that you have done some training already. The main thing here is that the adventure will be well-organized to high standards of safety with leaders who know what they are doing, usually including people from the locality who can share their unique insights into a remote or unusual place.

Absolute Africa Ltd
41 Swanscombe Road
Chiswick
London W4 2HL
www.absoluteafrica.com
Email: absaf@actual.co.uk

Tel: 020 8742 0226
Trekking and safaris in numerous locations in southern and eastern Africa.

Across the Divide Expeditions
Jubilee House
Fore Street
Thorncombe
Chard
Somerset TA20 4PP
www.acrossthedivide.com
Email: events@acrossthedivide.com
Tel: 01460 30456
ATD specializes in charity challenges including small groups trekking the Inca Trail in Peru for Cancer Research UK, or traversing Costa Rica on mountain bikes for Mencap, and staging some of the largest outdoor adventure events in Southern Africa for Pallotta Teamworks (USA).

Brathay Exploration Group
Brathay Hall
Ambleside
Cumbria LA22 0HP
www.brathayexploration.org.uk
Email: admin@brathayexploration.org.uk
Tel: 015394 33942
The Brathay Group has conducted more than 550 expeditions since its foundation in 1947 for young people in small groups on a variety of scientific discovery trips. Participants contribute towards the costs, but there are sponsorship funds for young people who are financially disadvantaged.

Discovery Initiatives
The Travel House
51 Castle Street
Cirencester
Gloucestershire GL7 1QD
www.discoveryinitiatives.com
Email: enquiry@discoveryinitiatives.com
Tel: 01285 643333

Inspirational journeys that provide an insight into culture and the natural world while supporting their long-term survival and conservation.

Explore Worldwide Ltd
1 Frederick Street
Aldershot
Hampshire GU11 1LQ
www.exploreworldwide.com
Email: info@exploreworldwide.com
Tel: 01252 760000
Small-group adventure travel with no frills but respect for local culture and the environment. The company was founded by three travel companions with a passion for adventure, now part of Holidaybreak plc.

High & Wild
1 Heritage Courtyard
Sadler Street
Wells
Somerset BA5 2RR
www.highandwild.co.uk
Email: adventures@highandwild.co.uk
Tel: 01749 671777
High & Wild is a travel firm that organizes and advises on expeditions, adventures and journeys of discovery for independent travellers and small groups, including Polar expeditions, Himalayas and jungle trekking in South America.

Himalayan Expeditions
184 Bishop Road
Bishopstone
Bristol BS7 8NB
www.himalayaclimb.com
Email: himalayanexpeditions@earthlink.net
Tel: 01179 087954
Full-service climbing and trekking adventures in the Himalaya including all transport and use of gear and porter services, for experts and beginners in high mountains.

Jagged Globe Mountaineering
The Foundry Studios
45 Mowbray Street
Sheffield S3 8EN
www.jagged-globe.co.uk
Tel: 0845 345 8848 (local call rate) from outside the UK +44 114 276 3322
Jagged Globe is a specialist mountaineering company that provides mountaineering expeditions and courses at all levels of ability from beginners to advanced climbers looking for new challenges. You can discuss your aspirations with experienced staff and expedition leaders, but don't ask them about mountain biking or kayaking trips!

Karakoram Experience
32 Lake Road
Keswick
Cumbria CA12 5DQ
www.keadventure.com
Email: info@keadventure.co.uk
Tel: 017687 73966
A real adventure company organizing treks and trips to 38 countries but particularly central Asia and the Himalayan mountain range, the Andes, Africa and beyond.

Mountain and Wildlife Ventures
Brow Foot
High Wray
Ambleside
Cumbria LA22 0JE
Tel: 01539 433285
Specialists in adventure and expedition planning for Scandinavia, including Nordic cross-country skiing treks.

Oceanic Society Expeditions
Fort Mason Center
Building E. Suite 230
San Francisco
CA 94123-1394
USA
OSE manages research projects around the world and promotes

the collection of scientific evidence for use in the protection of marine and land habitats. Natural history and volunteer-assisted research expeditions are led by OSE naturalists and use local guides where possible. More than thirty expeditions are offered each year.

Scientific Exploration Society
Expedition Base
Motcombe
Shaftesbury
Dorset SP7 9PB
www.ses-explore.org
Email: base@ses-explore.org
Tel: 01747 853353
Founded by John Blashford-Snell and colleagues after the Blue Nile expedition to Ethiopia, SES offers worldwide expeditions with a scientific, conservation or educational purpose but requiring no specialist experience or qualifications. Examples include exploring a remote tribal area of north-east India, archaeology and conservation projects in Panama, observation of forest elephants in Ghana and navigation of the Rio Grande gorge in Bolivia.

Trekforce Expeditions
34 Buckingham Palace Road
London SW1W 0RE
www.trekforce.org.uk
Email: info@trekforce.org.uk
Tel: 020 7828 2275
Science-related expeditions to Indonesia, including jungle training and natural history survey work alongside professional scientific researchers. Projects have included a Sumatran rhino survey, grasshopper studies and restoring a former British colonial fort.

World Challenge Expeditions
Black Arrow House
2 Chandos Road
London NW10 6NF
www.world-challenge.co.uk/
Tel: 020 8728 7200
World Challenge Expeditions enables young people aged 16 to 20 to travel in small groups to remote places to conduct basic environmental field trips. They are not strictly scientific research projects but involve tasks designed to build leadership skills and self reliance and an awareness of the natural environment. The website has a bulletin board where you can look for vacancies on an expedition already being planned.

Expedition Training Courses

4th World Adventure Ltd
The Barn
Upper Goddards Farm
Skirmett
Oxfordshire RG9 6TB
www.4thworldadventure.com
Email: info@4thworldadventure.com
Tel: 0845 1300 448

Active First Aid
The Old Stables
Snowdon Street
Llanberis
Gwynedd LL55 4HE
www.activefirstaid.co.uk
Email: katherine@activefirstaid.co.uk
Tel: 01286 870019

Adventure Lifesigns
www.adventurelifesigns.co.uk
Email: info@adventurelifesigns.co.uk
Tel: 01483 459139
Specialize in health and safety and expedition medicine training. Expedition Care Program courses are organized in various parts of the world including Belize, Central America, and Indonesia Asia.

Adventureworks
The Foundry Studios
45 Mowbray Street
Sheffield S3 8EN
www.adventureworks.co.uk
Email: info@adventureworks.co.uk
Tel: 0114 276 3322 or 0845 345
8850
Training courses for youngsters in
expedition preparation, moutaineer-
ing and Alpine skills, in the Peak
District, Scotland and the Alps.

Brathay Exploration Group
Brathay Hall
Ambleside
Cumbria LA22 0HP
www.brathayexploration.org.uk
Email: admin@brathayexploration.
org.uk
Tel: 015394 33942

Chapel Outdoors
The Chapel Group
65 Normanton Road
Basingstoke
Hampshire RG21 5QP
www.thechapelgroup.com
Email: enquiries@thechapelgroup.
com
Tel: 07879 654191
Tailor-made individual adventures
to in-depth expedition training
with experienced instructors
connected with Hampshire Scouts
Expeditions (HSX).

The Expedition Company Ltd
PO Box 17
Wiveliscombe
Taunton TA4 2YL
www.expedition.co.uk
Email: info@expedition.co.uk
Tel: 01984 624780
Outdoor courses, map reading,
community project expeditions
and adventure travel training for
teachers and students.

Expedition Medicine Company
Dr Sean Hudson
Jubilee House

Fore Street
Thorncombe
Nr Chard
Somerset TA20 4PP
www.expeditionmedicine.co.uk
Email: events@atd-expeditions.co.uk
Tel: 01460 30456
Expedition training for doctors,
based around the Expedition &
Travel Medicine for Medical
Professionals and the Raleigh
International Expedition Medic
Course. EMC concentrate on
providing specific technical infor-
mation on subjects as diverse as
high-altitude medicine, aero-
medical evacuations, cold weather
injuries and the management of
mass casualty scenarios.

ExpeMed
81–83 Victoria Road
Surbiton
Surrey KT6 4NS
www.voyageconcepts.co.uk/expem
ed.htm
Email: info@voyageconcepts.co.uk
Tel: 020 8399 9090
The Expedition Medicine training
course is now in its fourth year.
Doctors can gain skills and
invaluable teaching about their
role in remote expedition settings
where resources are few and far
between. The four-day course
concentrates on practical skills
with small-group teaching and
casualty scenarios.

**International School of
Mountaineering**
Hafod Tan y Graig
Nant Gwynant
Caernarfon LL55 4NW
www.alpin-ism.com
Email: ism@alpin-ism.com
Tel: 01766 890441
Alpine mountaineering training in
Switzerland and expeditions to
Peru and Kun Lun, China.

Life Support Training Services
128 Main Street
Haverigg
Millom
Cumbria LA18 4EY
www.lsts-safety.co.uk
Email: info@lsts-safety.co.uk
Tel: 01229 772708
LSTS specialize in offering
Remote Environment Health &
Safety training covering
Mountain, RYA, Remote
Environment First Aid, expedition
training and off-road and over-
land driver and vehicle skills.

Mediact
Brookside
Lightwood Avenue
Buxton
Derbyshire SK17 7BA
www.mediact.net
Email: firstaid@mediact.net
Tel: 01298 71827 / 0771 409 4029
First aid courses at Thornbridge
Outdoors in the English Peak
District.

More Adventures
Adventure House
Holme View
Ilkley
West Yorkshire LS29 9EL
www.moreadventures.com/expedtr.
htm
Email: info@moreadventures.com
Tel: 01943 609334
Wide range of training
programmes from adventure
weekends to Scottish winter
mountaineering and Nepal peak
trekking.

National Mountain Centre
Plas Y Brenin
Capel Curig
Conwy LL24 OET
Email: info@pyb.co.uk
Tel: 01690 720214
A comprehensive range of adven-
ture training courses in the
mountains of north Wales. The

Godfrey Jackson Memorial Fund
offers bursaries for young people
to train in snow and ice mountaineering in Scotland and the
Alps, and the centre administers
the Kathmandu Memorial
Bursary to fund expedition
training.

Plas Y Brenin
National Mountain Centre
Capel Curig
Conwy LL24 0ET
www.pyb.co.uk
Email: info@pyb.co.uk
Tel: 01690 720214

Raleigh International
27 Parsons Green Lane
London SW6 4HZ
www.raleighinternational.org
Email: volunteer@raleigh.org.uk
Tel: 020 7371 8585
Highly respected youth development charity providing training in
community projects and expedition life. Raleigh runs 11
project-based expeditions each
year to Chile, Costa Rica and
Nicaragua, Ghana, Namibia and
Sabah-Borneo. The training
concentrates on personal development, cultural awareness and
environmental and global issues.

**SEAT (School of Expedition and
Adventure Training)**
www.adventure-school.co.uk
Email: seat@adventure-school.co.uk
Courses in basic survival skills
and adventure activities based at
the Kinver Scout Camp.

UK Survival School Ltd
Seymour House
24 East Street
Hereford HR1 2LU
www.uksurvivalschool.co.uk
Email: info@uksurvivalschool.co.uk
Tel: 01432 376751
Courses to build the confidence
to tackle the most arduous and

challenging outdoor conditions, aiming to create a wider understanding of nature and providing essential knowledge and skills to sustain and save life. Jungle survival training is done in the Borneo rainforest and includes an ascent of Mount Kinabalu.

Wilderness Medical Training
The Coach House
Thorny Bank
Skelsmergh
Kendal
Cumbria LA8 9AW
www.wildernessmedicaltraining.
co.uk
Email: enquiries@wilderness
medicaltraining.co.uk
Tel: 01539 823183
Wilderness Medical Training is one of the leading UK providers of advanced expedition medical training for laypeople and professional medics. Operating since 1991, WMT has trained hundreds of expedition leaders and medics from dozens of organizations including World Challenge Expeditions, the Royal Geographical Society, Coral Cay Conservation and Raleigh International.

Government Sources of Information

An essential part of planning an expedition or adventure trip is to research the country you are going to, and to get the best advice available, particularly on lesser-known – and therefore more adventurous – destinations. The Foreign and Commonwealth Office (FCO) provides travel advice to the public by phone and on the Internet. The FCO website Country Advice section contains official travel advice on over 200 countries and there are also country-specific Travellers' Tips. When the Government issues warnings about visiting certain countries because of dangers arising from political unrest, terrorism or natural disasters, they will appear on this website.

FCO Travel Advice Unit
www.fco.gov.uk
Tel: 0870 606 0290

Department of Health Public Enquiries Office
Richmond House
79 Whitehall
London SW1A 2NL
www.doh.gov.uk
Email: dhmail@doh.gsi.gov.uk
Tel: 020 7210 4850
Tel: 0800 555777 free to order
Health Advice for Travellers booklet.

Fit For Travel
www.fitfortravel.scot.nhs.uk/
'Fitfortravel' is a public access website provided by the National Health Service in Scotland and provides health information for people travelling abroad from the UK.

The website is compiled and updated by a team of experts from the Travel Medicine Division at the Scottish Centre for Infection and Environmental Health.

Other governments now share their official country advice on the Internet and although some of the details are specific to their own citizens, there may be nuggets of additional information and news that could give you more insights into the region you intend to visit.

US State Department Bureau of Consular Affairs
http://www.travel.state.gov/travel_warnings.html

Center For Disease Control
www.cdc.gov/travel/index_htm
Information on worldwide disease and health risks for travellers.

CIA The World Factbook
www.cia.gov/cia/publications/factbook/index.html
An extensive resource of factual information on every country in the world.

Canadian Department of Foreign Affairs
www.voyage.gc.ca/dest/index.asp

Australian Department of Foreign Affairs and Trade
www.dfat.gov.au/consular/advice/advices_mnu.html

Embassy World
www.embassyworld.com
An Internet directory of embassies and consulates around the world. It is not a government-sponsored website and all information about visas and other requirements for travellers should be treated with caution, as regulations can change without notice and should be checked with the country's consular staff or official embassy websites.

Tourism Offices Worldwide Directory
www.towd.com/
Online directory of official tourist information sources, listing only official government tourism offices, visitor bureaus, chambers of commerce, and similar agencies which provide free, accurate and unbiased travel information to the public. No travel agents, no tour operators, no hotels.

National Representation in the UK

Embassies, high commissions and consulates can provide travellers with information and advice about the countries they represent, especially with regard to regulations about visas and other entry formalities. Many now have websites with the key information readily available online, including downloadable visa application forms. A high commission is the equivalent of an embassy, usually for countries that belong to the British Commonwealth.

It is important to remember that embassy staff work in the fields of politics, diplomacy, law and international trade and should not be thought of as sources of holiday or tourism information, except where it concerns regulations about visas and permissions to enter or stay in the country. The consular services are chiefly for the benefit of their own citizens living away from their home country. Some embassies provide a tourism website: this is particularly the case where travel and tourism is a significant part of the country's economy, and in this listing some of the websites are from the tourism ministry or the national tourism board of the country. In a few cases the website is provided by the country's embassy in Washington, USA.

Afghanistan Embassy
31 Princes Gate
London SW7 1QQ
www.afghanembassy.co.uk
Tel: 020 7589 8891

Albania Embassy
2nd Floor
24 Buckingham Gate

London SW1E 6LB
Tel: 020 7828 8897

Algeria Embassy
54 Holland Park
London W11 3RS
Tel: 020 7221 7800

American Samoa
External Territory of the USA and
represented abroad by United
States Embassies
Travel Information:
South Pacific Tourism
Organisation
PO Box 13119
Suva, Fiji
www.spto.org or www.tcsp.com
Email: info@spto.org
Tel: 00 679 330 4177

Andorra Embassy/Tourism
Delegation
63 Westover Road
London SW18 2RF
Tel: 020 8874 4806

Angola Embassy
22 Dorset Street
London W1U 6QY
Tel: 020 7299 9850

Anguilla
A British Overseas Territory, part
of the British West Indies.

Antigua and Barbuda High
Commission
15 Thayer Street
London W1M 5LD
Tel: 020 7486 7073

Argentina Embassy
65 Brooke Street
London W1K 4AH
Tel: 020 7318 1300
Consular Section (Visa Office):
27 Three Kings Yard
London W1K 4DF
Tel: 020 7318 1340

Armenia Embassy
25A Cheniston Gardens
London W8 6TG

www.armeniaemb.org
Tel: 020 7938 5435

Aruba
Represented by the Netherlands
Embassy
38 Hyde Park Gate
London SW7 5DP
www.netherlandsembassy.org.uk/
Email: London@netherlands-emba
ssy.org.uk
Tel: 0870 162 0856

Australia High Commission
Australia House
Strand
London WC2B 4LA
Tel: 0870 162 0822

Austria Embassy
18 Belgrave Mews West
London SW1X 8HU
www.austria.org.uk
Tel: 020 7235 3731

Azerbaijan Embassy
4 Kensington Court
London W8 5DL
www.azembassy.com
Tel: 020 7938 5482

Bahamas High Commission
Bahamas House
10 Chesterfield Street
London W1X 8AH
www.bahamas.com
Tel: 020 7408 4488

Bahrain Embassy
30 Belgrave Square
London SW1X 8QB
www.bahrainembassy.org
Tel: 0870 162 0824

Bangladesh High Commission
28 Queen's Gate
London SW7 5JA
Tel: 020 7584 0081

Barbados High Commission
1 Great Russell Street
London WC1B 3ND
www.foreign.gov.bb
www.barbados.org and

www.barmot.goy.bb
Email: barbados@foreign.gov.bb
Tel: 020 7631 4975

Belarus Embassy
6 Kensington Court
London W8 5DL
Tel: 020 7937 3288

Belgium Embassy
103 Eaton Square
London SW1W 9AB
www.belgium-embassy.co.uk/
Tel: 020 7470 3700

Belize High Commission
22 Harcourt House
19 Cavendish Square
London W1G 0PL
Tel: 020 7499 9728
Travel website: www.btia.org

Benin Embassy
Dolphin House
16 The Broadway Stanmore
Middlesex HA7 4DW
Tel: 020 8954 8800

Bermuda
A British Overseas Territory
(Crown Colony)
Visa enquiries:
Passport Office
Globe House
89 Eccleston Square
London SW1V 1PN
Tel: 0870 241 1902
Travel Information:
Bermuda Tourism
1 Battersea Church Road
London SW11 3LY
Tel: 020 7771 7001

Bhutan
No national representation in
the UK
Independent travel is not allowed.
Tours must be pre-arranged with
The Tourism Authority of Bhutan
PO Box 126
Thimpu
Bhutan
Tel: 00 975 223251

Enquiries about entry visas may
be made at the embassy in New
Delhi.

Royal Bhutanese Embassy
Chandragupta Marg
Chanakyapuri
New Delhi 110 021
India
www.kingdomofbhutain.com and
www.tourism.gov.bt
Email: bhutan@del2.vsnl.net.in
Tel: 00 91 11 688 9230

Bolivia Embassy
106 Eaton Square
London SW1W 9AD
www.europanas.com/
Tel: 020 7235 4248

Bonaire
Part of the Netherlands Antilles
and represented by the Royal
Netherlands Embassy
38 Hyde Park Gate
London SW7 5DP
Travel website: www.infobonaire.
com
Email:
Europe@tourismbonaire.com
Tel: 0870 162 0856

Bosnia and Herzegovina Embassy
5–7 Lexham Gardens
London W8 5JJ
Tel: 020 7373 0867

Botswana High Commission
6 Stratford Place
London W1C 1AY
www.southern-skies.co.uk/
Botswana.htm
Tel: 020 7499 0031
Visa information Tel: 09065 508
954 (calls cost £1 per minute)

Brazil Embassy
32 Green Street
London W1Y 4AT
www.brazil.org.uk
Email: info@brazil.org.uk
Tel: 020 7499 0877

Consulate General (Visa Office)
3rd & 4th Floor
6 St Alban's Street
Haymarket
London SW1Y 4SQ
Email: consulado@cgbrazil.org.uk
Tel: 020 7930 9055

British Virgin Islands
A British Overseas Territory
Visa Enquiries:
Passport Office
Globe House
89 Eccleston Square
London SW1V 1PN
Tel: 0870 241 1902
Travel Information:
British Virgin Islands Tourist
Board
15 Upper Grosvenor Street
London W1K 7PJ
(No personal callers)
www.bvitouristboard.com
Email:
infouk@bvitouristboard.com
Tel: 020 7355 9585

Brunei Darussalam High
Commission
19/20 Belgrave Square
London SW1X 8PG
www.bruneiembassy.org
Tel: 020 7581 0521

Bulgaria Embassy
186–188 Queen's Gate
London SW7 5HL
www.bulgarianembassy.org.uk
Email: info@bulgarianembassy.
org.uk
Tel: 020 7584 9433
Visa Section Tel: 09065 508 950
(calls cost £1 per minute)

Burkina Faso
No national representation in the
UK. Enquiries should be made
with the Embassy in Brussels.
Ambassade du Burkina Faso
16 Place Guy d'Arezzo
1180 Brussels
Belgium

http://burkinaembassy-usa.org
Email: ambassade.burkina@skynet.
be
Tel: 00 32 2 345 9912

Burma (Myanmar) Embassy
19A Charles Street
London W1X 8ER
Tel: 020 7629 6966

Burundi
No national representation in the
UK. Enquiries should be made at
the Embassy in Brussels.
Ambassade de la République du
Burundi
Square Marie-Louise 46
1000 Brussels LE
Belgium
Tel: 00 322 230 4535

Cambodia
No national representation in the
UK. Enquiries should be made at
the Embassy in Paris.
Royal Embassy of Cambodia
4 rue Adolphe Yvon
75116 Paris
France
www.embassy.org/Cambodia or
www.mot.gov.kh
Email: ambcambodgeparis@
mangoosta.fr
Tel: 00 33 1 45 03 47 20

Cameroon High Commission
84 Holland Park
London W11 3SB
Ministry of Tourism:
www.camnet.cm/mintour/tourisme
or www.mintour.gov.cm
Tel: 020 7727 0771

Canada High Commission
Visa Section:
38 Grosvenor Square
London W1 0AA
www.canada.org.uk
Tel: 09068 616 644 (calls cost
60p per minute)

Cultural Section:
Canada House
Pall Mall East
London SW1Y 5BJ
www.dfait-maeci.gc.ca/london
Email: ldn-cs@dfait-maeci.gc.ca
Tel: 020 7258 6600

Cape Verde
No national representation in the
UK. Enquiries should be made to
the Embassy in Brussels.
Embassy of the Republic of Cape
Verde
Avenue Jeanne 29
1050 Brussels
Belgium
www.virtualcapeverde.net
Email: emb.caboyerde@skynet.be
Tel: 00 322 643 6270

Cayman Islands
A British Dependent Territory
Government Office
6 Arlington Street
London SW1A 1RE
www.caymanislands.ky
Email: info-uk@caymanislands.uk
Tel: 020 7491 7772

Central African Republic
No national representation in the
UK. Enquiries should be made to
the Embassy in Paris.
Embassy of the Central African
Republic
30 rue des Perchamps
75016 Paris
France
Tel: 00 33 1 42 24 42 56

Chad
No national representation in the
UK. Enquiries should be made to
the Embassy in Paris.
Embassy of the Republic of Chad
65 rue des Belles Feuilles
75116 Paris
France
www.chadembassy.org
Tel: 00 33 1 45 53 36 75

Chile Embassy
12 Devonshire Street
London W1N 2DS
Tel: 020 7580 6392

China Embassy
49–51 Portland Place
London W1N 4JL
Tel: 020 7636 9375
Consular Section:
31 Portland Place
London W1N 3AG
www.chinese-embassy.org.uk
Email: press@chinese-
embassy.org.uk
Tel: 020 7631 1430
Consulate General (Visa office):
55 Corstorphine Road
Edinburgh EH12 5QG
Tel: 0131 337 9896

Colombia Embassy
Flat 3A
3 Hans Crescent
London SW1X 0LN
www.colombianembassy.co.uk/
homeing.htm
Email: mail@colombianembassy.
co.uk
Tel: 020 7589 9177

Comoros
No national representation in the
UK. Enquiries should be made to
the Embassy in Paris.
Embassy of the Federal Islamic
Republic of the Comoros
20 rue Marbeau
75016 Paris
France
Tel: 00 331 1 40 67 90 54
Travel Information:
Email: dg.tourisme@snpt.km

Congo Democratic Republic
(capital, Kinshasa) Embassy
38 Holne Chase
London N2 0QQ
Tel: 020 8458 0254

Republic of Congo (capital, Brazzaville)
No national representation in the UK. Enquiries should be made to the Embassy in Paris.
Embassy of the Republic of Congo
37 bis rue Paul Valéry
75016 Paris
France
Tel: 00 33 1 45 00 60 57

Cook Islands
Travel Information:
South Pacific Tourism Organisation
PO Box 13119
Suva, Fiji
www.spto.org or www.tcsp.com
Email: info@spto.org
Tel: 00 679 330 4177

Costa Rica Embassy
Flat 1, 14 Lancaster Gate
London W2 3LH
www.costarica-embassy.org/
Email: embassy@costarica-embassy.org
Tel: 020 7706 8844

Côte d'Ivoire (Ivory Coast)
Embassy
2 Upper Belgrave Street
London SW1X 8BJ
Tel: 020 7235 6991

Croatia Embassy
21 Conway Street
London W1P 5HL
Ministry of Tourism website:
www.mint.hr
Email: ministarstvo-turizma@zg.tel.hr
Tel: 020 7387 2022

Cuba Embassy
167 High Holborn
London WC1 6PA
Ministry of Tourism website:
www.cubatravel.cu
Tel: 020 7240 2488

Visa Information Tel: 0870 240 3675
(calls cost 60p per minute)

Curaçao
See Netherlands Antilles

Cyprus High Commission
93 Park Street
London W1K 7ET
Email: cyphclondon@dial.pipex.com
Tel: 020 7499 8272
Travel Information:
17 Hanover Street
London W1S 1YP
Tel: 020 7569 8800

Northern Cyprus (Turkish Republic of Northern Cyprus)
Office of the London Representative
29 Bedford Square
London WC1B 3EG
www.tourism.trnc.net/main/main-eng.htm
Tel: 020 7631 1920

Czech Republic Embassy
26 Kensington Palace Gardens
London W8 4QY
www.czech.org.uk
Email: london@embassy.mzy.cz
Tel: 0870 162 0831
Visa Information Tel: 09069 101 060
(calls cost 60p per minute)

Denmark Embassy
55 Sloane Street
London SW1X 9SR
www.denmark.org.uk
Email: lonamb@um.dk
Tel: 020 7333 0200

Djibouti
No national representation in the UK. Enquiries should be made to the Embassy in Paris.
Embassy of the Republic of Djibouti
26 rue Emile Ménier

75116 Paris
France
Tel: 00 331 47 27 49 22

Dominica High Commission
1 Collingham Gardens
London SW5 0HW
www.dominica.co.uk
Email: agnesa@dominica.co.uk
Tel: 020 7370 5194

Dominican Republic Embassy
139 Inverness Terrace
Bayswater
London W2 6JF
www.dominicana.com.do/
Email: general@embajadadom
london.demon.co.uk
Tel: 020 7727 6285
Visa Information Tel: 09065 508
945 (calls cost 60p per minute)

East Timor
East Timor became independent
from Indonesia in May 2002, but
does not yet have a national
representative office in the UK.
East Timor Embassy in USA
3415 Massachusetts Avenue NW
Washington DC 20007-0000
Email: embtlus@earthlink.net
Tel: 001 202 965 1515

Ecuador Embassy
Flat 3, 3 Hans Crescent
London SW1X 0LS
www.ecuador.org
Email: embajada.ecuador@btclick.
com
Tel: 020 7584 2648

Egypt Embassy
26 South Street
London W1Y 6DD
Email: etembuk@hotmail.com
Tel: 0870 162 0832
Consulate (Visa Office):
2 Lowndes Street
London SW1X 9ET
www.touregypt.net
Tel: 0870 162 0833

El Salvador Embassy
Tennyson House
159 Great Portland Street
London W1N 5FD
www.elsalvador.org
Tel: 020 7436 8282

Equatorial Guinea
No national representation in the
UK. Enquiries should be made to
the Embassy in Paris.
Embassy of the Republic of
Equatorial Guinea
29 Boulevard de Courcelles
75008 Paris
France
Tel: 00 33 1 01 56 88 54 54
Office of Tourism and Culture:
Via Monti Simbruni 1
00016 Monterotondo
Rome
Email: comtur-guineaec@flashnet.
it
Tel: 00 39 06 881 6486

Eritrea Embassy
96 White Lion Street
London N1 9PF
Email: eriemba@freeuk.com
Tel: 020 7713 0096

Estonia Embassy
16 Hyde Park Gate
London SW7 5DG
www.estonia.gov.uk or
www.visitestonia.com
Email: embassy.london@estonia.
gov.uk
Tel 020 7589 7690

Ethiopia Embassy
17 Prince's Gate
London SW7 1PZ
www.ethioembassy.org.uk
Email: info@ethioembassy.org.uk
Tel: 020 7589 7212

Falkland Islands
British Overseas Territory
Government Office
14 Broadway
London SW1H 0BH

www.falklands.gov.fk
Email: travel@falklands.gov.fk
Tel: 020 7222 2542

Faroe Islands
An Overseas Administrative
Division of Denmark.
Royal Danish Embassy
55 Sloane Street
London SW1X 9SR
www.denmark.org.uk
Email: lonamb@um.dk
Tel: 020 7333 0200

Fiji High Commission
34 Hyde Park Gate
London SW7 5DN
www.fiji.gov.fj and www.spto.
org
Email: fijirepuk@compuserve.
com
Tel: 020 7584 3661

Finland Embassy
38 Chesham Place
London SW1X 8HW
www.finemb.org.uk
Email: sanomat.lon@formin.fi
Tel: 020 7838 6200

France
French Guiana
French West Indies (The French
Overseas Departments of
Martinique and **Guadaloupe** with
St Martin and **St Barthelemy**)
Embassy of France
58 Knightsbridge
London SW1X 7JT
www.ambafrance-uk.org
Email: press@ambafrance.org.uk
Tel: 0870 162 0834
Visa Information Tel: 09065 540
700 (calls cost £1 per minute)

Gabon Embassy
27 Elvaston Place
London SW7 5NL
www.gabontour.com
Tel: 020 7823 9986

The Gambia High Commission
57 Kensington Court

London W8 5DG
www.visitthegambia.gm
www.gambiatourism.info
Email: gambia@gamhighcom.fsnet.
co.uk
Tel: 020 7937 6316

Georgia Embassy
Consular Section
4 Russell Gardens
London W14 8EZ
www.geoemb.org.uk/consular.htm
Email: geoemb@dircon.co.uk
Visa Information Tel: 0906
550 8927
(calls cost £1 per minute)

Germany Embassy
23 Belgrave Square
London SW1X 8PZ
www.german-embassy.org.uk
Email: info@german-embassy.org.
uk (not visa enquiries)
Tel: 020 7824 1300
Consulate (Visa Office):
1–6 Chesham Place
Belgrave Mews West
London SW1X 8PZ

Ghana High Commission
13 Belgrave Square
London SW1X 8PN
www.ghana-com.co.uk
Email: enquiries@ghana-com.co.uk
Tel: 020 7235 4142
Education, Visas and Trade:
104 Highgate Hill
London N6 5HE
Tel: 020 8342 8686

Greece Embassy
1A Holland Park
London W11 3TP
www.greekembassy.org.uk/
Email: consulategeneral@greek
embassy.org.uk
Tel: 020 7221 6467
Visa Information Tel: 09065
508 983
(calls cost £1 per minute)

Greenland
A self-governing Dependency of
Denmark
Royal Danish Embassy
55 Sloane Street
London SW1X 9SR
www.denmark.org.uk
Email: lonamb@um.dk
Tel: 020 7333 0200

Grenada High Commission
5 Chandos Street
London W1G 9DG
Tel: 020 7631 4277
http://grenadagrenadines.com
Email: grenada@highcommission.
freeserve.co.uk

Guadaloupe
Part of the French West Indies
and represented by the
Embassy of France
58 Knightsbridge
London SW1X 7JT
www.ambafrance-uk.org
Email: press@ambafrance.org.uk
Tel: 0870 162 0834
Visa Information Tel: 09065
540 700
(calls cost £1 per minute)

Guatemala Embassy
13 Fawcett Street
London SW10 9HN
www.embaguatelondon.btinternet.
co.uk
Email: embaguatelondon@
btinternet.co.uk
Tel: 020 7351 3042

Guinea Consulate General
137 Brent Street
London NW4 4GJ
Tel: 020 8457 2901

Guinea-Bissau
No national representation in the
UK. Enquiries should be made to
the Embassy in Paris.
Embassy of the Republic of
Guinea-Bissau
94 rue St Lazare
Paris 75009

France
Tel: 00 33 1 45 26 18 51

Guyana High Commission
3 Palace Court
Bayswater Road
London W2 4LP
www.guyanaca.com or
www.guyana.org
Tel: 020 7229 7684

Haiti
No national representation in
the UK.
Enquiries may be made with the
Haitian Embassy in Brussels.
Chaussée de Charleroi 139
Brussels 1060
Belgium
Tel: 00 322 649 7381

Honduras Embassy
115 Gloucester Place
London W1U 6JT
www.hondurasemb.org/
Email: hondurasuk@lineone.net
Tel: 020 7486 4880

Hong Kong
A Special Administrative Region
of China.
Embassy of China
49–51 Portland Place
London W1N 4JL
Tel: 020 7636 9375

Hungary Embassy
35 Eaton Place
London SW1X 8BY
www.huemblon.org.uk
Email: office@huemblon.org.uk
Tel: 020 7201 3440
Visa Enquiries Tel: 09065 508 936
(calls are charged at £1 per
minute)

Iceland Embassy
2A Hans Street
London SW1X 0JE
www.iceland.org.uk/
Email: icemb.london@utn.stjr.is
Tel: 020 7259 3999

India High Commission
India House
Aldwych
London WC2B 4NA
www.hcilondon.org
Tel: 020 7836 8484
Visa Information Tel: 09068
444 544
(calls cost 60p per minute)

Indonesia Embassy
38 Grosvenor Square
London W1K 2HW
Consular Section (visa office) for
personal callers:
38A Adam's Row
Mayfair
London W1X 9AD
www.indonesiatourism.com
Email: kbri@btconnect.com
Tel: 020 7499 7661

Iran Embassy
50 Kensington Court
London W8 5DB
Tel: 020 7937 5225
Visa Enquiries Tel: 0906 802 0222
(premium rate)

Iraq
No national representation
currently in the UK.

Ireland Embassy
17 Grosvenor Place
London SW1X 7HR
Tel: 020 7235 2171
Passport & Visa Office:
Montpelier House
106 Brompton Road
London SW3 1JJ
www.tourismireland.com
Tel: 020 7225 7700

Israel Embassy
2 Palace Green
London W8 4QB
www.israel-embassy.org.uk/london/
Email: cons-sec@london.mfa.
gov.il
Tel: 020 7957 9500

Italy Embassy
14 Three Kings Yard
London W1K 4EH
www.embitaly.org.uk/
Email: emblondon@embitaly.org.uk
Tel: 020 7312 2200

Jamaica High Commission
1–2 Prince Consort Road
London SW7 2BZ
Tel: 020 7823 9911

Japan Embassy
101–104 Piccadilly
London W1 J 7JT
www.embjapan.org.uk
Email: info@embjapan.org.uk
Tel: 020 7465 6500

Jordan Embassy
6 Upper Phillimore Gardens
London W8 7HB
www.jordanembassyuk.org
Ministry of Tourism website:
www.mota.gov.jo
Email: info@jordanembassy.uk.org
Tel: 020 7937 3685

Kazakhstan Embassy
33 Thurloe Square
London SW7 2SD
www.kazakhstan-embassy.org.uk
Email: kazak@imtr.net
Tel: 020 7581 4646
Visa Information Tel: 09065 508
978 (calls cost £1 per minute)

Kenya High Commission
45 Portland Place
London W1B 1AS
www.kenyahighcommission.com
Email: info@kenyahighcommission.
com
Tel: 020 7636 2371

Embassy of **Kenya**
2249 R Street, NW
Washington DC 20008
www.kenyaembassy.com/
Email: consular@kenyaembassy.com
Tel: 001 202 387 6101
Consulates in Los Angeles and
New York.

Kiribati
No national representation in the UK. Enquiries should be made directly to the President's office.
Office of the President
PO Box 68
Bairiki
Tarawa
Kiribati

Korea (South)
Embassy of the Republic of Korea
60 Buckingham Gate
London SW1E 6AJ
www.visitkorea.or.kr
Tel: 020 7227 5500
Consular Section Tel: 020 7227 5505

Korea (North)
Embassy of the Democratic People's Republic of Korea
73 Gunnersbury Avenue
Ealing
London W5 4LP
Tel: 020 8992 4965

Kuwait Embassy
2 Albert Gate
London SW1X 7JU
Tel: 020 7590 3400
Kuwait Information Centre:
Hyde Park House
60A Knightsbridge
London SW1X 7JX
www.kuwaitinfo.org.uk
Email: kuwait@dircon.co.uk
Tel: 020 7235 1787

Kyrgyz Republic (Kyrgyzstan)
Embassy
Ascot House
119 Crawford Street
London W1U 6BJ
www.kyrgyz-embassy.org.uk
Email: embassy@kyrgyz-embassy.org.uk
Tel: 020 7935 1462

Laos
No national representation in the UK.
Enquiries should be made to the Embassy in Paris.
Embassy of the Lao People's Democratic Republic
74 Avenue Raymond-Poincaré
75116 Paris
www.laoembassy.com
Tel: 00 33 1 45 53 02 98

Latvia Embassy
45 Nottingham Place
London W1U 5LR
www.latviatourism.lv
Email: embassy@embassyoflatvia.co.uk
Tel: 020 7312 0040

Lebanon Embassy
15 Palace Gardens Mews
London W8 4RB
www.lebanon-tourism.gov.lb
Tel: 020 7727 6696
Consular Section (Visas): 020 7229 7265

Lesotho
A kingdom and developing country completely surrounded by South Africa.
High Commission
7 Chesham Place
Belgravia
London SW1 8HN
Email: lhc@lesotholondon.org.uk
Tel: 020 7235 5686

Liberia Embassy
2 Pembridge Place
London W2 4XB
Tel: 020 7221 1036

Libya
Libyan People's Bureau
61–62 Ennismore Gardens
London SW7 1NH
Tel: 020 7589 6120

Liechtenstein
Embassy of Switzerland
16/18 Montagu Place
London W1H 2BQ
www.liechtenstein.li/lisite/html/
liechtenstein/index.html.en
Email: swissembassy@lon.rep.
admin.ch
Tel: 020 7616 6000

Lithuania Embassy
84 Gloucester Place
London W1U 6AU
www.urm.lt/full_e.php
Email: chancery@lithuanian
embassy.co.uk
Tel: 020 7486 6401
Visa Section Tel: 020 7486 6404

Luxembourg Embassy
27 Wilton Crescent
London SW1X 8SD
Tel: 020 7235 6961

Macau
A Special Administrative Region
of China
Embassy of China
49–51 Portland Place
London W1N 4JL
www.macau.gov.mo
Tel: 020 7636 9375

Macedonia Embassy
5th Floor
25 James Street
London W1U 1DU
Email: mkuk@btinternet.com
Tel: 020 7935 3842

Madagascar
No national representation in the
UK. Enquiries should be made to
the Embassy in Paris.
Embassy of the Republic of
Madagascar
4 Avenue Raphael
75016 Paris
France
www.embassy.org/madagascar/
Tel: 00 33 1 45 04 62 11

Malawi High Commission
33 Grosvenor Street
London W1K 4QT
Tel: 020 7491 4172

Malaysia High Commission
45 Belgrave Square
London SW1X 8QT
www.tourism.gov.my
Email: mwlondon@btinternet.
com
Tel: 020 7235 8033

Maldives High Commission
22 Nottingham Place
London W1M 3FB
www.visitmaldives.com
Email: maldives.high.commission@
virgin.net
Tel: 020 7224 2135

Mali
No national representation in the
UK. Enquiries should be made to
the Embassy in Brussels.
Embassy of the Republic of Mali
Avenue Molière 487
1050 Brussels
Belgium
www.maliembassy-usa.org
Tel: 00 32 2 345 7432

Malta High Commission
Malta House
36–38 Piccadilly
London W1V 0PQ
Tourism website: www.visitmalta.
com
Email: info@visitmalta.com
Tel: 020 7292 4800

Marshall Islands
No national representation in the
UK
www.rmiembassyus.org/

Mauritania Embassy
8 Carlos Place
Mayfair
London W1K 3AS
www.mauritaniembassy-usa.org
Email: ambarimlon@yahoo.com
Tel: 020 7478 9323

Mauritius High Commission
32 Elvaston Place
London SW7 5NW
www.mauritius.net
Email: londonmhc@btinternet.com
Tel: 020 7581 0294

Mexico Embassy
42 Hertford Street
Mayfair
London W1J 7JR
www.embamex.co.uk
Email: mexuk@easynet.co.uk
Tel: 020 7499 8586
Consular Section (Visa Office):
8 Halkin Street
London SW1X 7DW
Tel: 020 7235 6393

Micronesia
No national representation in the
UK. Enquiries may be made to
the Fiji High Commission in
London.
www.visit-fsm.org/

Moldova
No national representation in the
UK. Enquiries should be made to
the Embassy in Brussels.
Embassy of the Republic of
Moldova
Rue de Tenbosch 54
Brussels 1050
Belgium
Tel: 00 32 2 732 9300

Monaco Consulate General
4 Cromwell Place
London SW7 2JE
www.monaco.gouv.mc
Tel: 020 7225 2679
Consulates also in Edinburgh,
Birmingham, Manchester.

Mongolia Embassy
7 Kensington Court
London W8 5DL
www.embassyofmongolia.co.uk
www.mongoliatourism.gov.mn/
Email: office@embassyofmongolia.
co.uk
Tel: 020 7937 0150

Montserrat
A British Overseas Territory and
part of the British West Indies.
Monstserrat Government UK
Office
Lauderdale House
30B Wimpole Street
London W1G 8YB
Tel: 020 7224 5226

Morocco Embassy
49 Queen's Gate Gardens
London SW7 5NE
Tel: 020 7581 5001
www.mincom.gov.ma
www.visitmorocco.com
Email: mail@sifamaldn.org

Mozambique High Commission
21 Fitzroy Square
London W1T 6EL
Email: Mozalon@compuserve.com
Tel: 020 7383 3800

Myanmar (Burma) Embassy
19A Charles Street
London W1J 5DX
www.myanmars.net/mtt
Tel: 020 7499 8841
Visa Information Tel: 0906 550
8924
(calls cost £1 per minute)

Namibia High Commission
6 Chandos Street
London W1G 9LU
Email: info@namibiatourism.co.uk
www.namibiatourism.co.uk
Tel: 020 7636 2924

Nauru Honorary Consulate
Romshed Courtyard
Underriver
Near Sevenoaks
Kent TN15 0SD
www.nauruembassy.org/usa.html
Email: nauru@weald.co.uk
Tel: 01732 746061

Nepal Embassy
12A Kensington Palace Gardens
London W8 4QU
www.nepembassy.org.uk and

www.welcomenepal.com
Email: info@nepembassy.org.uk
Tel: 020 7229 1594

The Netherlands (Holland)
Embassy
38 Hyde Park Gate
London SW7 5DP
www.netherlands-embassy.org.uk/
Email: London@netherlands
embassy.org.uk
Tel: 0870 162 0856

Netherlands Antilles
Comprising the Caribbean islands
of Curaçao, Bonaire.
Saba, Sint Eustatius and Sint
Maarten.
Represented by the Embassy of
the Netherlands.
www.netherlandsantilles.com/

New Caledonia
A French Overseas Territory
represented by the Embassy of
France.
Travel information:
South Pacific
Tourism Organisation
PO Box 13119
Suva, Fiji
www.spto.org or
www.tcsp.com
Email: info@spto.org
Tel: 00 679 330 4177

New Zealand High Commission
New Zealand House
80 Haymarket
London SW1Y 4TQ
www.nzembassy.com
Email: nzembassy@newzealandhc.
org.uk
Tel: 020 7930 8422 (not visa
information)
Visa Information Tel: 09069 100
100 (calls cost £1 per minute)

Nicaragua Embassy
Suite 31
Vicarage House
58 Kensington Church Street
London W8 4DB

http://freespace.virgin.net/emb.
ofnicaragua
Email: emb.ofnicaragua@virgin.net
Tel: 020 7938 2373

Niger
No national representation in the
UK. Enquiries should be made to
the Embassy in Paris.
Embassy of the Republic of Niger
154 rue du Longchamp
75116 Paris
France
Tel: 00 33 1 45 04 80 60

Nigeria High Commission
9 Northumberland Avenue
London WC2N 5BX
www.nigeriahighcommissionuk.com
Email: enquiry@nigeriahigh
commissionuk.com
Tel: 020 7839 1244
Consular Section:
56 Fleet Street
London EC4Y 1BT
Tel: 020 7353 3776

Niue
Travel Information:
South Pacific Tourism
Organisation
PO Box 13119
Suva, Fiji
www.spto.org or
www.tcsp.com
Email: info@spto.org
Tel: 00 679 330 4177

Norway Embassy
25 Belgrave Square
London SW1X 8QD
www.norway.org.uk
Email: emb.london@mfa.no
Consular Section:
Email: Konsulat.london@mfa.no
Tel: 020 7591 5500
Consulate-General
86 George Street
Edinburgh
EH2 3BU
Tel: 0131 226 5701

Oman Embassy
167 Queen's Gate
London SW7 5HE
www.omantourism.gov.om
Email: omanembassy@fsnt.com
Tel: 020 7225 0001
Visa Information Tel: 0906 550
8964 (calls cost £1 per minute)

Pakistan High Commission
35–36 Lowndes Square
London SW1X 9JN
www.pakmission-uk.gov.pk
Email: tourism@isb.comsats.net.pk
Tel: 020 7664 9200

Palau
No national representation in the
UK. Enquiries should be made to
the Honorary Consul in the
Netherlands or to the Palau
Embassy in Washington DC.
Honorary Consul General
Kennemerstraatweg 51
1851 BA Heiloo
The Netherlands
Fax: 00 31 72 5339 539
www.visit-palau.com/
Email: apotheker@heylo.nl
Embassy of the Republic of Palau
1800 K St NW #714
Washington DC 20006
www.palauembassy.com
Email: info@palauembassy.com
Tel: 001 202 452 6814

Panama Embassy
Panama House
40 Hertford Street
London W1J 7SH
www.panaconsul.com
Tel: 020 7409 2255 (Consular
Section)

Papua New Guinea High
Commission
14 Waterloo Place
London SW1Y 4AR
Email: kduldn@compuserve.
com
Tel: 020 7930 0922

Paraguay Embassy
Third Floor
344 Kensington High Street
London W14 8NS
www.senatur.gov.py
Email: embapar@londrespy.
freeserve.co.uk
Tel: 020 7610 4180

Peru Embassy
52 Sloane Street
London SW1X 9SP
www.peruembassy-uk.com
Email: postmaster@peruembassy
-uk.com
Tel: 020 7235 1917
Consular Section (Visas)
Tel: 020 7838 9223
Email: consulate@peruembassy-uk.
com

Philippines Embassy
9A Palace Green
London W8 4QE
www.philemb.co.uk
www.wowphilippines.com.ph
Email: embassy@philemb.co.uk
Tel: 020 7937 1600

Poland Embassy
47 Portland Place
London W1B 1JH
Tel: 0870 774 2700
Email: polishembassy@polish
embassy.org.uk

Consulate-General
73 New Cavendish Street
London W1W 6LS
Tel: 020 7580 0476
www.polishembassy.org.uk
www.pnto.dial.pipex.com/index_
flash.shtml
Email: kgrp.londyn@btclick.com

Portugal Embassy
11 Belgrave Square
London SW1X 8PP
Tel: 020 7235 5331
Email: London@portembassy.co.uk
Consulate-General
Silver City House
62 Brompton Road

London SW3 1BJ
Tel: 020 7581 8722
Visa Information Tel: 0906 550
8948
(calls cost £1 per minute)
Email: mail@cglon.dgaccp.pt
www.portugalinsite.pt

Qatar Embassy
1 South Audley Street
London W1K 1NB
Tel: 020 7493 2200
British Council website:
www.britishcouncil.org/qatar/
index.htm

Romania Embassy
Arundel House
4 Palace Green
London W8 4QD
Tel: 020 7937 9666
Email: roemb@copperstream.co.uk
Ministry of Tourism website:
www.mtromania.ro
Consulates also in Los Angeles
and Chicago.

Russian Federation Embassy
13 Kensington Palace Gardens
London W8 4QX
Tel: 020 7229 2666
Email: office@rusemblon.org
Consular Section:
5 Kensington Palace Gardens
London W8 4QP
Tel: 020 7229 8027
Visa Information Tel: 09065 508
960 (calls cost £1 per minute)
www.intourist.co.uk

Rwanda Embassy
Uganda House
58–59 Trafalgar Square
London WC2N 5DX
www.ambarwanda.org.uk and
www.visitrwanda.gov.rw
Email: uk@ambarwanda.org.uk
Tel: 020 7930 2570

Saint Christopher and Nevis (St
Kitts & Nevis) High Commission
2nd Floor
10 Kensington Court

London W8 5DL
www.stkittsnevis.org
Email: sknhighcomm@aol.com
Tel: 020 7460 6500

Saint Lucia High Commission
1 Collingham Gardens
South Kensington
London SW5 0HW
www.stlucia.org
Tel: 020 7370 7123

Saint Vincent and the Grenadines
High Commission
10 Kensington Court
London W8 5DL
Email:
svghighcom@clara.co.uk.net
Tel: 020 7565 2874

Samoa
No national representation in the
UK. Enquiries should be made to
the High Commission in Brussels.
High Commission for the Inde-
pendent State of Samoa
Avenue Franklin D Roosevelt 123
1050 Brussels
Belgium
Tel: 00 32 2 660 84 54

San Marino
No national representation in
the UK.
State Tourism Office:
www.visitsan
marino.com
Email: statoturismo@omnway.sm

São Tomé and Principe
No national representation in the
UK. Enquiries should be made to
the Embassy in Brussels.
Embassy of the Democratic Repu-
blic of São Tomé and Principe
Square Montgomery
175 Avenue de Tervuren
1150 Brussels
Belgium
Tel: 00 322 734 8966

Saudi Arabia Embassy
30 Charles Street
Mayfair
London W1J 5DZ
www.saudiembassy.org.uk/
Tel: 020 7917 3000

Senegal Embassy
39 Marloes Road
London W8 6LA
www.senegalembassy.co.uk
Tel: 020 7937 7237

Serbia and Montenegro
Embassy
28 Belgrave Square
London SW1X 8QB
www.yugoslavembassy.org.uk
Email:
londre@jugisek.demon.co.uk
Tel: 020 7235 9049
Serbia: www.serbia-tourism.org
Montenegro: www.mturizma.cg.yu

Seychelles High Commission
2nd Floor, Eros House
111 Baker Street
London W1U 6RR
Tel: 020 7224 1660
Seychelles Tourist Office
36 Southwark Bridge Road
London SE1 9EU
www.aspureasitgets.com
Email: seychelles@hillsbalfour.com
Tel: 020 7202 6363

Sierra Leone High Commission
Oxford Circus House
245 Oxford Street
London W1D 2LX
www.slhc-uk.org.uk
Email: info@slhc-uk.org.uk
Tel: 020 7287 9884

Singapore High Commission
9 Wilton Crescent
Belgravia
London SW1X 8SP
www.mfa.gov.sg/london/
Email: info@singaporehc.org.uk
Tel: 020 7235 8315

Slovak Republic (Slovakia)
Embassy
25 Kensington Palace Gardens
London W8 4QY
www.slovakembassy.co.uk
Email: mail@slovakembassy.co.uk
Tel: 020 7313 6470

Slovenia Embassy
10 Little College Street
London SW1P 3SH
Tel: 020 7222 5400
Email: VLO@mzz-dkp.gov.si (not
for visa enquiries)
Slovenian Tourist Office
Email: info@slovenia-tourism.si
Tel: 0870 225 5305

Solomon Islands
No national representation in the
UK Enquiries should be made to the
High Commission in Brussels. High
Commission of the Solomon Islands
Avenue Edouard Lacombert
1040 Brussels
Belgium
Email:
siembassy@compuserve.com
Tel: 00 322 732 7085

Somalia
No national representation in the
UK. The Somali Embassy in
Washington closed in May 1991.
Embassy of Somalia
26 rue Dumont d'Urville
75116 Paris
France

South Africa High Commission
South Africa House
Trafalgar Square
London WC2N 5DP
www.southafricahouse.com
Email: general@southafricahouse.
com
Tel: 020 7451 7299

Spain Embassy
39 Chesham Place
London SW1X 8SB
Tel: 020 7235 5555

Consular Section:
20 Draycott Place
London SW3 2RZ
Tel: 020 7589 8989
www.mae.es and www.mir.es

Sri Lanka High Commission
13 Hyde Park Gardens
London W2 2LU
www.slhclondon.org/
Email: mail@slhc.globalnet.co.uk
Tel: 020 7262 1841

Sudan Embassy
3 Cleveland Row
St James's
London SW1A 1DD
www.sudan-embassy.co.uk
Tel: 020 7839 8080

Surinam
No national representation in
the UK. Enquiries should be
made to the Embassy in The
Hague.
Embassy of the Republic of
Surinam
Alexander Gogelweg 2
The Hague
2517JH
The Netherlands
Tel: 0070 365 0844

Swaziland High Commission
20 Buckingham Gate
London SW1E 6LB
www.swaziland.org.uk
Tel: 020 7630 6611

Sweden Embassy
11 Montagu Place
London W1H 2AL
www.swedish-embassy.org.uk/
Tel: 020 7917 6400

Switzerland Embassy
16/18 Montagu Place
London W1H 2BQ
www.swissembassy.org.uk
Email: swissembassy@lon.rep.
admin.ch
Tel: 020 7616 6000

Travel information:
Switzerland Tourism
Swiss Centre
10 Wardour Street
London W1D 6QF
www.myswitzerland.com
Tel: 020 7292 1550:
Freephone: 00800 100 200 30

Syria Embassy
8 Belgrave Square
London SW1X 8PH
Tel: 020 7245 9012
Visa Information Tel: 09065 508
935
(calls cost 60p per minute)

Tahiti
Part of French Polynesia, a French
Overseas Territory represented by
the Embassy of France.
Travel information:
South Pacific Tourism
Organisation
PO Box 13119
Suva, Fiji
www.spto.org or
www.tcsp.com
Email: info@spto.org
Tel: 00 679 330 4177

Taiwan
Taipei Representative Office
50 Grosvenor Gardens
London SW1W 0EB
www.gio.gov.tw/
Email: tro@netcomuk.co.uk
Tel: 020 7396 9152

Tajikistan
There is no national representa-
tion in the UK.
Travellers can apply for a visa at
the Russian Embassy in London
or at the Tajik Embassy in Berlin.
Tel: 00 49 30 34 79 300
Travel Information:
State National Tourism Company
Email: gafarov@cada.tajik.net
Tel: 00 992 23 14 01

Tanzania High Commission
43 Hertford Street
London W1J 7DB
www.tanzania-online.gov.uk
Email: balozi@tanzania-online.
gov.uk
Tel: 020 7499 8951

Thailand Embassy
29–30 Queen's Gate
London SW7 5JB
www.thaiinuk.com/thaiembassy.html
Email: thaiduto@btinternet.com
Tel: 020 7589 2944

Togo
No national representation in the
UK. Enquiries should be made to
the Embassy in Paris.
Embassy of the Republic of Togo
8 Rue Alfred-Roll
75017 Paris
France
www.republicoftogo.com/fr/home.
asp
Tel: 00 33 1 43 80 12 13

Tonga High Commission
36 Molyneux Street
London W1H 5BQ
www.tongatapu.net.to/ and
www.vacations.tvb.gov.to/
Email: fetu@btinternet.com
Tel: 020 7724 5828

Trinidad and Tobago High
Commission
42 Belgrave Square
London SW1X 8NT
www.visittnt.com/ and
www.gov.tt/
Email: tthc.info@virgin.net
Tel: 020 7245 9351

Tunisia Embassy
29 Prince's Gate
London SW7 1QG
Tel: 020 7584 8117

Tourism Office:
77A Wigmore Street
London W1U 1QF
Tel: 020 7224 5561

Turkey Embassy
43 Belgrave Square
London SW1X 8PA
www.turkishembassy-london.com
Email: turkish.embassy@virgin.net
Tel: 020 7393 0202
Consulate-General (Visa Office):
Rutland Lodge
Rutland Gardens
Knightsbridge
London SW7 1BW
www.tourist-offices.org.uk/turkey
Email: trcons@globalnet.co.uk
Tel: 020 7589 0949
Visa Information Tel: 09068 347
348 (calls cost £1 per minute)

Turkmenistan Embassy
2nd Floor South
St George's House
14–17 Wells Street
London W1T 3PD
www.turkmenistanembassy.org
Tel: 020 7255 1071

Turks and Caicos
A British Overseas Territory
www.turksandcaicostourism.com

Tuvalu Ministry of Tourism
Email: mttc@tuvalu.tv
Travel Information:
South Pacific Tourism
Organisation
PO Box 13119
Suva, Fiji
www.spto.org or www.tcsp.com
Email: info@spto.org
Tel: 00 679 330 4177

Uganda High Commission
58–59 Trafalgar Square
London WC2N 5DX
www.ugandaembassy.com
Tel: 020 7839 5783

Ukraine Embassy
60 Holland Park
London W11 3SJ
Consular & Visa Section:
Ground Floor
78 Kensington Park Road
London W11 2PL

www.ukremb.org.uk
Tel: 020 7243 8923
Ukrainian Consulate General
8 Windsor Street
Edinburgh EH7 5JR

United Arab Emirates Embassy
30 Prince's Gate
London SW7 1PT
Email: information@uaeembassy
uk.net
Tel: 020 7589 3434

United States of America
Embassy
24 Grosvenor Square
London W1A 1AE
www.usembassy.org.uk
Tel: 020 7499 9000
Recorded Visa Information Tel:
09068 200 290 (calls cost 60p
per minute)
Operator Service Visa
Information Tel: 09055 444 546
(calls cost £1.30 per minute)

Uruguay Embassy
2nd Floor
140 Brompton Road
London SW3 1HY
www.embassy.org/uruguay/
Email: emb@urubri.demon.
co.uk
Tel: 020 7589 8735

Uzbekistan Embassy
41 Holland Park
London W11 3RP
www.uzbekistanembassy.uk.net/
Email: info@uzbekistanembassy.
uk.net
Tel: 020 7229 7679

Vanuatu (formerly the New
Hebrides)
High Commission
C/o Department for Foreign
Affairs
Port Vita
Vanuatu
National Tourism Office of
Vanuatu
PO Box 209

Port Vila
Vanuatu
Email: info@tourism.vu
Tel: 00 678 22515

South Pacific Tourism
Organisation
PO Box 13119
Suva, Fiji
www.spto.org or www.tcsp.com
Email: info@spto.org
Tel: 00 679 330 4177

Vatican City Apostolic Nunciature
(No travel or tourism information)
54 Parkside
London SW19 5NE
Email: nuntius@globalnet.co.uk
Tel: 020 8946 1410

Venezuela Embassy
1 Cromwell Road
London SW7 2HW
Consular Section (Visa Office)
56 Grafton Way
London W1P 5LB
www.venezlon.demon.co.uk
Email: venezlon@venezlon.demon.
co.uk
Tel: 020 7584 4206

Vietnam Embassy
12–14 Victoria Road
London W8 5RD
www.vietnamembassy.org.uk
Email: consular@vietnamembassy.
org.uk
Tel: 020 7937 3222 (Consular
Section)

Yemen Embassy
57 Cromwell Road
London SW7 2ED
www.yemenembassy.org.uk
Email: info@yemenembassy.org.uk
Tel: 020 7584 6607

Zambia High Commission
2 Palace Gate
Kensington
London W8 5NG
www.zhcl.org.uk and
www.zambiatourism.com
Tel: 020 7589 6655

Zimbabwe High Commission
429 Strand
London WC2R 0JR
Tel: 020 7836 7755
www.zimbabwetourism.co.zw
Email: zimlondon@callnetuk.com

Visa Services Agencies

Applying for visas to visit some
countries can be time-consuming
and expensive, especially if you do
not live in London or a city that
has a consulate that can issue visas
for the country you intend to visit.
You can spend hours queuing to
make an application in person and
then find you must return another
day to collect your stamped passport. Visa service agencies are businesses that handle visa applications
and deal with the embassies on
your behalf. They provide a one-
stop-shop facility which could save
you time and energy when you
need visas for several countries for
a trip or if you are organizing
travel for a group. They make a
charge for administration, in addition to any embassy visa fees. In
some instances, the visa service can
help you obtain a visa support
document, usually an invitation or
confirmation of your travel
arrangements.

Andrews Travel House
23 Pembridge Square
London W2 4DR
www.andrews-consulting.co.uk
Tel: 020 7727 2838
Visa services covering 55 countries,
but specializing in visas and travel
support documents for visits to
Russia, Ukraine, Kazakhstan and
the other former states of the
Soviet Union, China, India,
Vietnam and Saudi Arabia. This
is the visa service used by the
staff of the British Council.

Asia Travel Group
Riverside House
160 High Street
Huntingdon
Cambs PE29 3TF
www.asia.co.uk
Email: visas@asla-select.co.uk
Tel: 01480 433783
Specialists in obtaining visas and
support documents for UK citizens
to visit Russia, Ukraine and other
states of the former Soviet Union.

Direct Passport & Visa Company
12 Chepstow Road
London W2 5BD
www.direct-visa.com/
Email: sales@russian-visa.co.uk
Tel: 020 7229 1412
Visa processing including 24-hour
service to obtain a Russian visa.

Thames Consular Services Ltd
Unit 4 The Courtyard
Swan Centre
Fishers Lane
London W4 1RX
www.thamesconsular.com
Tel: 020 8995 2492
Central London Office:
3rd Floor
35 Piccadilly
London W1J 0DW
Tel: 020 7494 4957
The company can provide infor-
mation and guidelines about visa
conditions for over 180 countries
and the website allows you to
download visa application forms
for over sixty countries.

Travcour (UK)
Tempo House
15 Falcon Road
Battersea
London SW11 2PJ
www.travcour.com
Tel: 020 7223 5295
The website contains information
about visa requirements for most
countries and you can download
the relevant application forms.

TVS The Visa Service Ltd
2 Northdown Street
Kings Cross
London N1 9BG
www.visaservice.co.uk
Email: info@visaservice.co.uk
Tel: 020 7833 2709
Long-established London visa and passport processing agency, now merged with Zierer Visa Service, the largest visa agency in the USA. This is the visa service recommended to participants in Charity Challenge overseas events.

Indian Visa 123
www.indianvisa123.co.uk
Email: info@indianvisa123.co.uk
Indian tourist visas for British citizens in under five days. compared with 15 days for postal applications direct to the Indian High Commission.

Magic Carpet Travel Ltd
Visas for tourist visits to Iran. The visa allows you to stay in Iran for up to 30 days at the discretion of the Iranian Foreign Ministry. Magic Carpet processes your application through its office in Tehran and you receive a reference number which enables you to get your passport stamped at the Iranian Consulate. The Iranian Foreign Ministry does not allow American passport holders to travel to Iran independently. US citizens must travel on escorted tours, as part of a tour group or on a tailor-made tour. An exact itinerary, to which you must adhere, is compulsory and all travel and accommodation must be arranged through Magic Carpet, including internal flights, car hire and guides. In the US, Iranian visas are dealt with by the Iranian Interest section of the Pakistani Embassy, 2209 Wisconsin Avenue, Washington DC; see the Iranian government's website at www.daftar.org for further information and online application forms.

WorkOz (UK)
Office address:
WorkOz Visa Section
16 Myrtle Tree Crescent
Sand Bay
Kewstoke
Weston Super Mare
BS22 9UL
www.australian-travel-visa.co.uk/
Email: info@workoz.com
Tel: 0870 240 7367
Travellers to Australia other than Australian or New Zealand citizens are required to have a visa, either stamped in the passport or in the form of an Electronic Travel Authority which can be obtained online from the Australian High Commission. A tourist visa is valid for three months but does not allow you to work even as a volunteer. To travel and work in Australia you will need a work visa. You can apply online for the Electronic Working Holiday Maker Visa and it will be granted within seven days and emailed straight to your inbox without having to send away your passport. You can apply for an Electronic Working Holiday Maker Visa if you meet the following criteria: you need to be aged between 18 and 30 years and 11 months; and you must be a citizen of Canada, Germany, Great Britain, Japan, Malta, Netherlands, Republic of Ireland, Norway, Denmark, Sweden or Republic of Korea. The visa is valid for 12 months from the first day you enter Australia.

Passport Visa Express
1911 North Fort Myer Drive
Suite 503
Arlington

VA 22209
www.passportvisaexpress.com
Email: info@passportvisaexpress.com
Tel: 888 596 6028
Passport Visa Express specializes in obtaining travel visas for US Citizens and foreign nationals travelling internationally to any country in the world. They have offices in the heart of Washington DC, San Francisco and Chicago, only minutes away from all of the foreign embassies and consulates. Passport Visa Express works directly with each embassy assisting you in expediting your visa application and can provide a same-day service in urgent cases. Applications can made online.

Travel Document Systems
925 15th Street NW
Suite 300
Washington DC 20005
www.traveldocs.com
Email: support@traveldocs.com
also
1 Embarcadero Center
Suite 500
San Francisco
CA 94111
Email: sfo@traveldocs.com
TDS is your 'one-stop shop' for visa and passport processing. They provide expedited visa processing for US citizens for countries which require an entry visa, and can also assist Canadians and US permanent residents of other nationalities with visas for most countries.

TDS specializes in travel that involves visas for more than one country. Their offices are located in both Washington DC and San Francisco just steps away from the embassies, consulates and the US Passport Agency.

UK Representation Abroad

The Foreign & Commonwealth Office (FCO) Country Advice
www.fco.gov.uk/
The FCO website has addresses, phone numbers and emails for all the British diplomatic missions around the world, British embassies, high commissions and consulates and you should make a note of the ones relevant to your plans. They could be important in an emergency or if you get seriously stuck. There is a British embassy in just about every capital city and there are British consulates in other major business cities in some countries.

Do remember that the main function of a British embassy is to be the eyes and ears of the British Government in another capital city. It looks after the interests of the United Kingdom in the host country for political and trade purposes, and is a point of contact for British people living or staying in the country. An embassy or consulate is not a tourist office and cannot provide help for travellers except in an emergency such as loss of a passport, crime, a serious security problem or an accident or natural disaster. The Foreign & Commonwealth Office recommends that in some countries visitors and travellers should report their presence to the British embassy. This is particularly the case where there is political unrest or a threat of natural disaster. It is certainly wise for leaders of groups to inform the British embassy about their plans especially if they are venturing into remote areas of a country. An email or phone call ahead of time could be valuable for getting the very latest alerts and advice about anything that could affect your plans. But remember, you should never consider the presence of British officials in a country as any substitute for adequate travel insurance to cover your journey and activities.

Banking Hours Worldwide

Bank opening hours vary around the world, so it's worth checking with the national tourist office of each country that you intend to visit before you leave home.

Don't forget to check for dates of national holidays because you can be sure the banks will be closed, except possibly at the airports. There is a country-by-country list of banking hours in the book, *Your Passport to Safer Travel*, published by Thomas Cook Publishing (Tel: 01733 416477).

With the expansion of the cash machine (ATM) network, getting hold of local currency is less of a problem than it used to be, and taking money out with a cash card is generally more economical than incurring charges for exchanging travellers' cheques at a bank counter. Visa has a website that allows you to search for the location of cash machines (ATMs) compatible with Visa cards http://visaatm.infonow.net/bin/find Now?CLIENT_ID=VISA&RGION

Worldwide Weather Information

The climate and season weather systems can have a bearing on decisions about when and where to go. For example, tornadoes, monsoons, typhoons, hurricanes and the like tend to be seasonal and affect some parts of the world more than others. Your early planning should include some research about the weather. This is a matter of taking precautions to ensure you don't get caught out with predictable stormy conditions that could ruin your trip, but on the other hand you may be a brave soul who is up for chasing tornadoes or observing milder climatic phenomena as the theme and purpose for travel. There are numerous resources on the Internet to help you. Here is a selection:

The Met Office website has a comprehensive world weather section with five-day forecasts and reports of extreme conditions around the globe. www.met-office.gov.uk

The BBC has a weather website with maps and at least 5,000 forecasts from around the world which can be selected from a menu of world regions. Includes articles on weather features such as the monsoon, the greenhouse effect and climate data for various countries. www.bbc.co.uk/weather/

CNN.com has a comprehensive and searchable weather section including five-day forecasts from around the world. www.cnn.com/weather

Weather Underground has worldwide weather maps and conditions data on towns and cities within selected countries. www.wunderground.com

The Weather Channel operates several websites including weather.co.uk, weather.com and

weather.com/brasil which has weather reports and maps specifically for Latin America.
www.weather.com

Marine Weather is an online service of weather reports covering the world's oceans.
www.marineweather.com

The US National Hurricane Center has an authoritative website on hurricanes, cyclones and all other tropical storms, including printable weather-tracking maps and forecasts.
www.nhc.noaa.gov

Hurricanes2003.com is another website devoted to hurricanes, cyclones and tropical storms. It has updates, warnings and predicted storm-tracking maps.
www.hurricanes98.com

Russia's Weather Server provides detailed condition reports and forecasts for Russia, the Baltic states and neighbouring countries, from data provided by the Russian HydroMet Centre. Registered users get immediate updates to its six-day weather forecast.
http://meteo.infospace.ru

The South African Weather Service website has weather reports covering southern Africa, and a list of telephone numbers for regional forecast and information centres. Phone 082 162 within South Africa for the Weatherline and 082 233 9000 for forecasts longer than seven days.
www.weathersa.co.za

The Bureau of Meteorology website offers detailed weather reports for Australia. You can get a two-day forecast and severe weather warnings for the main population centres by dialling 1196 anywhere in Australia. There are also telephone service numbers listed on the website for more detailed reports for each state.
www.bom.gov.au

Australian Severe Weather is an online resource devoted to tornadoes and tropical cyclones, and includes links to storm-chasing tours.
http://australiasevereweather.com

The University of Hawaii provides hourly weather forecasts and surfing condition reports on its website, along with more general weather and climate reports for the Pacific Ocean.
www.hawaii.edu/news/locaweather

Thunderbolt Tours organize storm-chasing adventure tours in the USA and Australia.
www.thunderbolttours.com
Email: support@thunderbolttours.com

The **Weather Photography** website has stunning pictures of weather effects and tips on taking your own pictures of atmospheric phenomena.
www.weather-photography.com/index.php

Recommended Websites

Travel planning

There are several Internet-based services for planning and booking flights, but they are mainly concerned with scheduled airlines on international routes for holidays and business travel. They do not show the flights and fares of low-cost airlines, for example, and you will need to consult the websites of each company. You may still need the help of a travel industry professional to find alternatives and for details of internal flights within any country. Travel agents and tour operators have access to more extensive computerized air timetables.

A2A Travel/Travelocity
www.a2b.com/home/home.asp
Comprehensive search engine for flights by scheduled airlines.

Ebookers
www.ebookers.com
An online travel agent service.

Expedia
UK: www.expedia.co.uk
USA: www.expedia.com
Online travel agent, now also covering charter flights as well as scheduled airlines.

Lastminute.com
www.lastminute.com
Holiday-orientated online travel service.

Opodo
www.opodo.co.uk
A pan-European travel company which acts as an air ticket consolidator, owned by a consortium of nine airlines and Amadeus, a travel industry distribution service.

Environment Concerns and Global Issues for Travellers

British Trust for Conservation Volunteers
36 St Mary's Street
Wallingford
Oxfordshire OX10 0EU
www.btcv.org
Email: Information@btcv.org.uk
Tel: 01491 821 600

Climate Care
58 Church Way
Oxford OX4 4EF
www.climatecare.org
Email: mail@climatecare.org
Tel: 01865 777 770
An Oxford-based campaigning group on environmental issues with a section on travel.

Cross-Cultural Solutions
UK Information Office
PO Box 7127
Quorn
Loughborough LE12 8ZX
www.crossculturalsolutions.org/uk/infoforuk.cfm
Email: infouk@crosscultural solutions.org
Tel: 0845 458 2781/2782
Based in Leicestershire, Cross-Cultural Solutions provide assistance to anyone from the UK who is interested in volunteering overseas.

Earthwatch Europe
267 Banbury Road
Oxford OX2 7HT
www.earthwatch.org/europe
Email: info@earthwatch.org.uk
Tel: 01865 318838
Scientific exploration breaks, lasting from 3–7 days, in some of the most beautiful locations in the British Isles – and now in Cameroon – helping with vital environmental research.

Green Globe 21
Contact Office UK
1 Heritage Courtyard
Sadler Street
Wells BA5 2RR
Tel: 07768 977191
A worldwide travel business organization promoting environmental concerns in the travel market.
Green Globe 21
C/o CAST
Puerto Rico

www.cha-cast.com
Green Globe Asia Pacific
GPO Box 371
Canberra
ACT 2601
Australia
www.ggasiapacific.com.au

Green Volunteers
PO Box 23
Sandy
Bedfordshire SG19 2XE
www.greenvolunteers.org
Email: network@greenvolunteers.
org
Tel: 01767 262481

Pacific Asia Travel Association (PATA)
www.travelwithpata.com/
The Pacific Asia Travel
Association is a non-profit partnership of businesses and the
recognized authority on Pacific
Asia travel and tourism. It is an
advocate of balancing growth
with responsible conservation
measures.

Rainforest Alliance
www.rainforest-alliance.org
Campaigning for better recognition of environment-friendly
travel facilities, such as the Smart
Voyager project which gives
travellers an assurance that boat
operators in the Galapagos
islands meet the requirements of
care for the environment, wildlife
and the well-being of local
communities.

World Tourism Organization
www.world-tourism.org
A global forum for travel and
tourism issues and a practical
source of know-how, set up by
the United Nations to promote
the development of responsible,
sustainable tourism as a means of
improving the prosperity of
poorer nations and protecting the
environment and cultural heritage.

The Red Sea Sustainable Tourism Initiative (RSSTI)
www.rssti.org
One of the first tourism
programmes in the Middle East
to adopt the principles of
sustainable development. Egypt
is planning for thousands of
new hotel rooms to be built
in the next 15 years around
the Red Sea and Sinai Peninsula.
The RSSTI is encouraging
the tourist industry to be
environmentally and socially
responsible in their development
projects.

Eco Resorts Kenya
www.eco-resorts.com
A collection of articles and
reports that provide some inspirational background reading and
ideas on the issues and principles
of eco-tourism.

Jamaican Community-based Tourism
www.tpdco.org/community_
tourism.aso
Articles describing projects in
Jamaica to bring more economic
benefit to village communities
through encouraging visitors and
sustainable tourism.

General Interest

The BMC (British Mountaineering Council)
177–179 Burton Road
West Didsbury
Manchester M20 2BB
www.thebmc.co.uk
Email: office@thebmc.co.uk
Tel: 0870 010 4878

The British Sub Aqua Club
Telford's Quay
South Pier Road
Ellesmere Port
Cheshire CH65 4FL
www.bsac.com

Email: postmaster@bsac.com
Tel: 0151 350 6200

Journeywoman
www.journeywoman.com
Online magazine created especially
for women travellers.

Suzy Lamplugh Trust
www.suzylamplugh.org
A resource for personal safety
advice including an extensive
country-by-country directory,
World Wise.

Turkey Travel Planner
www.turkeytravelplanner.com
Tom Brosnahan's website of information about Turkey.

How to See the World
www.artoftravel.com
An e-book on budget travel
around the world.

Travel-Library.com
www.travel-library.com
An online collection of personal
travelogues and destination
information.

Organizations, Societies and Travel Clubs

**Association of Independent Tour
Operators**
www.aito.co.uk
Email: info@aito.co.uk
Tel: 020 8744 9280
AITO members are small and
medium-sized travel businesses
who are encouraged to raise
awareness among staff, suppliers
and customers of the importance
of responsible tourism. The AITO
website is full of inspirational
travel themes and destinations in
lesser-known parts of the world,
covering adventure travel, cultural
tours and outdoor events and you
can order brochures online. Many

of the featured tours and holidays
are unusual and are not available
from well-known high street
travel firms.

ABTA
www.abta.co.uk
Tel: 0901 201 5050 (calls charged
at 50p per minute) The UK's
main trade association for tour
operators and travel agents.

ATOL
Consumer Protection Group
Civil Aviation Authority
K3 CAA House
45–59 Kingsway
London WC2B 6TE
www.caa.co.uk/cpg/atol
The Air Travel Organisers'
Licensing scheme operated by
the Civil Aviation Authority
to protect the interests of
consumers who make air
travel bookings.

IATA
Central House
Lampton Road
Hounslow
Middlesex TW3 1HY
www.iata.org
Tel: 020 8607 6262
The international air transport
trade body.

Travel Trust Association
www.traveltrust.co.uk
Email: info@traveltrust.co.uk
Tel: 0870 889 0577
Promotes consumer protection by
operating a Trust Account backed
by a fidelity insurance, to protect
travellers' money paying for travel
arrangements.

WEXAS
45 Brompton Road
London SW3 1DE
www.wexas.com
Email: mship@wexas.com
Tel: 020 7589 3315

The renowned travel club founded in 1970 mainly for students and expeditionary travel, with over 35,000 members.

Youth Hostels Associations

When it comes to looking for accommodation on the cheap, youth hostels stand out and for many good reasons. They are safe, secure and generally run along the principles of environmental good practice. Hostelling International is the trading name of the international federation of youth hostel associations and is a source of information about where to stay all over the world. Membership of your national association qualifies you for an international card which allows you to stay at a youth hostel in most other countries for the same price as local members. The hostel movement has expanded from its European core to embrace the world and fulfil the expectations of today's young people who have more money, more free time and greater mobility than ever before.

Youth Hostels Association (YHA)

YHA (England and Wales) Ltd
Trevelyan House
Matlock
Derbyshire DE4 3YH
www.yha.org.uk/

Scottish Youth Hostels Association (SYHA)

SYHA National Office
7 Glebe Crescent
Stirling FK8 2JA
www.syha.org.uk
Email: info@syha.org.uk
Tel: 01786 891400
The YHA and SYHA are part of the largest network of budget accommodation in the world, and it is not limited to youth.

Membership is open to anyone living in Britain or the rest of the European Union.

Hostelling International

International Youth Hostel Federation
1st Floor, Fountain House
Parkway
Welwyn Garden City
Herts AL8 6JH
www.iyhf.org/openHome.sma
Tel: 01707 324170
The website of the International Youth Hostel Federation is a mine of information about hostels worldwide. There are over 4,000 hostels in sixty countries and you can now book your stay online. There is no age limit – people of all ages may use hostels in the course of their travels.

Adventure Women

15033 Kelly Canyon Road
Bozeman MT 59715
USA
www.adventurewomen.com
Email: advwomen@aol.com
Tel: 001 406 587 3883
Toll Free in USA: 1 800 804 8686
Unconventional expeditions including diving, overland travel and Antarctic voyages for women over 30.

Railway Travel

Thomas Cook Publishing

PO Box 227
Coningsby Road
Bretton
Peterborough PE3 8XX
www.thomascookpublishing.com
and
www.thomascooktimetables.com
Email: publishing-sales@thomas cook.com
Tel: 01733 416477

Publishers of a range of travel guides, but best known for the European and overseas railway timetables which are essential reading for train-based adventures. Thomas Cook also publish railway maps.

Trans-Siberian Railway
www.trans-siberia.com/
The official website of Russia's great railway, in English, with an introduction to the towns and cities on the route and tips for stop-overs to break the monster journey and explore a fascinating country.

India by Rail
www.eindiatourism.com/india-rail/
A website promoting travel through India by train.

Routes International
www.routesinternational.com/rail.htm
An extensive list of worldwide train-related links.

Rail Passes
Rail passes are very good value for touring and adventure travel as they allow greater flexibility than point-to-point return tickets and give you the freedom to explore branch lines off your main route. There are also privileges such as special discounts for travel-related services and accommodation. There are no longer any age limits, but travellers over 26 pay more than young people for their passes.

InterRail
www.interrailnet.com
InterRail is perhaps the best known rail freedom pass covering Europe except Albania and the former Soviet states, but including also Morocco and the whole of Turkey. The global InterRail pass gives you the freedom of the national rail networks in all 29 participating countries, except your own home country, for up to one month. Europe is divided into zones covering three or four neighbouring countries each and it is possible to buy a limited range InterRail pass for one or more linked zones. Eurostar and the cross-channel ferries have a pass-holder discount fare for the journey between England and France or Belgium. Supplements must be paid on premium high-speed trains in Europe including Thalys, TGV, ICE and Talgo, but Germany no longer charges extra for journeys on IC/EC express trains. Some privately-owned railways in Switzerland recognize InterRail and other passes for free travel.

Sleeping car and couchette charges are not included nor are seat reservations, which may be compulsory on long-distance routes such as main-line trains in Spain, express trains in Norway and Sweden and German *Nachtzuge* (night trains).

There's a bonus if you are heading for Greece: the InterRail pass allows free travel in deck class on ferries between Italy, Greece and Corfu. Full details are on the InterRail website at www.interrailnet.com or from the agents listed below.

Eurailpass
www.eurail.com
This is similar in validity to the InterRail pass but applies to first-class travel and is only available to residents of countries outside Europe. EurRail includes most supplements for high-speed premium trains.

EuroDomino
The EuroDomino pass allows unlimited travel on the national rail network of any one country for a set number of days, from three to eight, within a month, so could be very economical for multiple location tours.

Balkan Flexipass
Unlimited rail travel in Bulgaria, Greece, Macedonia, Romania, Serbia-Montenegro and Turkey for up to 15 days within a month.

Benelux Tourrail
Unlimited travel on the rail networks of Belgium, Luxembourg and the Netherlands for five days in a month.

ScanRail Pass
Unlimited second-class travel in Denmark, Finland, Norway and Sweden, with discounts on bus and ferry services, available for up to 21 consecutive days or as a flexi-pass allowing five or ten days travel within two months.
    Details of freedom travel tickets for rail and bus travel in individual countries are described in the Thomas Cook European Timetable.

Agents for InterRail and Other International Rail Freedom Passes

Rail Pass Direct
A division of Thomas Cook Publishing (address above)
www.railpassdirect.co.uk
Email: railpassdirect@thomascook.com
Tel: 01733 402001
InterRail passes, timetables and maps supplied by mail order or online purchase.

Rail Europe
178 Piccadilly
London W1V 0BA
www.raileurope.co.uk
Tel: 08705 848 848
InterRail, single-country freedom passes and other train tickets and planning advice from rail travel consultants in person. The office gets very busy in the summer and you can experience a long wait especially in the afternoons.

Ffestiniog Travel
Harbour Station
Porthmadog
Gwynedd LL49 9NF
www.festtravel.co.uk
Email: info@festtravel.demon.co.uk
Tel: 01766 512400
A small travel business specializing in railway holiday packages and individual tailor-made rail adventures, and a comprehensive rail ticket and reservation service. A member of AITO and the Association of European Rail Agents. ATOL protected.

Deutsche Bahn UK
Suite 6/8
The Sanctuary
23 Oakhill Grove
Surbiton KT6 6DU
Tel: 08702 435363

European Rail Ltd
Tavistock House North
Tavistock Square
London WC1H 3HR
www.europeanrail.com
Tel: 020 7387 0444

International Rail
Chase House
Gilbert Street
Ropley SO24 0BY
Hampshire
www.international-rail.com
Tel: 0870 751 5000

RailChoice
15 Colman House
Empire Square
High Street
London SE20 7EX
(visit by appointment only)
www.railchoice.co.uk
Email: sales@railchoice.co.uk
Tel: 020 8659 7300

Stephen Walker Travel
Assembly Rooms
Market Place
Boston PE21 6LY
Lincolnshire
Email: swtlincs@aol.com
Tel: 08707 466 400

Trainseurope Ltd
4 Station Approach
March
Cambridgeshire PE15 8SJ
www.trainseurope.co.uk
Tel: 0900 195 0101 (calls cost
60p per minute refundable on
booking)

Ultima Travel
424 Chester Road
Little Sutton
South Wirral CH66 3RB
Tel: 0151 339 6171

Forsyth Travel Library
Westchester 1
44 South Broadway
White Plains
New York 10601
www.forsyth.com

Bus/Coach Travel

In addition to organized bus tours
and commercial coach-based holidays, buses run virtually
anywhere that there is a road and
are often a cheaper alternative to
trains where they exist. Many
countries have long-distance buses
that are air-conditioned as well as
more basic regional and local
services on which local people
rely for their everyday needs.
Australia, for example, has a
range of long-distance routes and
very comfortable buses. Iran,
Turkey, Pakistan, Sri Lanka and
the former Yugoslavia have
extensive bus services that are
more efficient than trains. Chile,
Mexico and China are criss-crossed
by bus routes, and there are many
options for cross-border travel,
for example in India, Bangladesh,
Myanmar and Thailand with the
possibility of extensions to
Singapore and Malaysia. The
tourist offices and websites of
individual countries can provide
more information. This list is
necessarily selective and illustrates
some of the more off-beat possibilities in a few countries to get
you to think about bus travel as
part of your adventure.

Busabout Europe
www.busabout.com
A website containing details of
flexi-passes for unlimited travel
on long-distance bus routes in
Europe and north Africa.

Eurolines
www.eurolines.com/
The European network of
international coach routes.

National Express
www.nationalexpress.com/neh.cfm
The consortium of British
intercity bus/coach services, and
partner in Eurolines.

Bus Éireann
www.buseireann.ie/site/home/
Expressway long-distance coach
services link cities and towns in
Ireland. You can buy National
Tickets online and show the
driver your email print-out when
you get on.

Greyhound Bus Lines
www.greyhound.com/
The legendary long-distance bus service of America and Canada.

Green Tortoise Adventure Travel (US)
www.greentortoise.com
Email: tortoise@greentortoise.com
Cheap and cheerful bus travel across America and up and down the West Coast with routes into Mexico and Central America. The buses are basic but are fitted with bunks to sleep on during overnight journeys.

Buslines Australia
www.buslines.com.au/
Email: buslines@buslines.com.au

Bus Australia
www.busaustralia.com/links.html.nt
Email: ken@busaustralia.com
Online directories of bus services in Australia including timetables of interstate services, such as the Firefly Express between Sydney, Melbourne and Adelaide and special fares for backpackers on the Greyhound Pioneer service between Sydney and Cairns along the east coast. Australia's Greyhound company is distinct from the American company of the same name. An alternative long-distance bus company is McCafferty's, website www.mccaffertys.com.au.

The Blue Banana tour bus is a favourite among backpackers in northern Australia, operating out of Darwin.

New Zealand TravelPass
www.travelpass.co.nz/welcome.html
Email: res@travelpass.co.nz
New Zealand Travelpass offers flexible coach travel for independent travellers, using Newmans Coach Lines and high-quality InterCity Coachlines.

Magic Travellers Network (New Zealand)
www.magicbus.co.nz
Email: info@magicbus.co.nz
Coach network that includes pickups at backpacker hostels and access to New Zealand's national parks and centres of activity and wildlife.

The Baz Bus (South Africa)
www.bazbus.co.za
Email: info@bazbus.com
South Africa's backpacker bus service serving over forty towns and cities with drop-offs at hostels and no time limit on the validity of your ticket.

Directorio.com.mx
www.directorio.com.mx/autobuses/
Online directory of bus companies in Mexico.

Fez Bus (Turkey)
www.feztravel.com/thefezbus.asp
Email: feztravel@feztravel.com
Hop-on, hop-off bus network covering Turkey's main towns and cities with pick-ups and drop-offs at youth and backpacker hostel locations. Cheap travel-pass deals are available including the Turkish Delight Pass with an option of two nights sailing on a Gulet yacht.

Iran Seyr-o-Safar Bus Service
Tel: Tehran 8732535
Iran's train network is very basic but there are plenty of intercity coaches and you can get around the country relatively cheaply. Seyr-o-Safar is one of the bus operators available.

JR Highway Bus Service
www.seejapan.co.uk/ftransport.html
Japan's intercity bus routes are operated by several companies including JR, the Japanese Railway, and go overnight, which

can save on travel and accommodation costs.

Nor-way Bussekspress
www.nor-way.no
Email:
ruteinformasjon@norway.no
Intercity routes in Norway,
including the 720 between Bod,
Fauske and Narvik in northern
Norway, where the bus is carried
on a ferry across some fjords along
the route. International routes
include direct services between Oslo
and Berlin, Warsaw and Hamburg.

Passenger Carrying Freighters

Long-distance passenger ships are
out of fashion because of the
advances in air travel and are
restricted to luxury cruises and
routine ferries. There are a few
sailings between Europe and South
Africa and a very infrequent
transatlantic service operated by
Cunard. Some cruise lines will sell
a ticket for a point-to-point voyage
on a cruise ship a few hours
before sailing, rather than have a
cabin empty for the duration of
the scheduled cruise.

One of the more off-beat
adventure possibilities is to sail
the high seas on a cargo ship. It's
the no-frills alternative to
cruising. You don't have the
luxury of a fashionable cruise
liner and your ship will dock at a
commercial quayside with few of
the facilities of a passenger
terminal. The medical services will
not be up to the standards of
commercial passenger ships so
there may be health and age
restrictions. But you get to some
wonderful parts of the world and
the journey itself will be the
adventure as you share the
conditions and privations of the
people who run the ship. Paying
passengers on freighters are
treated as guests and usually dine
with the master or captain of the
ship, but on some you just muck
in with the crew at meal times.

Andrew Weir Shipping handles
bookings for cruises with Bank Line
(Round the World in 120 days –
monthly service with four ships).
St Helena Line Ltd (Portland
UK/Ascension/St Helena/South
Africa www.rms-st-helena.com)
and United Baltic Corporation
(Felixstowe/Continent /Finland).
Andrew Weir Shipping
Dexter House
2 Royal Mint Court
London EC3N 4XX
www.aws.co.uk/
Tel: 020 7265 0808

ABC Passenger Shipping Guide
Monthly list of companies that
offer freighter transport for
passengers.
Reed Travel Group
Dunstable
Beds LU5 4HB
Tel: 01582 600111
The Cruise People Ltd offers
cargo ship voyages from one
week to 126 days in duration,
and now represents almost 400
freighters carrying passengers
worldwide.
http://members.aol.com/CruiseAZ/
freighters.htm
Tel: 020 7723 2450

Canada Maritime (Trans-Atlantic
between UK/Continent &
Montreal)
UK Head Office:
North Kiln
Felaw Maltings
Felaw Street
Ipswich IP2 8HE
www.canmar.com
Tel: 01473 696680

North America Headquarters:
La Tour Xerox
Place Alexis Nihon
Suite 1150
3400 de Maisonneuve Boulevard
West
Montreal
Quebec
Canada
H3Z 3E7
Tel: 001 514 934 5133

Contship Containerlines
(Tilbury/Australia/NZ/USA/Tilbury)
Ipswich
Email: info@ips.contship.com
Tel: 01473 232000

DG & G Cruise & Ferry Guide
DG & G Travel Information
Dukeminster House
Church Street
Dunstable
Bedfordshire LU5 4HU
A quarterly listing of passenger
shipping services worldwide.

**Ford's Freighter Travel Guide &
Waterways of the World**
Ford's lists travel agents who
specialize in freighter travel.
19448 Londelius Street
Northridge CA 91324
USA
Tel: 001 818 701 7414

'Freighter'
Freighter Cruises
180 South Lake Avenue
335 Suite Pasadena
CA 91101
USA
Tel: 001 818 449 3106
A handbook of cargo passenger
services. They are also booking
agents for most lines.

Freighter Travel News
Monthly newsletter of the
Freighter Travel Club
3524 Harts Lake Road
Roy WA 98580
USA

Grimaldi (Adriatic to South
America and East Africa)
Via Marchese Campodisola 13
80133 Naples, Italy
www.grimaldi.napoli.it/
Email: switchboard@grimaldi.
napoli.it
Tel: 00 39 081 496111

Hamilton Shipping Ltd
Belfast
Email:
sales@hamiltonshipping.com
Tel: 028 90533 200

Lykes Lines (Trans-Atlantic US
Gulf/Med & US Gulf/South
America)
European Head Office
East Grinstead
Tel: 01342 336 336

P&O Nedlloyd Containers
(Tilbury/South Africa)
Northfleet Hope House
Site 41
Tilbury Docks
Tilbury
Essex RM18 7HX
Tel: 01375 812200

Safemarine (Tilbury/South Africa)
Pathfinder
PO Box 461
Southampton SO15 2ZE
www.safemariner.co.uk and
http://mysaf.safmarine.com
Email: pathfinder@safemariner.co.uk
Tel: 023 8084 3333

Strand Cruise Centre
Charing Cross Shopping
Concourse
Strand
London WC2N 4HZ
www.strandtravel.co.uk/strand
voyages/sv_freighter.asp
Email: voyages@strandtravel.co.uk
Tel: 020 7836 6363

TravLtips Cruise & Freighter Travel Association
http://travltips.com/
Email: info@travltips.com
The website includes freighter cruise listings, including round-the world trips. The Association also publishes a magazine about travel on cargo ships with sailing schedules and stories by freighter travellers. TravLtips also makes reservation arrangements for barges and tall ships.

Hitchhiking Organizations

Allostop
www.allostop.com
Email: allostop@mlink.net
Subscription-based and environment-friendly ride-sharing association that puts you in contact with drivers to share fuel costs on long journeys, and to cut down the number of motor vehicles on the road.

Allostop
4317 Rue Saint Denis
Montreal H2J 2K9
Quebec
Canada
Tel: 00 1 514 985 3032

Allostop
8 rue Rochambeau
Paris
Tel: 00 33 1 53 20 42 42

Autopass
21 Rue Patou
59800 Lille
Tel: 00 33 3 20 14 31 96

Mitfahrzentrale
Lammerstrasse 4
8 Munich 2
Tel: 00 89 19440

Mitfahrzentrale
Danngasse 1a
1080 Wien/Vienna
Austria
Tel: 00 222 408 2210

Mitfahrzentrale
Kapuzinerstrasse 14A
4020 Linz
Austria
Tel: 00 732 78 27 20

Freewheelers
www.allostop.com/English/default.htm
UK-based online ride-sharing community in association with Allostop.

Autostop Navigator
www.autostopguide.com
Internet resource for hitchhikers.

Digihitch
www.digihitch.com
Extensive US-based Internet forum for hitchhiking news and discussion.

Hitchhikers
www.hitchhikers.org/
Internet message board that brings together drivers and hitchers.

Suite 101 Hitch-hiking
www.suite101.com/welcome.cfm/hitch_hiking
Online community and discussion group.

Vilnius Hitch-hiking Club
www.autostop.It/main.php
Organizes events and collaboration with foreign hitch-hikers in the Baltic states and Russia.
VHHC
Umedziu st 98–19
Vilnius
Lithuania

Internet Cafes

You need never be out of touch if you can access the Internet in a cyber cafe, and the network is growing all the time, even in some remote and unexpected corners of the world, such as Everest Base Camp. As the technology develops, new means of getting online are becoming widespread, including Internet and email terminals in public telephone kiosks. As a result, a list in a book of public access cyber cafes can only ever be a snapshot of the spread of the facilities at the time of writing. It is, in effect, out of date as soon as it is printed and you may well discover new Internet access points on your travels. A number of airlines are even experimenting with in-flight Internet facilities and you can send emails from your laptop at 30,000 feet using a server built in to the aircraft's communications system. United Airlines was the first to offer an onboard email service on its American domestic routes. British Airways, Lufthansa, Scandinavian, Cathay Pacific and Japan Airlines are also trying out or are committed to introducing an in-flight Internet service based on satellite communications. The service is not cheap at the moment and is aimed at business people with urgent messages to send while on the move.

If your project is designed to feed back information and reports to your home base on a regular basis, then clearly you need to plan for independent mobile facilities and there are gadgets to link a laptop to a mobile or satellite phone to give you Internet usage anywhere in the world. But for the occasional electronic postcard home, or for reassurance that you can be in contact in an emergency, it would be nice to know that there's an Internet cafe or kiosk not too far away.

It's worth spending a few minutes of your planning time to consult a website to locate Internet cafes on your projected route.

Internet CyberCafe Database
http://cybercafe.katchup.co.nz/search.asp
Fully searchable database of cyber cafes and worldwide public Internet access points, with a facility to add more as you find them.

Cybercafes.com
www.cybercafes.com/
A database of over 4,000 Internet cafes in 140 countries. You can subscribe to receive email updates when new ones open.

Cybercaptive
http://cybercaptive.com/
A search engine with a database of over 6,000 Internet cafes, public Internet access points and kiosks around the world.

Cyber Café Listings
www.jcoston.bizland.com/cybercafesfr.htm
A list of 125 cyber cafes mainly in ports and airports around the world.

Netcafeguide.com
www.netcafeguide.com
4,500 Internet cafes listed country-by-country.
The following list shows a few examples of the spread of public access Internet points in some of the more remote regions of the world or just curious locations, though more may be opening up and some closing down, depending on the demand.

Graffiti Wall

www.ricksteves.com/graffiti/
archives/cybercafes.html
A message board full of tips from
travellers on cyber cafes they have
found and used, sponsored by
travel writer Rick Steves.

Naukri.com

www.naukri.com/infoedge/cyber/
c000019.htm
Internet cafe locations in Calcutta,
India.

Philippines – Universe Cafe

www2.mozcom.com/~trigern1/
An expanding chain of Internet
cafes in the Philippines.

Thailand

Chiengkhan
Open daily 09.00 to 23.00
315/1 Soi 10 Chiengkhan district
town
Loei Province
Near the MeKong River

Tobago

The Clothes Wash Cafe
Store Bay Road
Crown Point
A combination of coin-operated
laundry and public Internet
access.

Web Oz

www.weboz.net.au/
Directory of cyber cafe locations
in Australia.

Zambia – Businet Internet Cafe

Open 08.00 to 19.00 Mon to Fri;
08:30 to 14:30 Saturday
Lewis Construction
The Workshop
Kabelenga Road
Lusaka

Phone Cards

A phone card enables you to
make a call worldwide from any
phone and is particularly useful in
regions not served by the GSM
mobile phone network. You dial a
freephone number and then key
in an account number and PIN
before dialling the number you
wish to call. The cost will appear
on your monthly bill at home.

BT Chargecard

www.payphones.bt.com
Email: cardserve.helpline@bt.com
Tel: 0800 345 144
You make calls from almost any
fixed-line phone worldwide and
pay through your home telephone
account or by credit card.

eKit Phonecard

www.yha.ekit.com/ekit/Info/
infoabout
An international phone card
recommended by the YHA. It also
gives you access to a voicemail
service which helps people at
home to keep in touch and you
can listen to email messages over
the phone even if you are out of
range of an Internet service.

Millennium Global Calling Card

www.card4anywhere.com/
A prepaid international phone
card that you can use on a
touch-tone phone, including
mobiles, in any of 55 countries.
The cards have an initial credit
value of £15, and a list of call
charges from various countries is
available at www.CallCalc.com.

Roaming Internet Service

Net2Roam
www.net2roam.com/downloads.
html
Tel: 08700 110 188
You can download a piece of
software to enable your laptop or

PDA to dial up an Internet connection virtually anywhere in the world. The subscription costs around £1 per week.

Telco Electronics Ltd
www.telcoelectronics.co.uk
Tel: 07000 701999

Satellite Communications

In the more remote parts of the world or out at sea you can be miles away from a mobile phone cell. For your added safety or to keep in regular touch with base you can now rent a satellite phone for your expedition. This list is just a selection of companies offering the service, but the personal telecoms market is expanding rapidly and new companies start up all the time. Iridium Satellite services, including hand-held satellite phones, are supplied through service partner companies.

Applied Satellite Technology
AST Airtime Limited
Burlingham House
Hewett Road
Gapton Hall Estate
Gt Yarmouth
Norfolk NR31 0NN
www.satcomms.com/iridium.php
Email: sales.enquiries@ast-uk.com
Tel: 01493 440011
AST provided Pen Haddow with satellite communication services for his solo expedition to the North Pole.

Mobell Satellite Phone Rental
The Winding House
Walkers Rise
Rugeley Road
Hednesford
Staffordshire WS12 0QU
www.mobell.co.uk/satellite_phones.asp

Email: website.enquiries@mobell.com
Tel: 01543 426999
Satellite phone rental and international mobile phone hire to keep in touch worldwide. The company has offices in the UK, USA and Japan.

SatCom Distribution Ltd
Unit 5, Centre One
South Portway Business Park
Salisbury SP4 6BU
Wiltshire
Tel: 01722 410800

Stratos
London Office:
6th Floor
3 Finsbury Square
Moorgate
London EC2A 1AE
www.stratosglobal.com
Tel: 020 7562 4826 (0800–2000 GMT)
Tel: 020 7562–4827 (after hours)

Specialist Magazines

The range of travel magazines is expanding and some now have websites associated with them, so you can have access to articles in publications abroad. Some larger branches of WHSmith at main railway stations tend to have a bigger choice of specialist magazines on their shelves, and shops such as Stanford's import travel publications from the USA.

ActivPursuits
www.activpursuits.com
ActivPursuits is a new type of adventure magazine, published exclusively online, covering exploration and discovery, climbing, trekking, adventure racing, kayaking, diving and much more. Publishing online means it can deliver news and reports ahead of

printed magazines and at lower cost with articles written by some of the world's leading adventure writers, including first reports of adventures and expeditions. The website has an archive of all previously published articles, which makes it a growing resource of adventure information and inspiration.

AT – Adventure Travel Magazine
PO Box 6254
Alcester
Warwickshire B49 6PF
Email: alunadtrav@btinternet.com
Tel: 01789 488166

Australian Geographic
PO Box 321
Terrey Hills
NSW 2084
Australia
www.australiangeographic.com.au
Email: order@ausgeo.com.au
Tel: 00 61 2 9473 6700
Articles on life in the more remote parts of Australia.

Canadian Geographic
Royal Canadian Geographical Society
39 McArthur Avenue
Vanier
Ontario K1L 8L7
Canada
www.canadiangeographic.ca
Email: rcgs@canadiangeographic.ca
Tel: 001 613 745 4629
Tel: Free Tel: 1 000 267 0824.

Explore
54 St Patrick Street
Toronto
Ontario M5T 1V1
Canada
www.explore-mag.com
Tel: 001 416 599 2000

The Explorers Journal
The Explorers Club
46 East 70th Street

New York NY 10021
http://explorers.org/publications/the_explorers_journal.php
Email: exjournal@aol.com
Tel: 001 212 628 8383
Magazine promoting exploration and field sciences; free to members.

Geographical Magazine
Unit 11, Pall Mall Deposit
124 Barlby Road
London W10 6BL
www.geographical.co.uk
Email: magazine@geographical.co.uk
Tel: 020 8960 6400
The monthly magazine of the Royal Geographical Society.

Globe
The Globetrotters Club
BCM/Roving
London WC1N 3XX
www.globetrotters.co.uk
The magazine of a non-commercial travel club run by volunteers.

The Great Outdoors (TGO)
Newsquest Magazines Ltd
200 Renfield Street
Glasgow G2 3QB
www.smg.plc.uk/tgo
Email: tgo.sales@magazines.newsquest.co.uk
Tel: 0141 302 7700
Magazine for hill-walking, backpacking and overseas trekking.

Journeywoman
50 Prince Arthur Avenue
Toronto M5R 1B5
Canada
www.journeywoman.com
Email: editor@journeywoman.com
Tel: 001 416 929 7654
Online magazine mainly for women travellers with travel stories, tips and safety advice.

Lonely Planet Travel Journal
Lonely Planet Publications
72–82 Rosebery Avenue
London EC1R 4RW
Email: go@lonelyplanet.co.uk
Tel: 020 7841 9000
Occasional printed magazine
drawing on the extensive
resources of LP, plus a monthly
email newsletter available by
subscription on the Lonely Planet
website.

National Geographic
Geographic Traveler Magazine
1145 17th Street NW
Washington DC 20036–4688
USA
www.nationalgeographic.com
Email: traveler@nationalgeographic.
com
Tel: 001 813 979 6845
Renowned journal packed with
stunning photographs, now
supplemented with a bi-monthly
travel magazine.

Outside Magazine
400 Market Street
Santa Fe
New Mexico 87501
www.outsidemag.com
Email: outsideonline@outsidemag.
com
Adventure travel magazine with
an extensive website.

RoughNews
Rough Guides Ltd
80 Strand
London WC2R 0RL
www.roughguides.com
Tel: 020 7010 3000
An occasional magazine from the
publishers of the highly respected
Rough Guides.

The South American Explorer
South American Explorers Club
Casilla 3714
Lima 100
Peru

www.samexplo.org
Email: explorer@saexplorers.org
Tel: (US) 001 607 277 0488
Quarterly magazine of a non-profit
organization promoting responsible
travel in South America.

Trail
Emap Active Ltd
Bretton Court
Bretton
Peterborough PE3 8DZ
Email: trail@emap.com
Tel: 01733 264666
Monthly outdoor activity maga-
zine focused on mountains and
high-level walking in the UK and
abroad.

Travel Africa
Travel Africa Ltd
4 Rycote Lane Farm
Milton Common
Oxford OX9 2NZ
www.travelafricamag.com
Email: jason@travelafricamag.com/
Tel: 01844 278883
Quarterly independent magazine
and a well-illustrated website,
devoted to travel in Africa with
an emphasis on eco-tourism,
wildlife and conservation.

Traveller
Wexas Ltd
45–49 Brompton Road
London SW3 1DE
www.traveller.org.uk
Email: traveller@wexas.com
Tel: 020 7589 3315
Serious travel writing quarterly
magazine free to members of
Wexas.

Traveller's Voice
www.travellersvoice.com
Quarterly online magazine with
practical information on adventure
travel and eco-tourism, half on
Canada and half on international
travel.

Wanderlust Magazine
PO Box 1832
Windsor
Berkshire SL4 1YT
www.wanderlust.co.uk
Email: info@wanderlust.co.uk
Tel: 01753 620426

Awards and Grants

Adventure travel and expeditions can cost a lot of money because by their nature they do not benefit from the economies of scale in mass tourism to popular holiday destinations, so it pays to shop around for some funding to support a trip that you can show will be worthwhile. No one is going to pay for you to sit on a beach for a fortnight but a journey with a purpose is a different matter and there are numerous trusts, charities and other funding bodies that can sponsor your effort to discover the world, or at least a small corner of it. This list is related to Chapter 10 on fundraising and sponsorship and you should take the advice in it about writing letters appealing for funds. In all cases the eligibility criteria will be quite strict, so try not to waste anyone's time with an inappropriate request.

The Adventure Trust for Girls
1 Bicton Villas
Exmouth
Devon EX8 1JW
A fund set up to help girls aged 11–18 from the Exmouth area in their quest for adventure.

Adrian Ashby-Smith Memorial Trust
c/o Mr Jan Ivan-Duke
39 Sutherland Drive
Newcastle-under-Lyme

Staffordshire ST5 3NZ
Support for people under 40 years of age on their first expedition.

African Bird Club Awards
African Bird Club
c/o BirdLife International
Wellbrook Court
Girton Road
Cambridge CB3 0NA
www.africanbirdclub.org/club/
awards.html
Supports small conservation projects in Africa. There is an annual ABC Expedition Award of £1,000 (US$1,500).

Andrew Croft Memorial Fund
The River House
52 Strand-on-the-Green
London W4 3PD
Tel: 020 8994 6359
Grants for young people (under 30) to participate in expeditions to the Arctic, for research and the benefit of Arctic communities.

Andy Fanshawe Memorial Trust
181 Abbeydale Road
Sheffield S7 2QW
www.thebmc.co.uk/gripped/grip/
fanshaw.htm
Email: afmt_adm.@hotmail.com
Tel: 0114 236 5589
Andy Fanshawe was one of Britain's leading mountaineers and made a point of helping young climbers. After his death in 1992, a Trust was set up to continue his work, and it provides money for young people who can't otherwise afford to visit the world's high peaks. If you are under 26 and lack funding for a climbing expedition or other outdoor adventure, you could qualify for a grant to cover half the costs of your expedition, up to a maximum of £500, to enable you to reach your goal and fulfil a dream. The Andy Fanshawe Memorial Trust can also help you

to find a training course so long as it is for your own personal development and not because you want to gain a professional qualification. In other words, there is money available to help with the costs of an adventure.

British Cave Research Association Research Fund
Bill Tolfree
BCRA Research Fund
6 Ledsgrove
Ipplepen
Newton Abbot
Devon TQ12 5QY
www.bcra.org.uk
Email: research-fund@bcra.org.uk
Grants for scientific projects in any field of caving.

Jim Bishop Memorial Trust
c/o Young Explorers Trust
10 Larch Close
Bingham
Nottinghamshire NG13 8GW
Small grants (around £50) for individuals under 19 years old taking part in adventure activities.

BP Conservation Programme Awards
Programme Manager
BirdLife International
Wellbrook Court
Girton Road
Cambridge CB3 0NA
www.bp.com/conservation/
Email: bp-conservation-programme @birdlife.org.uk
Tel: 01223 277318
Open to teams (not individuals) of students planning conservation research projects of a global priority.

British Airways / RGS-IBG Travel Bursaries
Grants Co-ordinator
Royal Geographical Society (with the institute of British Geographers)
1 Kensington Gore
London SW7 2AR
Email: grants@rgs.org
Tel: 020 7591 3000
Bursaries for tourism-related fieldwork or research outside the UK. For postgraduates registered with a UK Higher Education institute.

British Canoe Union
John Dudderidge House
Adbolton Lane
West Bridgford
Nottinghamshire NG2 5AS
www.bcu.org.uk
Grants for international canoeing expeditions only; considerable canoeing experience and experience of previous expeditions required. An Expeditions for Youth Fund is also administered by the BCU, which gives small grants (around £50) to help young people undertake basic expeditions by canoe.

British Ecological Society
Education and Careers Committee
British Ecological Society
26 Blades Court
Deodar Road
Putney
London SW15 2NU
www.britishecologicalsociety.org
Email: general@ecology.demon. co.uk
Tel: 020 8871 9797
Grants for projects overseas intended to widen the ecological experience of participants. For sixth-form students the expedition must be within the British Isles.

British Mountaineering Council
177–179 Burton Road
Manchester M20 2BB
www.thebmc.co.uk/
Email: office@thebmc.co.uk
Tel: 0870 010 4878
Support for projects finding new routes or British firsts in the world's mountain ranges.

British Sub-Aqua Jubilee Trust
c/o British Sub-Aqua Club
Telford's Quay
South Pier Road
Ellesmere Port
South Wirral CH65 4FL
www.bsac.com
Email: postmaster@bsac.com
Tel: 0151 350 6200
Awards for diving-related projects or expeditions, amateur or professional, using aqua-lung technique.

Ralph Brown Expedition Award
Grants Co-ordinator
Royal Geographical Society (with The Institute of British Geographers)
1 Kensington Gore
London SW7 2AR
www.rgs.org
Email: grants@rgs.org
Tel: 020 7591 3000
A major annual award for the leader of a research expedition associated with the study of inland or coastal wetlands, rivers, or the shallow marine environment. Applicants must be over 25.

Carnegie Trust for the Universities of Scotland
Cameron House
Abbey Park Place
Dunfermline
Fife KY12 7PZ
www.carnegie-trust.org
Email: jgray@carnegie-trust.org
Tel: 01383 622148
Grants for supervised field research expeditions by undergraduates of Scottish universities.

Winston Churchill Memorial Trust
15 Queen's Gate Terrace
London SW7 5PR
www.wcmt.org.uk
Tel: 020 7584 9315
Grants in various categories, including the Mike Jones Award

for canoeing, and usually one on exploration and adventure. British citizens only.

Monica Cole Research Grant
Grants Co-ordinator
Royal Geographical Society (with The Institute of British Geographers)
1 Kensington Gore
London SW7 2AR
www.rgs.org
Email: grants@rgs.org
Tel: 020 7591 3000
A grant for a female geographer to do field research overseas. Undergraduates and postgraduates are eligible.

Commonwealth Youth Exchange Council (CYEC)
7 Lion Yard
Tremadoc Road
Clapham
London SW4 7NQ
www.cyec.org.uk/
Email: Mail@cyec.demon.co.uk
Tel: 020 7498 6151
Supports educational visits by groups of young people aged 16–25 to a British Commonwealth country. Grants cover up to 35 per cent of the international travel costs. The CYEC website is very informative and full of ideas for planning a stimulating adventure into another culture across the world.

Connect Youth International
The British Council
10 Spring Gardens
London SW1A 2BN
www.connectyouthinternational.com
Tel: 020 7389 4030
Funds for young people aged 15–25 to undertake exchanges between Britain and other countries in West, Central and East Europe, the USA and Japan.

CoSCAN Travel Awards
Dr Brita Green
103 Long Ridge Lane
Nether Poppleton
York YO26 6LW
Grants to encourage exchange
visits by young people aged 15 to
25 from the UK and Ireland and
the Scandinavian countries.

Augustine Courtauld Trust
The Clerk
The Augustine Courtauld Trust
Red House
Colchester Road
Halstead
Essex CO9 2DZ
www.augustinecourtauldtrust.org
Support for expeditions to the
Arctic or Antarctic.

**Darwin Initiative for the Survival
of Species**
Darwin Initiative Secretariat
www.darwin.gov.uk
Email: darwin@defra.gsi.gov.uk
Tel: 020 7944 6205
A major funding initiative for
projects on the biodiversity needs
of developing countries, open to
British institutions, organizations
and individuals.

Edinburgh Trust No. 2
The Duke of Edinburgh's Office
Buckingham Palace
London SW1A 1AA
Grants for all expeditions that
have the backing of a recognized
society.

Nick Estcourt Award
c/o The Secretary
24 Grange Road
Bowdon
Altrincham
Cheshire WA14 3EE
Grants for expeditions attempting
an objective of mountaineering
significance, such as a previously
unclimbed face.

Explorers Club Exploration Fund
Support for scientific field
research and exploration.

**Explorers Club Youth Activity
Fund**
Explorers Club
46 East 70th Street
New York NY 10021
USA
www.explorers.org
Email: youth@explorers.org
Tel 212 628 8383
Grants for high school or under-
graduate students to do field
research with a qualified scientiest.

**Fauna and Flora International
(100 per cent Fund)**
Great Eastern House
Tenison Road
Cambridge CB1 2TT
www.fauna-flora.org
Tel: 01223 571000
Support for projects that directly
help endangered species of flora
or fauna. Not suitable for
undergraduate projects.

2111 Foundation for Exploration
86 Catharine Street
Cambridge CB1 3AR
Email: Foundation@2111.org
Grants to expeditions that use
space technology, such as using
remote-sensing data, satellite
communications, and expeditions
undertaking fieldwork in the
interests of space exploration.

The Fuchs Foundation
British Antarctic Survey
High Cross
Madingley Road
Cambridge CB3 OET
Contact the Secretary
www.nbs.ac.uk/public/fuchs/fuchs.
html
Email: k.reid@bas.ac.uk
Tel: 01223 221607
To help young people who would
otherwise be precluded for

reasons of family background or financial status, undertake organized adventurous outdoor activity. Individual applications only.

Georgina Travers Award
Eagle Ski Club
Eastlea
Felix Lane
Shepperton
Middlesex TW17 8NN
www.eagleskiclub.org.uk/gtform.
html
Tel: 01932 248628
Small grants (about £150) for ski mountaineering expeditions and training courses.

Ghar Parau Foundation
Secretary: David Judson
Hurst Barn
Castlemorton
Malvern
Worcestershire WR13 6LS
www.bcra.org.uk/gpf/
Email: d.judson@bcra.org.uk
Tel: 01684 311057
Grants for original exploration, photography and survey of caves, especially in little-known or remote locations. Evidence of experience, ability and research required.

Reg Gilbert International Youth Friendship Trust
The Appeals' Secretary
Rathlyn, Blatchbridge
Frome BA11 5EE
Somerset
www.GIFT.care4free.net
Email: GIFT@care4free.net
Grants to encourage international friendship mainly through home-stays in which young people aged 14–25 become deeply involved in the daily life of the host family abroad.

Gordon Foundation
PO Box 214
Cobham

Surrey KT11 2WG
Email: Gordon.Foundation@bt internet.com
Tel: 01483 456347
Grants for people under 30 to undertake educational travel involving physical challenge or endeavour, or the performing arts.

The Fred Harper Memorial Trust
Weston Cottage
West Way
Crayke
York Y061 4TE
Grants for projects that promote training in the skills for safe mountain walking and climbing.

RJ Harris Charitable Trust
Thring Townsend Solicitors
Midland Bridge Road
Bath BA1 2HQ
Travel grants for people living in Bath and Wiltshire.

The Institute of Biology
Georgina Day
Institute of Biology
20 Queensberry Place
London SW7 2DZ
www.iob.org
Grants for student expeditions overseas with a biological aim or a clear biological component.

Journey of a Lifetime Award
Grants Co-ordinator
Royal Geographical Society
(with the Institute of British Geographers)
1 Kensington Gore
London SW7 2AR
www.rgs.org
Email: grants@rgs.org
Tel: 020 7591 3073
A bursary is on offer to someone who is undertaking a journey that will inspire an interest in peoples and places and who has the ability to communicate their experiences through the medium of radio broadcasting. The winner

will receive training in sound-recording techniques from the BBC. A resulting programme or series will be produced for BBC Radio 4.

The Kenneth Smith Scholarship & The Memorial Adventure Fund
The Alpine Ski Club Awards Sub-Committee
Mrs Jay Turner
22 Hatton Court
Hatton of Fintray
Aberdeenshire AB21 0YA
www.alpineskiclub.org.uk
Email: grants@alpineskiclub.org.uk
Small grants to help skiers and mountaineers to improve their touring and ski mountaineering skills and qualifications, and to support expeditions and tours.

David Loake Memorial Scholarship
c/o Crampton Pym & Lewis
47 Willow Street
Oswestry
Shropshire SY11 1PR
A scholarship to enable people from Shropshire, Powys or Clwyd to travel overseas on projects in agriculture, environmental sciences, rural development, conservation or veterinary studies.

The Merlin Trust
Valerie Finnis VMH
The Merlin Trust
The Dower House
Boughton House
Kettering
Northamptonshire NN14 1BJ
www.merlin-trust.org.uk
Tel: 01536 482279
Grants for young horticulturalists aged 18 to 35 to visit gardens or natural plant habitats anywhere in the world.

Mount Everest Foundation
WH Ruthven
Gowrie
Cardwell Close
Warton
Preston PR4 1SH
www.met.org.uk
Email: bill.ruthven@ukgateway.net
Grants for British and New Zealand expeditions or research in high mountain regions. Also awards Alison Chadwick Memorial Grant 'to further British and Polish women's mountaineering in the greater ranges.'

Mountaineering Council of Scotland
The Old Granary
West Mill Street
Perth PH1 5QP
www.mountaineering-scotland.org.uk
Tel: 01738 638227
Grants for expeditions by MCS members whose objective is adventure and excellence in mountaineering.

National Geographic Society
Expeditions Council
1145 17th Street NW
Washington DC 20036–4688
USA
www.nationalgeographic.com
Financial support to cover field costs of exploration and related technologies that provide new information about areas either largely or completely unknown. The programme is editorially driven and projects must have the potential for a compelling written and visual record. New Explorers grants are also awarded each year to talented and emerging explorers.

The Pain Adventure Trust
10 Victoria Road
Exmouth
Devon EX8 1DL
Tel: 01395 263270/223774
Funding for males aged 11–21 living in East Devon to help in their quest for travel and adventure.

People's Trust for Endangered Species
Unit 15
Cloisters House
Cloisters Business Centre
8 Battersea Park Road
London SW8 4BG
www.ptes.org
Email: enquiries@ptes.org
Funding for expeditions by students whose projects are concerned with the conservation of endangered species.

Polartec Challenge
Ruthann Brown
PO Box 582
Jackson NH 03846
USA
www.polartec.com
Email: brownr@maldenmills.com
An international grant programme designed to encourage the spirit and practice of outdoor adventure.

The Reserve Forces Ulysses Trust
Directorate Reserve Forces & Cadets
Applications Secretary
Room 711A
MOD
St Giles Court
Northumberland Avenue
London WCH 8LD
Financial support for expeditions worldwide undertaken by units of the Reserve Forces, University OTC or cadets.

Shipton/Tilman Grant
WL Gore & Associates Inc.
105 Vieve's Way
Elkton MD 21922
USA
www.gore-tex.com
Sponsorship programme established as a tribute to the explorers Eric Shipton and Bill Tilman, to encourage expeditions that demonstrate the principles of travelling in small compact teams without porters and excessive bulk. The

expedition must be self-propelled, environmentally sound and cost-effective.

Neville Shulman Challenge Award
Grants Co-ordinator
Royal Geographical Society
(with The Institute of British Geographers)
1 Kensington Gore
London SW7 2AR
www.rgs.org
Email: grants@rgs.org
Tel: 020 7591 3073
Grants to support exploration of the planet while promoting personal development through the intellectual or physical challenges involved in undertaking expeditions.

Frederick Soddy Trust/Geographical Association Expedition Grants
25 Henry Burt Way
Burgess Hill
West Sussex RH15 9UX
Grants of up to £500 for schools and other group expeditions to study a human community and life in a particular area.

The Captain Scott Society
Spirit of Adventure Award for individual or expedition displaying similar 'spirit of adventure' so nobly demonstrated by Captain Scott and The British Antarctic Expedition of 1910. Average grant £1,000.
Sir Vivian Fuchs Young Adventure Award
for young person aged between 11–19.
The Expeditions Secretary
The Captain Scott Society
c/o United Services Mess
Wharton Street
Cardiff CF1 2AG
For further info contact either Brian Thorpe (029 2056 2549) or Julian Salisbury (029 2075 4830)

Sports Council for Wales
Sophia Gardens
Cardiff CF11 9SW
Email: publicity@scw.co.uk
Tel: 029 20 300 500
The Sports Council for Wales
supports the principle of grant aid
for overseas expeditions which
will enhance the development of a
sport. Consideration will be given
to Welsh-based expeditions.

Talgarth Environment Fund
Talgarth Environment Group
Unit 4, Great House Barn
New Street
Talgarth
Powys LD3 0AH
Provides grants for applicants to
participate in expeditions related
to conservation and the environ-
ment. Applicants must live within
15 miles of Talgarth and be aged
under 40.

Trans-Antarctic Association
c/o Scott Polar Research Institute
Lensfield Road
Cambridge CB2 1ER
Grants for fieldwork in Antarctica
by nationals of the UK, South
Africa, Australia and New
Zealand.

Paul Vander-Molen Foundation
Michael Coyne
92 Belgrave House
Wanstead
London E11 3QP
Grants between £200 and £1,000
to provide opportunities for
people with disabilities to enjoy
and participate in adventurous
activities. Open to individuals,
schools, clubs and expeditions.

Gino Watkins Memorial Fund
The Secretary
Gino Watkins Memorial Fund
Committee
Scott Polar Research Institute
Lensfield Road

Cambridge CB2 1ER
Grants for expeditions to polar
regions.

The Whitley Laing Foundation
50 Queensdale Road
London W11 4SA
www.whitleyaward.org
Email: info@whitleyaward.org
Tel: 020 7602 3443
An annual award scheme for field
projects that will make a contribution to nature conservation in
developing countries. Awards
cover use of renewable energy,
technology, human rights issues
and general conservation work.

Wilderness Award
Inglewood
New Road
High Littleton
Somerset BS39 6JH
www.wildernesslectures.com
For an individual undertaking an
unusual and exciting project in a
wilderness area. He or she will
give a lecture in the following
year's Wilderness Lectures Series.
Charity expeditions are not
eligible.

Edward Wilson Fund
c/o Scott Polar Research Institute
Lensfield Road
Cambridge CB2 1ER
Small grants for expeditions to
polar regions.

Young Explorers Trust
Ted Grey
Stretton Cottage
Wellow Road
Ollerton
Newark
Notts NG22 9AX
www.yet2.demon.co.uk
Email: ted@yet2.demon.co.uk
Tel: 01623 861027
Grants for expeditions by people
under 20 years old (not usually
undergraduate expeditions)

involved in discovery and exploration in remote areas. Aims can include community projects, fieldwork and/or physical adventure (climbing/sailing, etc.). New groups and ones with disadvantaged members are encouraged to apply.

Fundraising Advice

Funding Exploration: The Future of Discovery in the 21st Century
by William F. Vartorella Craig & Vartorella Inc.
PO Box 1376
Camden
South Carolina 29020-1376
USA.
Email: globebiz@camden.net

Directory of Grant Making Trusts.
Charities Aid Foundation
Kings Hill
West Malling
Kent ME19 4TA
Tel: 01732 520000
An extensive catalogue of funding resources, featuring grants for organizations and individuals.

The Complete Fundraising Handbook
The Directory of Social Change
24 Stephenson Way
London NW1 2DP
Tel: 020 7209 5151

Ideas Annual
Scottish Community Education Council
Rosebury House
Haymarket Terrace
Edinburgh EH12 5EZ
Tel: 0131 313 2488

Travel Insurance

It is most important to check that your insurance policy covers you for all that you are likely to be involved in during an expedition or adventure trip. Normal holiday insurance does not usually cover hazardous activities such as mountaineering or winter sports such as ski trekking. There may be extra charges also for a policy to give you full medical and health cover in some countries. In remote areas, where you could be a long distance from a hospital, the cost of medical evacuation should be included in the insurance policy in case you need to be flown to a medical centre in a neighbouring country. Being under-insured can work out very costly if things go wrong; as always, better to be safe than sorry.

If you are using low-cost or discount air fares, also check the conditions for cancellation or curtailment and ensure that you are covered by insurance for any extra costs of getting home.

It is your responsibility to provide complete information to insurers when you take out your policy. You must ensure that all statements you make on proposal forms, claim forms and other documents are full and accurate.

Activinsura
www.activinsura.co.uk
Tel: 0870 066 7655
Backpacking and adventure travel insurance cover.

Ault Insurance Group
Kinder House
Lombard Street
West Bromwich B70 8SD
www.ault.co.uk
Tel: 0121 553 4791

Insurance arrangements that will take into account individual circumstances.

BMC British Mountaineering Council
Member Services
FREEPOST MR9759
Manchester M20 7AD
www.thebmc.co.uk
Email: insure@thebmc.co.uk
Tel: 0870 010 4878
Insurance especially for mountaineering, trekking and expedition travel.

Buddy
www.buddyindepth.co.uk
Tel: 0870 905 6569
Winter sports and diving insurance cover.

Campbell Irvine Limited
Insurance Brokers
Alma House
Alma Road
Reigate
Surrey RH2 0AX
Tel: 01737 223687
The insurance brokers for Pen Haddow's 2003 solo expedition to the North Pole.

Columbus Travel Insurance
www.columbusdirect.com
Tel: 0845 330 7076

Coverworks
www.coverworks.com
Tel: UK 01270 625431

Foundry Travel Insurance
www.foundrytravel.com
Email: info@foundrytravel.com
Tel: 0114 275 5806

Navigator Travel Insurance
www.navigatortravel.co.uk
Email: enquiries@navigatortravel.co.uk
Tel: 0870 241 0576
Worldwide travel insurance especially designed for backpackers and independent travellers, covering gap-year travel, working holidays and hazardous activities such as skydiving, scuba diving, trekking, white-water rafting, bungee jumping, surfing and windsurfing. Cover is available for up to two years. No excesses on policies of six months' duration or longer. Special rates available for itineraries which include Australia or New Zealand.

Outbacker
www.outbackerinsurance.com
Tel: 0871 711 5253

Snowcard Travel
www.snowcard.co.uk
Email: enquiries@snowcard.co.uk
Tel: 01327 262805
Specialist activity and winter sport insurance.

Sportscover Direct Ltd
33 Corn Street
Bristol BS1 1HT
www.sportscover.co.uk
Email: contact@sportscover.co.uk
Tel: 0845 120 6400
Sport and leisure travel insurance.

STA Travel
Priory House
6 Wrights Lane
London W8 6TA
www.statravel.co.uk
Tel: 0870 1600 599
Sixty branches over the UK.

TIA Travel Insurance Agency
Email: info@travelinsurers.com
Tel: 020 8446 5414

Travel Insurance Club
www.ticdirect.co.uk
Tel: 01702 423398
Insurance cover for working holidays and backpacking.

Trekker
www.flexicover.com
Tel: 0870 990 9292
Travel insurance for backpackers.

WEXAS International
45–49 Brompton Road
London SW3 1DE
www.wexas.com
Email: mship@wexas.com
Tel: 020 7589 3315
Comprehensive travel insurance deals for members of the association.

Worldwide
www.worldwideinsure.com
Tel: 01892 833338

Medical Care, Advice and Supplies

UK citizens are entitled to free or reduced-cost emergency medical treatment in countries of the European Economic Area (the European Union plus Iceland, Liechtenstein and Norway) but you will need to have a completed Form E111. This is available in the booklet, *Health Advice for Travelers*, from the Department of Health, Email: doh@prolog.uk.com, Tel: 0800 555777.

The UK has reciprocal agreements with about forty countries outside the EU for urgently needed medical treatment at reduced cost or, in some cases, free on the same terms as residents. The range of services may be more restricted than under the UK National Health Service. You will need to produce evidence that you are a resident of the UK, such as a passport or driving licence. You should have adequate insurance to cover any costs.

It's advisable to consult a vaccination centre about six to eight weeks before you travel, so that you can discuss your plans and get the right jabs for your needs. Some need time to work around your blood system before being fully effective. In some parts of the world yellow fever is prevalent and you will need to carry a certificate to prove you have been immunized, along with your passport. Always consult a doctor or a travel clinic for up-to-date advice on pre-travel vaccinations.

The American Society of Tropical Medicine and Hygiene
www.astmh.org/scripts/clinindex.asp
A directory of travel clinics in eighteen countries.

British Airways Immunization Centre
156 Regent Street
London W1
Tel: 020 7439 9584
Open Mon–Sat: no appointment required.

British Airways Travel Clinics
Located in various centres around Britain.
Tel: 01276 685 040 for details.
213 Piccadilly
London W1
Tel: 0845 600 2236
Walk-in service open Mon–Sat.

Victoria Plaza
Victoria Station
London SW1
Tel: 020 7233 6661
Open daily.

Bill Medical Centre
46 Wimpole Street
London W1G 8SD
Tel: 020 7569 5000
Open Mon–Fri.

Center for Disease Control and Prevention
www.cdc.gov
International Travelers Hotline:
1877 394 8747

Comprehensive worldwide travel health advice for American travellers abroad. The CDC produces the publication, *Health Information for international Travel.*

Department of Health Public Enquiries Office
Richmond House
79 Whitehall
London SW1A 2NS
www.doh.gov.uk
Email: dhmail@doh.gov.gsi.uk
Tel: 020 7210 4950
Tel: 0800 555777 free to order publications on travel health.

Fit For Travel
www.fitfortravel.scot.nhs.uk/
Online travel advice, including vaccinations, provided by the NHS in Scotland.

Fleet Street Travel Clinic
Tel: 020 7353 5678

Health Canada
www.TravelHealth.gc.ca
Online list of travel health and vaccination facilities across Canada.

The Health Network Pharmacy
www.healthnetwork.com.au
Email: pharmacy@healthnetwork. com.au
Advice and travel medical kit in Australia.

Hospital for Tropical Diseases
4 St Pancras Way
London NW1 0PE
Tel: 020 7637 6099
Comprehensive range of pre-travel vaccinations and post-travel check-ups.

Travel Clinic Healthline
Tel: 09061 33 77 33 (calls charged at 50p per minute)

International Association for Medical Assistance to Travellers
www.iamat.org
417 Center Street
Lewiston NY 14092
USA
Tel: 001 716 754 4883 and
40 Regal Road
Guelph
Ontario N1K 1B5
Canada
Tel: 001 519 836 0102
Advice on immunization requirements and worldwide health risks.

International Society of Travel Medicine
www.istm.org
Addresses and contact details for travel clinics around the world.

Malaria Healthline
Tel: 09065 508 908 (calls charged at £1 per minute)

Lisson Grove Medical Centre
3–5 Lisson Grove
Mutley
Plymouth PL4 7DL
Tel: 01752 205556
Open Wed–Thur 9am–6pm, Fri 9am–1pm

MASTA – Medical Advisory Services for Travellers Abroad
Head Office
Moorfield Road
Yeadon
Leeds LS 19 7BN
West Yorkshire
www.masta.org
Tel: 0113 238 7575
Travellers' Health Line: 0906 8224 100
(calls charged at 60p per minute)

Travel Health Centre
52 Margaret Street
London W1W 8SQ
Travel Clinic Location Line: 0870 6062 782
(calls charged at UK national rate)

MASTA operates travel clinics around the UK which provide advice, vaccinations and products such as insect repellents, mosquito nets and first aid and medical kits. MASTA can provide you with a health brief on the countries you intend to visit covering hazards, immunization requirements and malaria protection.

MDtravelhealth.com

www.mdtravelhealth.com
A comprehensive American website devoted to travel health information and resources.

Nomad Travel

3–4 Wellington Terrace
Turnpike Lane
London N8 0PX
www.nomadtravel.co.uk
Email: sales@nomadtravel.co.uk
Tel: 020 8889 7014
Nomad Travel Clinic
43 Queens Road
Bristol BS8 1QH
Tel: 0117 922 6567
Medical supplies, insect repellents and vaccinations for individual travellers and expedition groups.

The Travel Doctor

www.traveldoctor.co.uk
Online travel medical advice from two doctors based in South Wales with a wide range of experience in trekking and expeditions around the world.

Travel Medicine Program

www.TravelHealth.gc.ca
Advice and information for travellers from Health Canada.

Travelpharm.com

www.travelpharm.com
Email: info@travelpharm.com
Tel: 01404 815437
Online shop for first-aid kits, anti-malarial drugs and other medical supplies and advice.

US Department of State Medical Information for Americans Travelling Abroad

http://travel.state.gov/medical.html
The website contains advice, links to further information, travel medical insurance for US citizens and emergency air ambulance (Med-Evac) services.

World Health Organization (WHO)

www.who.int/ith
Travel health information including outbreaks of infectious diseases worldwide.

Water Purification Systems

The best advice for travellers is to drink only water that you know is safe, such as from sealed bottles, after boiling or filtering and treatment with iodine or chlorine tablets. Filters should be regarded as routine tools for use in extreme conditions and remote locations where the only water is from natural sources such as streams or springs, or as an additional precaution when carrying water drawn from a tap when you are not certain of the quality. The products listed are described fully on websites and are available in most outdoor supplies shops and for online purchase.

Aqua Pure Traveller

www.aquapurefilters.com/ and www.homehealth-uk.com/
Personal water purifier system – a filter and water bottle in one. The APT removes sediments and waterborne pathogens such as *E. coli*, Giardia and Cryptosporidium.

British Berkefeld Water Filters
www.h2owarehouse.com/british-
berkefeld/index.html

Katadyn
www.katadyn.ch
Swiss-made range of water-purifying filters and bottles.
Stocked in the UK by Gearzone
www.gear-zone.co.uk

Lifesystems
Calleva Park
Aldermaston
Berkshire RG7 8EN
www.lifesystems.co.uk
Email: mail@lifesystems.co.uk
Tel: 01189 811433
Makers of water-purifying prod-
ucts including chlorine tablet and
iodine droplets. The website
includes a search facility for your
nearest stockist.

MSR Miniworks
www.msrcorp.com
Compact water filter.
UK Distributor:
First Ascent
Units 4/5
Limetree Business Park
Matlock
Derbyshire DE4 3EJ
Email: info@firstascent.co.uk
Tel: 01629 580484

Potable Aqua Travel Kit
www.wpcbrands.com/brands/
potable/potablemain.html
Iodine-based water-purification
tablets and collapsible bottle.

Puritabs
Chlorine-based effervescent water-
purification tablets, for use with a
filter. Available from pharmacies.

Sources of Maps and Travel Books

AA Publishing
Forum House
Priestly Road
Basingstoke
Hants RG21 2EA
www.theaa.com/index.html
Tel: 01256 491538

A & C Black
Blue Guides Travel Books
37 Soho Square
London W1D 3QZ
www.acblack.com
Email: travel@acblack.com
Tel: 020 7758 0200

Blackwell Map & Travel
Bookshop
50 Broad Street
Oxford OX1 3BQ
www.bookshop.blackwells.co.uk/
Email: mail.ox@blackwell.co.uk
Tel: 01865 792792

Bradt Travel Guides
19 High Street
Chalfont St Peter
Bucks SL9 9QE
www.bradt-travelguides.com
Email: enquiries@bradt-travelguides.
com
Tel: 01753 893444

Cadogan Guides
Highlands House
165 The Broadway
London SW19 1NE
www.cadoganguides.com
Email: info@cadoganguides.com
Tel: 020 8544 8053

Cicerone
2 Police Square
Milnthorpe
Cumbria LA7 7PY
www.cicerone.co.uk
Email: info@cicerone.co.uk
Tel: 01539 562069
Pocket-sized guides to mountain

walking and trekking. Distributed in Australia through MacStyle Media and in North America through Alpenbooks and Midpoint Trade Books Inc.

Harper Collins Publishers
77–85 Fulham Palace Road
London W6 8JB
www.fireandwater.com/genres/maps.asp
Tel: 0870 900 2050
US: www.harpercollins.com

Harper Collins US Mail Address
10 East 53rd Street
New York NY 10022
Tel: 212 207 7000
Maps, atlases and travel literature. Publishers of *The Times Atlas of the World*.

Lonely Planet
www.lonelyplanet.com
A wide variety of travel and destination guides and an informative website.

Rough Guides
www.roughguides.co.uk and www.roughguides.com
Rough Guides publishes travel books on more than 150 destinations around the world and user-friendly, modern-language phrase books, designed for independent-minded travellers on any budget.

Stanfords
12–14 Long Acre
London WC2E 9LP
www.stanfords.co.uk
Email: customer.services@stanfords.co.uk
Tel: 020 7836 1321
29 Corn Street
Bristol BS1 1HT
Tel: 0117 929 9966
39 Spring Gardens
Manchester M2 2BG
Tel: 0161 831 0250

Stanfords is the leading map specialist and is famous for its vast range of maps from all parts of the world.

Thomas Cook Publishing
PO Box 227
Units 19–21
The Thomas Cook Business Park
Peterborough PE3 8XX
www.thomascookpublishing.com
Email: publishing-sales@thomascook.com
Tel: 01733 416477
Guidebooks and the renowned European and worldwide railway timetables.

The Travel Bookshop
13 Blenheim Crescent
London W11 2EE
www.thetravelbookshop.co.uk
Email: post@thetravelbookshop.co.uk
Tel: 020 7229 5260
A truly specialist travel bookseller. The bookshop featured in the Hugh Grant film *Notting Hill*.

Ulysses Travel Publications
4176 St-Denis Street
Montreal
Quebec H2W 2M5
www.ulyssesguides.com
Email: info@ulysses.ca
CanadRel: 514 843 9448
Maps, atlases and travel guides in stores and online sales. Specialists in guidebooks covering North America.
European sales:
Roundhouse Publishing Ltd
Millstone
Limers Lane
Northam
North Devon EX39 2RG
Email: roundhouse.group@ukgateway.net
Tel: 01237 474474

Vacation Work Publications
9 Park End Street
Oxford OX1 1HJ
www.vacationwork.co.uk
Email: sales@vacationwork.co.uk
Tel: 01865 241 978
Guidebooks to summer or gap-year
work and travel, with the latest job
information and contacts on the
website.

Wilderness Press
1200 5th Street
Berkeley CA 94710
USA
www.wildernesspress.com/
Email: mail@wildernesspress.
com
Tel: 001 510 558 1666
Outdoor adventure travel Guides
to North America.

YHA Adventure Shops
Shops all over Great Britain.
Suppliers of maps, guidebooks
and equipment.
Head Office Tel: 01784 458625
Mail Order Tel: 01159 505172

Specialist Reference Libraries

British Library Map Collections
96 Euston Road
London NW1 2DB
www.bl.uk
Email: maps@bl.uk
Tel: 020 7412 7702
A collection of about five million
maps relating to the history of
British cartography from all parts
of the world. Access by BL
reader's pass.

**British Library Oriental and India
Office Collections**
Printed volumes and manuscripts
in the languages of Asia, North
Africa, the Near and Middle East
plus records of the East India
Company and British government
in India until 1947. Access by BL
reader's pass.

**Foreign and Commonwealth
Office Library**
King Charles Street
London SW1A 2AH
www.fco.gov.uk
Tel: 020 7270 3925
Collection of books and other
reference material relating to
countries covered by the FCO,
particularly colonial history and
early works on travel mainly in
Commonwealth countries and
former British colonies.

French Institute Library
Institut Française
17 Queensbury Place
London SW7 2DT
Tel: 020 7838 2148
Resources on French cultural
interests.

Goethe-Institute Library
50 Princes Gate
Exhibition Road
London SW7 2PH
Email: Library@London.goethe.org
Tel: 020 7596 4040
Library specialising in German
affairs.

Instituto Cervantes
102 Eaton Square
London SW1W 9AN
www.cervantes.es
Email: biblon@cervantes.es
Tel: 020 7201 0757
Library specializing in Spain and
Latin America.

Italian Institute Library
39 Belgrave Square
London SW1X 8NX
www.italcultur.org.uk
Tel: 020 7235 1461
Collection relating to Italian
cultural interests, mainly in
Italian.

National Library of Scotland
George IV Bridge
Edinburgh EH1 1EW
www.nls.uk
Email: enquiries@nls.uk
Tel: 0131 226 4531
Houses special collections on
polar studies and exploration,
notably the papers of Louis
Baume, Graham Brown and Sir
James Mann Wordie.

**National Meteorological Library
and Archive**
London Road
Bracknell
Berkshire RG12 2SZ
www.metoffice.com
Tel: 01344 854841
Collection of books and papers
on worldwide climatology.

PA News Centre
Central Park
New Lane
Leeds
West Yorkshire LS11 5DZ
www.pa.press.net
Email: palibrary@pa.press.net
Tel: 0870 830 6802
Public access to the newspaper
cuttings collection of the Press
Association, dating back to 1928.

Polish Library
238–246 King Street
London W6 0RF
Email: polish.library@posk.org
Tel: 020 8741 0474
Closed Sun, Tue and Thur. Refer-
ence collection on all aspects of
Polish history and culture.

**Royal Geographical Society with
The Institute of British
Geographers**
1 Kensington Gore
London SW7 2AR
www.rgs.org
Tel: 020 7591 3000
Foremost collection of books and
other papers on expeditions and
exploration.

**United Nations Information
Centre**
Millbank Tower 21st Floor
21–24 Millbank
London SW1P 4QH
www.unitednations.org.uk
Email: info@uniclondon.org
Tel: 020 7630 1981
Open Mon–Fri
Full stock of publications and
documents from the UN.

Language Study

It would be all too easy to overlook the possibilities for adventure
in taking a language course. Living
in the country where the language
is spoken is a very effective way of
learning because you are forced to
practise. In addition there is the
opportunity to get out and about
and meet people and see something of another country.

Caledonia Languages Abroad
www.caledonialanguages.co.uk
Email: courses@caledonialanguages.
co.uk
Tel: 0131 621 7721
Language courses throughout the
year.

EducaCentre
22 Sinopskaya emb.
St Petersburg 191167
Russia
www.ed.spb.ru/
Email: mail@educacentre.net
Tel: 00 7 812 327 0373
Russian language courses in St
Petersburg.

EuroTalk Interactive
315–317 New Kings Road
London SW6 4RF
www.eurotalk.com
Tel: 020 7371 7711
Freephone in UK: 0800 018 8838
Self-study language learning
CD-Roms covering 80 languages.

French Institute
17 Queensbury Place
London SW7 2DT
Tel: 020 7581 2701

Goethe Institut
50 Princes Gate
Exhibition Road
London SW7 2PH
www.goethe.de/london
Email: mail@london.goethe.org
Tel: 020 7596 4000
German language courses.

i-to-i International Projects
9 Blenheim Terrace
Leeds LS2 9HZ
Tel: 0870 333 2332
Training network for volunteers
to teach English as a foreign
language.

Language Courses Abroad Ltd
67 Ashby Road
Loughborough
Leicestershire LE11 3AA
www.languagesabroad.co.uk
Tel: 01509 211612
Courses in Europe and South
America.

Oideas Gael
Gleann Cholm Cille
County Donegal
Republic of Ireland
www.oideas-gael.com/
Email: oifig@oideas-gael.com
Tel: 00 353 74 97 30 248
Courses in Irish language and
culture.

SIBS
SIBS Ltd
Beech House
Commercial Road
Uffculme
Devon EX15 3EB
www.sibs.co.uk
Email: trish@sibs.co.uk
Tel: 01884 841330
Language study in the country
where it is spoken.

Index